Pacific Odyssey

Connections

Pacific Odyssey
Connections

ARTHUR C. FARRINGTON

Sunflower University Press®

1531 Yuma • P.O. Box 1009 • Manhattan, Kansas 66505-1009 USA

Cover design concept by Karen (Farrington) Berghorst.

ISBN 0-89745-264-X

Sunflower University Press is a wholly-owned subsidiary
of the non-profit 501(c)3 Journal of the West, Inc.

This book is dedicated to the readers. I hope you are amused and enlightened a bit concerning the United States Marine Corps — and I hope you might enjoy an odyssey or two yourself.

— *Semper Fidelis*

Contents

Foreword

*H*AVING BEEN transported across the great Pacific twelve times from June 1942 through June 1968, the title of this work just seems right. I hope that my family, friends, and others interested in some of the adventures of a U.S. Marine will enjoy this account. This is not fiction. The actions are written as I saw, recorded, or remember them.

Since graduating from high school in June of 1940, I believe that I have remained true to my aims for a good life: to be proficient at whatever I chose to do, to enjoy it, and to get paid well. I believe that I was successful at my various assignments, was well satisfied with my work, and was compensated sufficiently. I thoroughly enjoyed both the military life (except, of course, the times in war when I was afraid or freezing) and, upon my retirement, the substitute teaching.

My first publication, *The Leatherneck Boys: A PFC at the Battle for Guadalcanal,* included many on-the-spot diary recordings, because at that time my duty was as a trainer on a twin 20mm Oerlikon antiaircraft gun and I had the time and opportunity to write. But my antiaircraft duty comes to an abrupt end early in this work, as do my direct observations from our invasion of Cape Gloucester on New Britain Island, just east of New Guinea.

After I had finished this manuscript, America once again became involved in a war — this time a "War on Terrorism." On September 11, 2001, the twin towers of the World Trade Center in New York City were destroyed by international terrorists, and the Pentagon in Washington, D.C., was attacked; in all, including a plane almost simultaneously downed in Pennsylvania, over 3,000 people were killed.

A poem from my mother's World War I photo album, author unknown, pasted below a picture of her "soldier-boy" beau, seemed to me apropos of our boys' mission in this new war. Mother would be pleased; she passed away at the age of 105, on November 30, 2000.

Gone to the Colors

The Kid has gone to the Colors,
And we don't know what to say;
The Kid we have loved and cuddled,
Stepped out for the Flag today.
We thought him a child, a baby,
With never a care at all,
But his country called him man-size,
And the Kid has answered the call.

He paused to watch the recruiting,
Where, fired by the fife and drum,
He bowed his head to Old Glory,
And thought that it whispered "Come!"
The Kid, not being a slacker,
Stood forth with patriot-joy
To add his name to the roster —
And, God, we're proud of the boy!

The Kid has gone to the Colors;
It seems but a little while
Since he drilled a schoolboy army

In a truly martial style,
But now he's a man, a soldier,
And now we lend him a listening ear,
For his heart is a heart all loyal,
Unscourged by the curse of fear.

His dad, when we told him, shuddered;
His mother — God bless her! cried;
Yet, blessed with a mother-nature,
She wept with a mother-pride,
But he whose old shoulders straightened
Was Grandad — for memory ran
To years when he, too, a youngster,
Was changed by the Flag to a man.

Arthur C. Farrington, 2002

xii

Private 1st Class Arthur C. Farrington, 283222, enlisted in the U.S. Marine Corps in Washington, D.C., on April 2, 1940. He retired at Camp Joseph H. Pendleton, California, on December 31, 1970. Note the Rifle Expert badge.

Introduction —
"Connections"

*O*N JUNE 12, 1942, my train pulled out from the water tower in Tent City, our camp near Jacksonville, North Carolina. We were bound for World War II. My diary entry reads:

> Tokio, Here We Come. Shoved off for WWII at 6:30 P.M.

After the events of my first book, *The Leatherneck Boys: A PFC at the Battle for Guadalcanal,* a series of "interim actions" occurred and thus I have included one as an introductory connection to this work. Others appear as short "vignettes" that expand on the story. I have also added the following, a few lines from my World War II diary, which I think reflected my own and the country's mindset regarding "decisions" made in wartime:

> Today is 2 Jan 42. Yesterday quite a few Marines traveled up to Durham, North Carolina, to see the Oregon

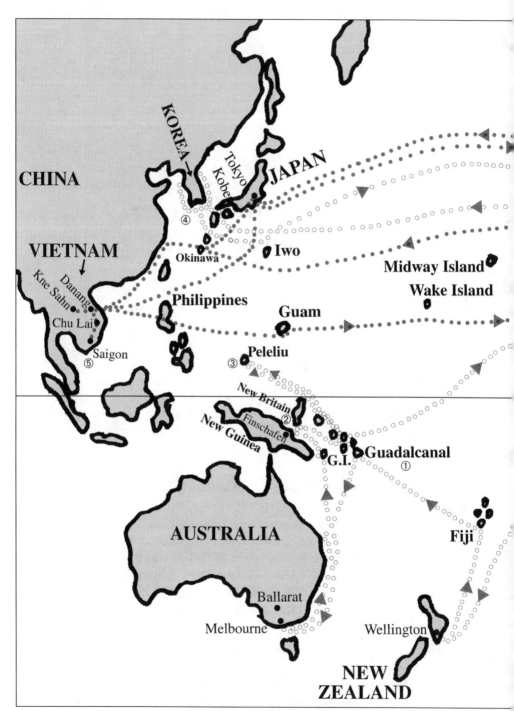

Pacific Odyssey Itinerary of Twelve Passages

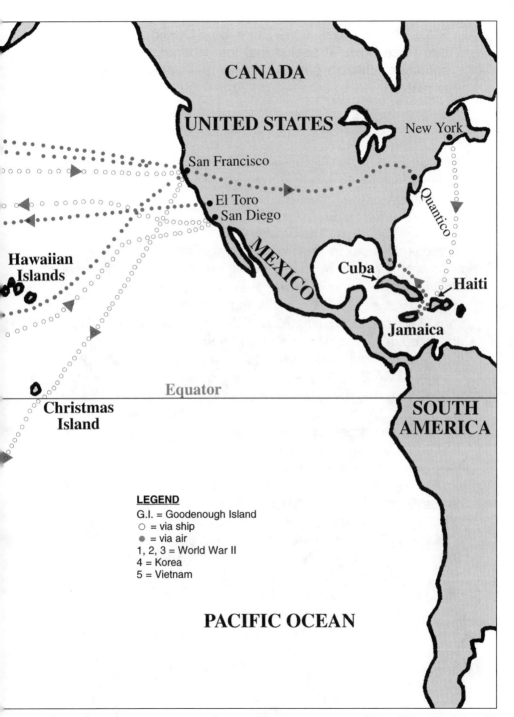

CANADA

UNITED STATES

New York

San Francisco

El Toro
San Diego

Quantico

Hawaiian
Islands

MEXICO

Cuba

Haiti

Jamaica

Equator

Christmas
Island

SOUTH
AMERICA

LEGEND
G.I. = Goodenough Island
○ = via ship
● = via air
1, 2, 3 = World War II
4 = Korea
5 = Vietnam

PACIFIC OCEAN

(Plus two roundtrips from Japan to Quantico, Virginia; stop-overs on Wake, Midway, and Hawaii.)

State "Beavers" defeat the Duke "Blue Devils" 20 to 16 in the "Rose Bowl." It seems that the Japanese had made someone "chicken out" of holding it in Pasadena, California!

By August 1942, I was on Guadalcanal Island, British Solomon Islands, in the Southwest Pacific theater of war. My subsequent vignette recorded that experience.

Souvenir?

Suddenly there in the blue sky they came from the west-northwest, 27 twin-engine Mitsubishi Ki-21 Sally bombers of the Imperial Japanese Army. Their origins were the landing fields of Rabaul, New Britain Island; their target was Henderson Field on Guadalcanal, British Solomon Islands. They appeared deceptively like a string of pearls, yet struck fear into the hearts of all who dared to observe their approach. I remember well how later I would slide down in my theater seat in Melbourne as the newsreels showed the planes approaching Darwin, Australia, in the identical formation.

We, on the target, did not fear the makers of the surrounding contrails — the Zero fighters accompanying the bombers. They were in the domain of our Grumman F4F Wildcat fighters, if any were on station. But suddenly the bombers' white bellies darkened as the bomb bays were opened on the incoming vector. Within seconds was heard the terrible screams of the anti-personnel bombs, the rushing of the 500-pounders, and a roar like falling freight-train cars made by the 1,000-pound bombs. We popped up to a scene of fire, smoke, and dust, and then a glorious sight greeted us. Our Wildcats had scored, and one bomber was trailing smoke right over the field and heading straight into the jungle near our 1st Engineer Battalion. The single, very large tail rudder, comparable to that of our B-17 Flying Fortress, distinguished this Sally from the Japanese Imperial Navy's newer twin-engine

A Grumman F4F4 fighter, No. 15. The aircraft was shot down on October 15, 1942, by three Zeros upon returning to Henderson Field in company with a PBY Catalina flying boat.

Grumman name-plate.

Mitsubishi Betty, which was also frequently used as a torpedo-bomber.

Most of the Marines were souvenir hunters, sometimes to a fault, so naturally a couple of our Marines from A Battery of the 1st Special Weapons Battalion, nearest the crash, charged to the site. They later told us that they noticed a Marine poking with a stick in the stomach of one of the dead Japanese airmen. In answer to what he was doing, he turned around and with a detached "Asiatic" stare stated that he was "just looking around." We had experienced such outlandish stares from some Marines who had served in the Far East before the war, and they were scary. But we soon got used to them after a little more time on "The Island," as Guadalcanal was called. In fact, upon leaving there for Australia on January 5, 1943, I noticed that, indeed, the 1st Marine Division included a few more men qualified to be termed "Asiatic."

The 15th of October 1942 was the day after the first naval battle of Guadalcanal, and two large *Maru* (Japanese transports) had beached themselves and were unloading troops just to the west of the Matanikau River, a good distance off, on the west side of the airfield.

The Japanese had gained air superiority after early attacks by our Douglas SBD Dauntless aircraft (SB = scout bomber, D = Douglas), as well as by eleven U.S. Army Air Forces B-17 Flying Fortresses from New Hebrides.

Around noon, over the palms arising from Henderson Field, a PBY Catalina flying boat appeared, surrounded by ten F4F Wildcats. The PBY had an aerial torpedo affixed under each wing, and it was headed toward the Matanikau River. We watched it go into a shallow dive surrounded by Zeros and through intense antiaircraft fire. A large smoke cloud appeared — scratch one *Maru* — and the PBY made a big, slow, looping turn and dived again.

We had a man atop a large antenna giving a blow-by-blow description of the events, because our view was blocked by the palm trees. As I was making my way back from the 3rd Defense Battalion mess with my chow, I saw the extremely slow PBY pass a few hundred feet overhead surrounded by Zeros. He made it, with many wounded heroes aboard. In my opinion, then and now, they all should have received the Medal of Honor.

Corporal Arthur C. Farrington
"Down Under" in 1943.

Arthur Farrington posing for friend Ellie
Marchbank in Melbourne, Australia.

The author posing in front of the Eureka
Stockade Memorial in Ballarat, wearing the
marksmanship badge and American Defense
ribbon with star, for service in Cuba before
World War II.

Arthur C. Farrington's father was also a U.S. Marine. Private Arthur C. Ferrington (note the different spelling), 104882, enlisted from Greenleaf, Wisconsin, on December 15, 1917 (born August 1, 1895; died June 1954). He was honorably discharged in Washington, D.C., on August 15, 1921. He reimbursed the USMC for four month's pay for his early release. Note also the Rifle Sharpshooter badge.

Arthur C. Ferrington, the author's father, a Buck Sergeant in the U.S. Marine Corps, on a downtown street in Washington, D.C., in barracks cap, high-necked blouse, jodhpurs, puttees (leggings), and high-topped dress shoes. The hands-in-pocket pose prompted the Marine Corps to later require officers to carry gloves and a silver-tipped swagger stick; senior NCOs carried gold-tipped sticks.

Two good-looking Marine Sergeants, the author's father, Arthur C. Ferrington (left), and one of the original Marinettes: both Sharpshooters with the Model .03 Springfield rifle.

Kittabel McMinn Farrington, the author's mother, in a 1919 photo, upon her graduation from Baylor University. She married the author's father in 1920 and subsequently worked in the World War II war effort in Washington, D.C. She retired after 30 years of government service, in 1960.

A Wildcat also appeared, with three Zeros on his tail! Sergeant Stinson and Private 1st Class Leffler opened up right in front of me with our twin 20mm guns and, according to my diary, "saved Grumman." I noted that the pilot had made a "beautiful landing on our field with flat tire and shot oil line."

As this second fighter strip was not yet completed, we just knew that the Wildcat was bound to crash in the deep and soft sand. That's why, my diary adds, "The landing was beautiful. Stopped near our hole." With tears in his eyes, the short Lieutenant told us that this had been his first time up and, as ordered, he had expended all of his ammunition on the Japanese soldiers aboard the transports, in the water wading ashore, and on the beach; and, thus, he was unable to defend himself.

My diary notes that he said the "AA had saved him." He thanked us, and asked the squad to guard his plane, as he would be back for it.

By Thursday, October 29, 1942, we hated his Grumman, as the Jap artillery used it as an aiming stake to zero in on the 11th Marine Artillery batteries set up near us. We raided the plane, looking for food naturally, but came up with only what

This is the type of Walrus spotter plane from the HMAS *Canberra* that was orphaned on Saturday night, August 8, 1942, when its ship was sunk by the Japanese Imperial Navy in Iron-Bottom Sound off Guadalcanal Island, British Solomon Islands. The aircraft was taxiing just beyond the wave line off Red Beach the next morning as the author's unit was headed up the coast trail toward the Japanese airfield.

was in the pilot's rubber boat for survival — a canteen of water, fish hooks, line, red cloth (bait), a folding knife, a Navy whistle, and some flares. I still have the whistle.

I am positive, these many years after the war, that the decision to station the 1st Marine Division in the state of Victoria, southern Australia, in 1943, after the Guadalcanal Campaign, was the best that could have been made. All our needs were met: training, refitting, regaining our health, great food, wonderful girls, appreciation — and, of course, Ballarat beer and Carlton Bitter.

Most of the 1st Marine Division was billeted in six-man tents in Melbourne and its environs while our tanks, artillery, and my outfit, the 1st Special Weapons Battalion (antiaircraft and anti-tank), was tented in the City Park (Victoria Park) of Ballarat, about 75 miles north of Melbourne. It was the middle of the Australian summer, but we were still cold at night in comparison to the temperature we had experienced at the Equator, and I slept under six warm blankets on a straw tick until my blood thickened.

Liberty for a long while was from 1300 to 0700 hours. Great beer and stout were the beverages of choice, and steak and eggs and meat pies topped the menu. Of course, if you ate in camp, you knew from the aroma that mutton was being continually served.

Ballarat had been a famous gold-mining town, and so I had a star made of Ballarat gold for my American Defense Ribbon, hammered out by a jeweler downtown on Dana Street. A few famous battles had been fought there — the Eureka Stockade for example.

We were able to get along with the Aussie girls, as they emulated the language of American movie stars in many cases. We could understand them much better than we could the Australian and New Zealand soldiers and airmen, who used such coarse language interspersed with so many unknown slang words that they were virtually unintelligible. The frequent dances at the Masonic lodge, and St. Patrick's and St. Alipius parishes, and the Old Time Dances (barn dances) provided the opportunity to meet and date many of the beautiful sheilas (girls).

Ellie Marchbank, the author's friend in Melbourne, Victoria, Australia, in 1943.

   While in Ballarat, however, I spent a month in an Australian military hospital with malaria. The VADs — Voluntary Aid Detachment — were great nurses who put up with no horseplay, even dumping over bunks with men in them when things got out of hand. We also had other pretty AWAS nurses (Australian Women's Army Service), as well as doctors and aides. Our medicine was liquid quinine, Atabrine, and an unknown pill. Many of my girlfriends and buddies visited, and we were allowed out on liberty in blue trousers, white shirt, and red tie so that no pub owners would serve us beer. (Needless to say, that did not work.)

We were paid fifteen Australian pounds every two weeks. I bought a Quale bicycle for twelve pounds, and when we left in September I gave it to a girlfriend. I also bought a Brewer tennis racquet for four pounds, five shillings (one shilling equaled sixteen cents, so one pound equaled $3.20).

I played quite a bit of tennis with my best friend, R.D. Phillips, Private 1st Class Leffler, and once with platoon Sergeant Hogan. At the conclusion of the match with Hogan, I had to duck his thrown Aussie racquet, which broke in two at the throat when it smashed into a fence. He had planned on beating me ever since our service in Cuba — but no go!

Once the winter of '43 arrived in April and May, tennis ceased, and Bubbles and Margaret MacDonald, two lovely Australian young ladies, took R.D. and me sailing in their boat on Ballarat Lake (Lake Wendouree) — the hardest and most injurious work that anyone can do in the name of "having fun." Never again!

Poor old R.D. was later sent home from the war with what was officially listed as a "strain." I have never seen nor heard from or about him since.

My diary of March 6, 1943, notes:

6 Mar 43. Aussie soldiers who have been in Tobruk for 2 yrs. have returned. [*They were the famous Desert Rats of Tobruk.*] Nazis dropped propaganda telling them that while they were fighting, the U.S. soldiers were taking their girls. [*Too right, we were doing our best, although we were not soldiers — we were Marines!*]

They gave Marines 'til 1:00 Sat. night to get out of Melb.

Marines given 100% liberty in dungarees [*in work clothes, instead of our Class A dress uniforms*].

Score [*number of troops*] in Hospital — Aussies = 72, Marines = 7.

7 Mar 43. Fight in Melb. continuing.

8 Mar 43. Score of Aussies over 200.

We in Ballarat were given no liberty or passes to Melbourne. We heard that the dungaree-clad Marines wore their Sam Browne belts with heavy brass buckles to counteract the hobnailed boots of the "Diggers" — the Australian soldiers.

Reggie (Arthur C. Farrington), Ellie Marchbank, and Roy Harmon in Melbourne, Australia, 1943.

Below: This Japanese occupation bill, to be spent in Australia, was worth eight cents American at the time.

It was a cold winter Down Under, but we live-fired our .50-caliber Browning machine guns, our twin 20mm Oerlikon cannons, and our newly acquired 40mm Bofors antiaircraft guns out over the water down in Geelong. The lack of good restrooms in that cold led to what appeared to be a battery of "underdeveloped" twelve-year-olds in the showers once we returned to our camp in Ballarat — if you get my drift. It was bad enough that the showers were outdoors, but in my life I have never anywhere seen snowflakes the size of the palm of your hand!

We had many wild adventures while in Australia, but I just can't forget our maneuvers in the countryside. The flies were God-awful. They had absolutely no respect for the short-tailed sheep, and did not understand being "brushed off." We learned this very early on to our disgust. To the flies, we were sheep with no way to be rid of them. After flailing away for a while, to no effect, we would soon smack our arms and faces and *voilà*, a hand and face covered with their remains. You either had to bear with them going for your eyes and mouth, or diligently try to brush them away.

We boarded the HMAS (His Majesty's Australian Ship) *Manoora* in the winter of 1943 for landings on Victoria's shores. Some 58 years later, on September 3, 2001, the HMAS (substitute *Her* for *His*) *Manoora* took aboard 438 Afghani refugees for transport to New Guinea! Was it the same ship, or a namesake?

While Down Under, we were issued Australian-made Eisenhower jackets and U.S. Army trousers, shoes, and other clothing to tide us over until some U.S. Marine Corps gear arrived. The jackets were great, and I still wear mine. The 1st Marine Division patch was issued and sewed onto the right arm, but later orders were issued to move it to the left. The Aussie girls really knew how to stitch, and the patches looked beautiful with the red embroidered borders.

Our .03 Springfield rifles were turned in, and we were reissued M-1 Garands and M-1 carbines. The Colt .45 pistol stayed, as did the BAR (Browning automatic rifle). The flame-thrower and 2.36 rocket launcher (bazooka) were added to our arsenal. The hand grenades were painted green rather than orange.

We were now ready to go after the Japs again.

Clive Turnbull's *A Concise History of Australia* (1965) notes:

> Scarcely anything material remains to remind Australians
> of this period when huge numbers of American troops were

quartered in their country. . . . It's possible that in the years to come pieces of rusted bulldozer, Coca-Cola shards and miraculously preserved beer-cans will find an honored place in Australian village museums as a reminder of that period in the twentieth century when it seemed that a new Rome was on the march. (*pp. 162-163*)

Sergeant Stinson was still our squad leader at this time, but our jobs had changed a little, due to converting from the 20mm Oerlikon to the 40mm Bofors gun. As a newly promoted Corporal (I always have considered it a "sympathy" warrant), I was assigned the distinctive duty of setting the range on a machine called a "director." One man was on each side of the director; their eyes were on scopes fitted with crosshairs. Their duty was to keep the target in the center of the crosshairs; mine was to set the range ahead of the target so that the aircraft would run into the stream of shells that the loader would provide and the gunner would fire. Unlike the 20mm, these shells would self-destruct if they missed the target. Now, A Battery had 40mm guns for bombers, and twin 20mm and .50-caliber machine guns for strafing and dive-bombing Japanese aircraft.

As we had much down time, I was able to keep a diary of sorts until the breakup of the 1st Special Weapons Battalion about May 20, 1944.

We left Ballarat at 1130 hours Wednesday morning, September 22nd, 1943, and arrived at Station Pier, Melbourne, at 1330 hours. We set up cots on the pier and immediately began loading ship. We worked three days and nights, and finally on Saturday we boarded the Liberty Ship *Boutwell*. Battery A set up our 40mm and 20mm guns topside, and we were given our last shore leave. Corporal W. A. "Woody" Wood and I then went ice skating at St. Kilda's Luna Park.

Chapter 1

New Guinea —
The Marines Are Coming

*O*N SUNDAY, September 26, 1943, we pulled out into Melbourne Bay. My diary describes the scene and what we subsequently experienced.

Girls on piers crying and waving.

Left Melbourne at 4 A.M. with 8 other ships. Aussie cans [*destroyers*], corvettes & sub chasers along.

Tues. At sea! Merchant Marine really makes the dough. If a bomb lands within a mile they receive $125.00 bonus.

Fri. At sea! Not anyone sick hardly. Gun watch 9-3. Avro Ansons [*Australian reconnaissance bomber*], Beauforts [*Australian torpedo-bombers*], and Vultee Vengeances [*American dive-bomber*] around.

Sat. At sea! Saw whales. Lots of tropical islands. Pretty decent chow.

Sun. At sea! PBYs around [*PBY Catalina flying boats — we didn't know for certain if they were the U.S. Navy's or the Australian Navy's.*]

Mon. At sea! [*Arrived at*] Townsville, Queensland, Australia 10:30 A.M. Anchored in bay.

Tues. At sea! Left Townsville.

Wed. At sea! Saw Red Cross ship [*Australian*] TASMAN.

Fri. At sea! Sighted New Guinea. Passed Milne Bay. [*The 5th Marine Regiment (the "5th Marines") was staged here and the 7th Marine Regiment (the "7th Marines") was staged farther up the New Guinea coast at Oro Bay.*]

[**Fri.**] 10-11 A.M. All ships . . . but three Liberty Ships [*passed*]. [*Arrived at*] 7:00 P.M. Goodenough Is. Air Raid. 8-10 P.M. Island's third. Beaufort bomber and gas truck hit on airport 10 mi. to N.

Sat. Unloading ship. [*The 1st Marine Regiment was staged here on Goodenough Island, about 50 miles off the eastern tip of New Guinea in the D'Entrecasteaux Group.*]

Sun. Unloading ship. Hitchhiked to future camp & went around airport. Bostons, Beauforts, Beaufighters, Kittyhawks, Tiger Moth, Dragonfly, Boomerang. [*The Bostons and Kittyhawks (P-40) were American-made, the rest were Australian or New Zealand-made.*]

Mon. Finished unloading ship. Tents set up 4 mi. N. of airport. Working parties.

Tues. Setting up camp. Have to wear all clothes. Can't roll sleeves up due to a typhus scare.

Sun. Visited Gook Village with Woody. 3 Pict. Send to Jack, Gov't Boy, Goodenough. [*Jack was one of the natives on Goodenough Island. He was in the employ of the Australian government, representing it with the tribes, and thus was called the "Government Boy." I finally sent the pictures a few years ago, but never did hear if Jack received them. I'm sure that they got into the right hands, however.*]

Sunday, 28 October. Roll sleeves up.

Saturday, November 6. Dug in 40s at beach.

Sunday. Fired 42 rds. 40mm ammo.

Thursday, 11 November. My 21st Birthday. Really

good. Guys sang Happy Birthday all day. All the turkey I could eat!

Friday. Saw "Reveille with Beverly." [*This is the first time that we saw Frank Sinatra. How could the girls back home go crazy over that skinny guy? Ann Miller was in the picture too, and she is still around.*]

24 Nov. Fired 30 rds. 40mm [*high-explosive (HE) and armor-piercing (AP)*] at beach. Knocked hell out of target on water. Direct tracking. Rain.

Thanksgiving. Received Xmas [*package*] from Mom & Dottie. [*Dottie was a girl that my mother had befriended back in Washington, D.C. She had a heart condition and died before I returned home.*]

Sunday, 28 November. Saw Gary Cooper, Una Merkle [*actress*], Phyllis Brooks [*actress*], & Andy Acari [*musician*] at 1st Marines. Ate chow & put on good show. Rain. Damn good. 1st Division patches given to them. [*The entertainers had flown directly to Goodenough Island. The show was in a pouring rain and Gary Cooper told jokes, sang, and danced. It was really a pleasure for us to see the real "Sergeant York."*]

29 Nov. Smith in C Btry. died from typhus (Jap river fever). [*He had been a good friend of mine in the D.C. Marine Reserve Battalion. He was from Takoma Park, Maryland, a suburb of Washington, D.C.*] In field with 40s, leggings, & sleeves down.

3 Dec. Saw "Barkie's" show. [*Private Barkheimer had organized, written, and produced — with a lot of help — a musical show while we were stationed in Ballarat. It was really great with original songs, jokes, and musical numbers. Barkie had been in burlesque, had been married to the second Betty Boop voice-over girl, and had been around the world doing shows with his two sisters.*] 32nd Div. Army Band, best in [*Southwest Pacific*], and Aussie as a girl [*in the show*]. Damn good. Good music.

4 Dec. Fired .30 carbine. Good rifle.

6 Dec. Saw Barkie's show again at 71 Wing (USAAF).

Below: "Margie" and her son, on Goodenough Island.

Above: Arthur C. Farrington and the Headman with the "Fuzzie Wuzzies" on Goodenough Island in the D'Entrecasteaux Group (meaning "Between the Castles"), off the tip of eastern New Guinea, October 17, 1943. Next to the Headman is his brand-new wife.

Below: The Goodenough Island villagers with Corporal "Woody" Wood, in the rear, in the "uniform of the day," and Jack, the "Government Boy," saluting.

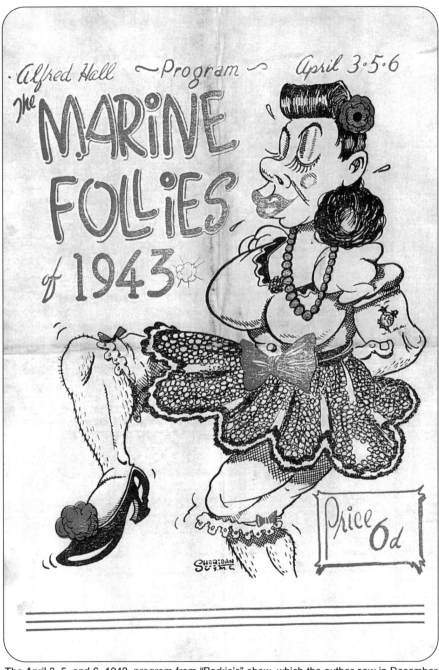

The April 3, 5, and 6, 1943, program from "Barkie's" show, which the author saw in December of 1943 on Goodenough Island.

The United States Marine Corp
"MARINE FOLL

Scenery:
Cpl. B. W. Shaffer, Cpl. W. J. Sheridan, Cpl. R. L. Gordon, Pfc. F. D. Walsh, Pvt. J. R. Scott, Pvt. T. Kane.

Wardrobe:
Pfc. E. Rieck, Pvt. C. L. White, Pvt. W. J. Conley.

Electricians:
Pfc. P. Berger, Sgt. S. Diamond, Sgt. J. Fernicola.

Make Up and Costumes:
Cpl. J. C. Mathis, Pfc. T. Robbins.

Producer - Chaplain

Director - -

Publicity Manager -

  - Assistant

Dances by Pvt. J
Comedy Skits by Pvt.

Tickets and Programs

Overture - - Cpl. Larry Sharkey and Orchestra

Prelude to Pagliacci - - - Cpl. E. W. Konecny

Master of Ceremonies - - Pvt. J. F. Berry, Jr.

Cpl. Larry Sharkey and Orchestra

Night Club Scene
    Ten stately, shapely Queens of the Chorus.
    Strip Tease, featuring that cute, curvacious charmer, Jacqueline.
        Cpl. J. C. Mathis

Tenor Solo - - - - - Pvt. J. Schmidt

Presenting the perfect argument for a two ocean navy - Pfc. L. D. Smith

Two jive artists in the groove with original tune by Pvt. C. White
    "The Jitterbug is jivin' for the Red, White and Blue"
        Sung by Pfc. L. Crawford with his dancing partner
            Pvt. H. G. Goralski

Sobriety - - - - Pvt. W. Barkhiemer

Glee Club featuring "One Lovely Tomorrow" by Pvt. C. White
        Directed by Cpl. R. D. Stewart

Comedy Skit   *"You don't have to be a Barber to be a Clip Artist"*
        Pvt. Berry, Pvt. Barkhiemer,
        Pvt. Hanson, Cpl. Mathis

Tenor Solo - - - - - Pfc. F. D. Walsh

Comedy Skit   *"A Day in a Rural Court House"*
    Pvt. Berry, Pvt. Barkheimer, Pvt. Kane, Cpl. Mathis

Guadalcanal Scene - *Featured Soloists in this scene*
    "Here I sit by a Bomb Proof Pit"
    Pvt. J. Schmidt, Sgt. J. Maynard, Cpl. B. Chapman

presents for your approval the

..ES OF 1943"

JAMES J. FITZGERALD

Lt. J. C. TURNACLIFF

.   Lt. G. S. NIXON

Directors -

.F. BERRY, Jr.

W. F. BARKHIEMER

.   Pvt. W. J. CONLEY

Art Work :

Cpl. W. W. Sheridan, Cpl. B. W. Shaffer.

Properties :

Sgt. H. Pelletier, Cpl. C. F. Lewandoski, Pvt. A. G. Saatzer, Pvt. W. D. Quigley, Pvt. A. M. Ortiz, Pvt. D. I. Duvall

Sound Effects

Mr. B. Secctrene, M. G. - J. W. Matchett, Cpl. W. Heffley, Pvt. J. Rhodes (A.I.F.)

Tap Routine - - - - -	Pvt. Berry
Hawaiian Scene	*The Del Monte Hawaiian Maidens and Queen of the Hula*
	Pvt. W. Barkhiemer

There will be a 15 Minute Intermission—Stay sober now.

Tapping Challenge - -	Pvt. Berry and Pvt. Barkhiemer

Hillbilly Group

Straight from the hills of Kentucky where corn comes in gallon jugs.

Featuring Pfc. F. Eckler

Under the Sea in a Nazi Sub.

With Commander Skunkfoatze

Featuring Pvt. T. Kane

How to secure a Husband - -	Pvt. Berry, Pvt. Duvall, Pvt. Barkhiemer, Cpl. Mathis
Tenor Solo - - - -	Cpl. E. W. Konecny
The Great Household Mystery	Pvt. Barkhiemer, Pvt. Duvall, Pfc. Smith, Cpl. Mathis
Accordion Solo - - -	Cpl. G. Nehoda

Finale

     Glee Club

     Rifle Team

     Rifle Exhibition - Cpl. Lewandoski, Pvt. Duvall

     Monologue - Lt. Turnacliff

     Salute to Fighting Men

National Anthems.

Acknowledgements

The Cast Gratefully ackowledges the co-operation of the Commanding Officers of all Units.

We thank the Men who stood duty for us while we were preparing "The Follies".

We extend our gratitude to the various persons and organizations in this vicinity who are in no small way responsible for the success of this Show.

To anyone who in any way helped us, whether it be Singing, Dancing, Coaching, Advertising, no matter what it might be, to you goes our fervent "Semper Fidelis".

Furniture by Tunbridges.   Flags by Harry Davies.

Ushers by V. W. S. C.

Scenery from Her Majesty's Theatre and Lt. W. Sutherland, A.M.F.

Stage Lighting and Spot by Mr. J. R. Blight.

Corsets by Lucas.

GLEE CLUB directed by Cpl. R. D. Stewart

Pfc. J. Krueger, Pfc. L. Crawford, Pfc. F. McDonald, Pvt. D. Heard, Pfc. M. Harrison, Pvt. W. Oddo, Pvt. J. Schmidt, Sgt. J. Maynard, Cpl. B. Chapman, Cpl. T. Mazarella, Cpl. W. Palmer, Pvt. W. Dixon, Pvt. O. Hefti, Pfc. G. Chapman, Pfc. F. Walsh.

DRILL TEAM

Pvt. A. Saatzer, Cpl. C. Lewandoski, Pvt. A. Ortiz, Pfc. D. Richardson, Pfc. M. Tutin, Pfc. B. Howard, Pfc. H. Martin, Pfc. R. Knapp, Pfc. C. Presnell, Sgt. H. Pelletier, Cpl. J. Walker, Cpl. K. Bales, Pvt. D. Duvall, Pfc. T. Robbins, Pvt. W. Quigley, Pfc. G. Bunch.

ORCHESTRA

Cpl. L. Sharkey, Pfc. J. Davidoff, Pfc. H. Beasley, Pvt. E. Hefti, Sgt. P. Muraine, Pfc. H. Harman, Pfc. C. Brooks, Cpl. G. Nehoda, Pvt. F. Eckler, Pfc. N. Cannon, Pfc. W. Putz, Pfc. F. Leibensberger.

CHORINES

Pvt. H. Goralski, Cpl. J. Mathis, Cpl. C. Lewandoski, Pvt. D. Duvall, Pvt. J. Hanson, Sgt. A. Pascale, Pfc. L. Smith, Cpl. C. Hurley, Cpl. K. Bales, Pvt. H. Clarke, Pfc. T. Robbins.

HILLBILLYS

Pfc. H. B. Harman, S. Sgt. P. F. Cisne, Pvt. E. Hefti, Sgt. C. J. Cotney, Pvt. F. Eckler.

FIGHTING MEN

U.S. M.C.—Cpl. K. W. Soncrainte   U.S. Navy—Sgt. J. Maynard
U.S. Army—Pfc. F. G. Hall
Australian Navy—Sgt. A. Pascale   Australian Army—Pfc. J. H. Scholz
Australian Air Force—Pfc. E. G. Fisher

Waller & Chester Pty. Ltd., Printers.

8 Dec. Goodbye. We are to leave in next three days on LSTs (Landing Ship, Tank) as part of the 21st Combat Team, 2nd Bn.1st Mar. 550 men on lighter, 2 for platoon, 2 40s & 2 .50s on one &1 40 & 2 20s on one. 24-hour trip. 2 days sea rations.

9 Dec. Taking rolls, khaki, cots, & tents. To Finschafen? [*New Guinea*] Not direct to action. [*The trip up the New Guinea coast to Finschafen was via LST; the lighters (LCTs — Landing Craft Tank) were to come later for our assault on New Britain Island.*]

That's all, folks. Dec 9 1943 A.C.F.

While we were in Australia, the following poetic tribute to the U.S. Marines appeared in a local newspaper:

Thanks for the Memories

Dedicated to the United States Marines [1st Marine Division]
Words by Audrey Gullet and Diana Gibson [Australians]

> To the U.S.M.C., Thanks for the Memory
> of coloured campaign bars
> Blossoms and Stars
> Of Rum and Cokes
> And Moron jokes
> And driving in Staff Cars
> (How lovely it was)
>
> Thanks for the Memory
> of castles in the Air
> Fingers in my hair
> Of Collins street
> And kisses sweet
> and
> Those medals that you wear
> (How lovely it was)

Thanks for the memory
Of evenings in your clubs
M. P.'s around the pubs
Of . . . drunks and fights
And . . . dreadful types
And . . . whirling jitterbugs
(How lovely it was?)

For manys the times that we feasted
and manys the times that we fasted
Gee it was swell while it lasted
We did have fun and no harm done — So
Thanks for the memory
Of sunburn on the shore
Lunch from 12 to 4
You might have been a headache
But you never were a bore
(How lovely it was)

Oh, manys the time that we flirted
I don't think we'll regret it
I know I shall never forget it
I loved you so
But there I go . . . So
Thanks for the memory
Of really good swing bands
Of Artie Shaw and Eleanor
And scribbling in the sand
How lovely it was!

Thanks for the memory of tidy little flats
Trying on your hats
And overcoats
And fishing boats
Of cozy fireside chats
Letters with little secrets
That couldn't be sent by Daywire
Too bad it had to go haywire
But that's all right, I sleep at nite

Thanks for the memory
Of St. Kilda's Esplanade
You took me home and . . . and stayed
Of Luna Park
And Gardens dark
Those football games you played
How lovely it was

Thanks for the memory
Of visits to the Zoo
Those crazy things you'd do
Of Southern drawls
Long distance calls
And dreams that won't come true
How lovely it was

Thanks for the memory
Of all that might have been
The things we might have seen
Of Texas Bare . . . And old Times Square
And . . . Life in New Orleans
How lovely it was

I was so sad when we parted
Although I knew you didn't care, Dear
I'd hopes all our dreams we might share, dear
But now I know
I was just snowed
But . . . Thanks for the memory
Of troops who'd been in strife
Kids who enjoyed life
Of love affairs, and foolish cares
And photos of your wife
How lovely it was!

Thanks for the memory
Of "Serenade In Blue"
That little beard you grew

I'm awfully glad I met you
And all the others too
I know I never should have hoped
That you could love me too
But all the same darling
Thanks to you so much!

Everywhere I go, except Korea, I plant vegetables. In Vietnam it was tomatoes, corn, and lima beans. When I left Goodenough Island, my lima beans were gigantic. I often wonder if besides bananas, sugar cane, coconuts, taro roots, papayas, heart of palm, and other edibles the natives on that tropical island are today blessed with lima beans.

10 Dec. Left Goodenough Is. Boarded LST #204 at 11:30 P.M. Fine ship. (380 ft. long, 75 ft. wide. Draught 7-10 ft. Mounted guns on deck.

11 Dec. 4 LSTs pulled out. 5:00 P.M. S.E.

12 Dec. Reached Buna [*New Guinea*]. Anchored in bay.

13 Dec. Left with 3 patrol boats. 4:00 P.M.

14 Dec. Beached 4 miles below Finschafen. 7 LSTs. Unloaded & set up tents in dense jungle. Front lines 26 mi. N.

19 Dec. Plane dropped 10 bombs. Killed some. P-47s, P-39s, & C-47s here [*Thunderbolts, Airacobras, Skytrains — "Gooney Birds"*]. 3 or 4 raids a night. Swimming in ocean 600 yds. every day. Sun tan. [*This is where we collected many beautiful hermit-crab shells. A match under the rear end would force an eviction, and we would provide a new home with a .45-caliber bullet brass shell case. You should have seen all the .45-caliber brass scuttling around in the surf! I also rescued 100 pages of a Papua, New Guinea, religious text with pictures, which I have attempted to translate over the years with little success.*]

Abe Podolsky (in a 1941 photograph taken in New River, North Carolina).

Playing Black Jack. Up to 23 pounds. [*We still used Aussie money.*]

22 Dec. Loaded gear on 4 recons [*small Ford reconnaissance trucks*]. . . . To beach. Issued jungle hammocks, 30-day supply Atabrine, Halazone [*for water purification*], and salt tablets. Also 3 K-rations & 3 D-rations. [*This D-ration was a large ersatz chocolate bar, which was good eaten or mixed with water to make a chocolate drink.*] Sent $75 Bond home from 40th Bn. C.B.s [*"Fighting Seabees" — Construction Battalion, attached to the 1st Marine Division*].

24 Dec. Rolled bed rolls and stored them, mosquito nets & excess gear. [*Our gear was now stored in Melbourne, Goodenough, and Finschafen.*]

25 Dec. [*Christmas Day*] Hiked to beach and jetties at 9:30 A.M. [*As the diary indicates, it took me forever to use military time — 0930 hours.*] I was assigned as a Runner [*messenger*] for Combat Team 21. Small box of Red Cross raisins for dinner. Johnson's 40 [*Bofors 40mm antiaircraft gun, with no truck to pull it*] on LCT #1, Castor's 40, Butler's 20, & Squire's .50 & two trucks with Lt. Alford on LCT #3. Graeff's 40, Truelove's 20, & Finney's .50 with two trucks. Caples & me on LCT #4. Boarded

14

4. Jesu kêtu ŋamalac 95

5. Simeoŋ agêc Ana seoc biŋ lasê kêpi ŋapalê Jesu.
(Luka 2, 21-40.)

1. Bêc 8 gêjaŋa, gocgo sêsa ŋapalê tau ma sê ênê ŋaê Jesu. Sêmoa e woke 6 gêjaŋa ma sêkôc eŋ sêja Jelusalem sebe natêtôc eŋ êndêŋ Apômtau to sêkêŋ da êtôm biŋ naŋ gêc Apômtaunê biŋsu gebe moŋgôm luagêc me balôsi ŋalatu luagêc.

Ŋac teŋ gêŋgôŋ Jelusalem ŋaê **Simeoŋ**, naŋ ŋac-gêdêŋ ôliandaŋ Anôtô gêôŋ Isilaeleneŋ biŋmalô gêmoa ma Ŋalau dabuŋ gêjam eŋ auc to gêwa sa gêdêŋ eŋ gebe ênam kauc gêmac e êlic Apômtaunê Kilisi acgom, tec Ŋalau kêkac eŋ kêsô lôm gêja. Josep agêc Malia sêkôc latuŋi Jesu sêsô sebe nasêŋgôm êtôm biŋsu ŋamêtê, ma Simeoŋ kêsip Jesu gêsac lêma ma kêlanem Anôtô gebe **Apômtau, galoc ôkôc nêm ŋacsakiŋ aê to têtac ma-lôgeŋ jawac êtôm nêm biŋ, gebe matocanô galic nêm moasiŋ ŋam.**

Tama agêc têna sê taêŋ biŋ naŋ kêpi ŋapalêŋa ma Simeoŋ gêjam mec êsêagêc ma kêsôm gêdêŋ têna Malia

Above and opposite: Pages from the Papua, New Guinea religious text, which the author found near Finschafen, New Guinea.

atom. Ma Juda sêjô eŋ awa gebe aêacma biŋsu gêc tec abe eŋ ênaŋa êtu biŋ taŋ kêsam tau kêtu Anôtônê latu.

4. Pilata gêŋô e kêtêc tau ŋanô jakêsô andu sêmêtôc biŋŋa gêja kêtiam ma kêsôm gêdêŋ Jesu gebe aôm aŋga ondoc e Jesu gêjam tau tôŋ. Tec Pilata kêsôm gêdêŋ eŋ gebe aôm gôjam taôm tôŋ aê me. Gôlicgac, aê katu ŋatau embe jasôm teŋ oc sêŋgamboac aôm su, ma embe jasôm teŋ oc sênac aôm ôpi ka. Ma Jesu gêjô eŋ awa gebe **embe Anoto lôlôcŋa êkêŋ êwiŋ atom, aôm oc ôtu aêŋoc ŋatau atom.**

Pilata gêŋô biŋ tonec ma gêjam daŋ gebe êŋgamboac eŋ su. Ma Juda sêmôêc sêôc aucgeŋ gebe embe ôŋgamboac ŋac tonec su oc kaisalanê ŋac aôm atom. Teŋ embe êŋgôm tau êtu konigi oc etoc tau sa êndêŋ kaisala, aêacma konigi masi, kaisala taugeŋ. Pilata gêŋô biŋ tonec su jakejoŋ Jesu kêsa awê, go gêŋgôŋsic gêŋgôŋ lêpôŋ sêmêtôc biŋŋa ma kêkic ênê biŋ gebe sênac eŋ êndu.

76. Sêjac Jesu kêpi ka.
(Matai 27, 31-38. Malaka 15, 20-28. Luka 23, 26-38. Joaŋ 19, 16-24.)

1. Lau siŋwaga sêsu Jesu susu e su, go sêkwalec ŋakwê asôsamuc su ma sêkêŋ eŋ kêsô taunê ŋakwê jasejoŋ eŋ sêja sebe sênac eŋ êpi ka. Sêsêlêŋ sêmoa e dêdac ŋac teŋ ŋaê Simoŋ aŋga Kuleŋ naŋ kêsa aŋga kôm gêmêŋ ma sêkac eŋ gebe êôc Jesunê kakesotau.

Lau taêsam têdaguc eŋ ma lauo ŋagêdô taêŋwalô eŋ ŋasec ma têtaŋ sêwiŋ sêja. Tec Jesu kêsa tau ôkwi ma

LCT 372 at 2 P.M. Shoved off at 4:00 P.M. On board: One amphibian tractor, one water trailer, two Jeeps, two re-cons [*trucks*], a 20, a 40, & supplies. Slept on deck. [*If you wished to relieve yourself, you had to hang out over the side, which was very exciting.*]

26 Dec. [A*t home in D.C., this was Christmas evening, 5 P.M.*] Up at 5:45. Ate K-ration. About 40 B-24s over towards Cape Gloucester airports. B-25s, -26s, P-47s, -39s & -38s around all day.

[*At this time my platoon was attached to the 2nd Battalion of the 1st Marine Regiment (Colonel Masters' Bastards — the Commanding Officer of the 2nd Battalion, 1st Marine Regiment) for the assault on Cape Gloucester between Tauali and Sag Sag on the west coast of New Britain. Our mission was to cut the trail to the southeast, prohibiting Japanese reinforcements coming from that direction — Arawe and Gasmata — coastal cities on New Britain Island.*]

We are about 7 miles off shore and watched ships shell up Gloucester way, also some Jap barges caught at sea. 11 B-25s bombed and strafed Sag Sag near our landing beach. 1st Wave hit at 8:00 A.M. 23 B-24s over, 9:00 A.M. Sat around in hot sun. We landed at 2:00 P.M. No opposition to landing. 3 Japs killed. Beach 5 ft. wide & bad. Amphibs pulled guns ashore. [*With*] 3 others [*I*] walked unawares 10 yards the other side of front lines. Began digging in 10 ft. from low tide. Guard. Plane dropped flare.

27 Dec. Rain all day. Wet most of time here on in. Bs [*bombers*] and Fs [*fighters*] over all day. Front lines set up 150 yds. N., 500 yds. E., & 800 yds. S. 37s, 50s, 30s [*37mm, .50-caliber, and .30-caliber small guns*], BARs, etc. Strong.

28 Dec. Rain every day constantly. Eat damn good 2 meals. Put in gun [*dug in the 40mm*]. Meals daily at 2nd Bn. Galley 20 yards away. Put [*dug*] in director [*the large box on legs with crosshairs for aiming the 40mm*] and generator [*to provide power for the director and gun*]. 7th

Marines at Cape Gloucester successful. Pushing S. to airport. Skirmishes here. Oriented and ready for anything.

29 Dec. Working party all day.

30 Dec. Japs attacked to E. at 3:00 A.M. after wind and rain storm. [*They*] cut wire, reformed, grenades, & charged our front lines but thrown back. Japs [*had*] .30 m.g. [*heavy machine gun*]. 2 Tenaru men went after, beat 'em over head with m.g. [*The Tenaru River men from Guadalcanal had wiped out the Ichiki Detachment at the Tenaru River battle on Guadalcanal.*] Mowed down Japs behind [*their*] lines. Daybreak. Marines bayoneted all dead and dying Japs but 4. Counted 74 Japs dead & buried. 6 Marines (dead). No count on mortar casualties. 5 snipers 50-100 yds. Kept us awake all night. 3 shot during night. 130 of 73rd Regiment Japs (Bataan & China) accounted for. Buried at 4 P.M. Test fired at 6 P.M. 2 rds. OK 5th [*Marines*] landing behind 7th [*up at the Cape*].

31 Dec. Quiet all night. 2 snipers killed last eve. Slept on beach. [*Our jungle hammocks were fine, but due to the Japanese mortar and artillery fire most of us dug a slit trench and hung the hammock down in it. The only trouble with this was that during a downpour the trench would fill up and we would be evicted.*] Repaired gun pit. Jap artillery registered 50 yards off shore. 7th [*Marines*] captured airport. Tank attack [*helped capture*]. 11th [*our artillery regiment*] moved 5 Packs [*75mm pack howitzers*] up E. ridge. [*I watched this take place in mud and muck up the steep ridge, with many men and ropes involved. It was no easy task manhandling the pieces into position, but thank God they did.*] Hear 11th 105s at Cape Gloucester. 2 Jap prisoners in hospital killed by Thompson sub-machine gun [*when they were*] escaping! 2 P.T. boats came in.

1 Jan. 1944. New Year's Day. No action last nite! Got cat's eyes [*beautiful small stones that look like a cat's eye*] on beach. Jap 70mm mt. [*mounted on wheels*] guns put 3 H.E. [*high-explosive*] shells 200-300 yds. in front of our gun! [*They*] moved into [*our*] mortar range to improve trajectory. [*Our*] 81mm mortars [*three*] fired 73 rds. in square at 2,300-2,400 yds. I observed fire. Japs knocked off. LCMs [*Landing Craft, Medium*] to Gloucester often. Japs fire artillery at the 7th [*Marines*] on airport! Russians on Lithuanian border. U.S. Navy [*will be*] as big as world's [*— biggest in the world*] in 1945.

2 Jan. Jap 2MB [*twin-engine bomber*] over last nite. Sick bay for New Guinea ear fungus. 2nd Bn 5th [*Marine Regiment*] (E Co.) walked here from Gloucester. 3 days. 1 casualty by own man. Saw old AA [*antiaircraft*] man (Tennessee Grimes). 11th Packs shelled Sag Sag at 2 P.M. 5th said M-5 Shermans [*tanks*] (really M-4s) attacked pillboxes perfectly. 5th on barges to . . . ? [*They went south for a landing.*]

3 Jan. Jap "Mavis" flying boat(?) [*four-engined*] over. Dropped load on Gloucester. 12th Defense [*Battalion, attached to 1st Marine Division*] AA & Searchlights. 11th shelled Sag Sag at 2 P.M. Sun out all day. Corn fritters, pancakes, beans, hominy, sausage, ketchup, hash, soup, prunes, fruit, corned beef. Sick bay, fungus, hurt like hell. [*The corpsman would scrape the scabs off, paint the area with alcohol, and blow powdered sulpha into my ears.*]

4 Jan. "Mavis" over again. Sick Bay. G. R. Weiland (later killed on Peleliu) & "Whitey" left by boat for Gloucester.

5 Jan. Left Guadalcanal a year ago today. Rain all nite. Big storm. Bulldozer pulled 40 [*mm cannon*] out of pit. No guard tonite.

6 Jan. Rain all nite. Cat eyes. Diarrhea. Reading *Guadalcanal Diary* [*by Richard Tregaskis*].

7 Jan. Working party all day. Big mortar and grenade battle last nite. No Japs. Set up gun. 3 K-rations.

8 Jan. Up early. Gear & gun to LCMs. . . . I left Sag Sag area 4:00 P.M. on recon truck with Porcher, Anderson, and a corpsman. We rode 23 miles to Gloucester.

At about this time, I heard that Sergeant Bradbeer from the Detroit 17th Battalion Marine Reserves (which had combined with the Washington, D.C., 5th Battalion in 1940), now was a Lieutenant and chief scout of the 1st Marine Division and had thoroughly evaluated our landing areas as an Alamo Scout. (Alamo was the code word for the Sixth Army.) He had done this in September, three months before our landings. Another outstanding man from the 17th Battalion was Lieutenant Rust, who as a Staff Sergeant had used me as his runner back in 1940. Later, we both were promoted to Warrant Officer and served together for the last time at Camp Joseph H. Pendleton, California, in 1956.

Our gun position consisted of our 40mm and a .50 caliber. We were in positions on Borgen Bay, north of the landing area at Cape Gloucester, with the last at the foot of Hill 660. I re-enlisted for four years on Cape Gloucester with Major Raymond G. Davis, the 1st Special Weapons Battalion Commanding Officer, doing the honors.

I also collected many souvenirs including a Japanese .25-caliber sniper rifle, which I was able to send home. I visited all the front lines, including Target Hill, Hill 660, and Walt's Ridge.

But here, I have to cover one three-day action of the 5th Marines.

21 Jan. Patrol going along shore [*in boats*] other side of bay. [*This was Borgen Bay and our gun position was just across from the action.*] Patrol ran into opposition. [*Enemy*] shells dropped by boats.

22 Jan. Amphibious truck [*DUKW or "Duck"*] with 108 self-propelled rockets (10 lbs. TNT) just shelled hell out of beach & 1st Bn., 5th hit beach. 11th shelled ahead of them all day. Duck repeated same. Some sight. 155s [*howitzers*] shelled barges in rivers.

23 Jan. Rocket-firing boat shelled point after 12-15 B-26s (Martin "Marauders") or A-20s (Douglas "Havocs") skip-bombed and strafed for about ½ hr. You could see the bombs hit the water and skip into their targets. Two Sherman tanks went up the beach shelling pillboxes and riding over them. We could see them and Infantry advance clean to the point. Jap mortars or 77s began shelling bay

Cpl. Arthur C. Farrington, USMC.
"D" Btry., 1st. Spl. Wps. Bn.
First Mar. Div., FMF.
% Fleet P.O., S.F., Cal.

Dear Mom,

I have just a few minutes before chow so this has to be short if I want to mail this today. This is my shipping over money. I received a new record book beginning April 1st. and so this is all the money I had coming. Enclosed is $220.00. Let me know if it all arrives okay.

How many of my packages have you received now. I got one from you day before yesterday with the candy in the red cake box. It's darn good.

_____ the other day Mom and I saw a little Army nurse. She was on _____ and she had a shoulder holster and .45, a ball cap, second louie's bar, dungarees, and boots.

Well, that's all for now.
                              Love, Reggie

A censored letter from Arthur Farrington sent from New Britain Island in April 1944 to his mother. He had just "shipped over" for four more years in the U.S. Marine Corps.

around boats and beach. One landed 50 yards in front of our gun. Action all day.

23 Apr. The transports USS *Adams, Hayes, Jackson,* one other, and two cargo ships anchored off shore loaded with Army from Guadalcanal. [*Over the next few weeks the 1st Marine Division left New Britain Island. The scuttlebutt was that we were going to New Ireland but we headed for the Solomon Islands.*]

29 Apr., Saturday. Arrived Pavuvu Island, Russell Island Group, British Solomon Islands. Set up in Palm groves on Pavuvu Bay. Coconuts, barracuda, sharks, crocodiles. MUD, movies, K- & 10-in-1 rations for 3 days [*one 10-in-1 package could feed ten men for one day*]. Saw three movies and some training films. Scuttlebutt: Going home. [*Special Weapons*] busting up A Btry. by May 20. Turned all gear in (incl. rifles) except pack, belt, canteen, & first-aid pack. My infected toe healing. MUD. Old guys (Guadal vets) got choice of outfits. Antiaircraft & tanks going to Amphibious Force. I selected 11th Marines.

Personally, I had a ball in the Solomons. I was very successful on the IQ test (which later helped me matriculate at UCLA). I played volleyball (spraining my ankle on D-Day, June 6th); encountered my first "colored" Marines; saw my first War Dogs (ferocious Dobermans); saw Jerry Cologna waving out the window of a Piper Cub as it was landing with Bob Hope; went to engineer school to become my platoon's demolition, bazooka, or flame-thrower man (I chose demolitions); and was able to remain a member of the 1st Marine Division as a fire-team leader in K-3-7 (K Company, 3rd Battalion, 7th Marine Regiment) when the 1st Special Weapons Battalion was broken up on May 20, 1944.

Some 260 officers and 4,600 enlisted men were rotated back to the States, and replacements came in. The rest of us "old guys" would have to make our third campaign, for according to the III Amphibious Corps personnel officer, "There just aren't enough men in the Marine Corps." But, we were told, the Corps now had women (WRs — Women Reserves).

And, thus, not only were we remaining friends and buddies (peons) from 1940-1941 divided up between the 1st, 5th, and 7th Marine Infantry Regiments and the 11th Artillery Regiment, Tanks, etc., but now we were among strangers and new replacements. It was like starting over. However, *now finally*, no more heavy equipment to haul around, clean, and maintain. All I had was my M-1 rifle and pack, with just one added piece of gear — a demolition pack loaded with half-pound TNT blocks, 2½-pound blocks of C-3 and C-4 plastic explosives, primacord (a thick cord/wire with explosives inside), fuze, fuze lighters, No. 8 blasting caps, and "tire tape" (regular repair tape).

I enjoyed Pavuvu. Bill D. Ross describes it totally in Chapter 3 of *Peleliu, Tragic Triumph: The Untold Story of the Pacific War's Forgotten Battle* (1991), as does George McMillan in Chapters 16 and 17 of *The Old Breed* (1949).

10 May. Replacements (1,500) came in on USS *McCormick* from the States (East Coast) via New Caledonia. 16 colored marines. [*I had already met some earlier arrivals at Weapons Company, 7th Marine Regiment, as I described in* **The Leatherneck Boys**, *page 162.*]

11 May. Ekins, Deegan, & I looked over replacements and talked to colored Marine. Smart, used Marine slang, & likes the Corps. He gave us dope on States (Pachuco riots in California, rationing, 4-Fs, women in the service, etc.).

13 May. Bernetchey & I talked to replacements. Colored guy from 14th & U Streets (in D.C.).

14 May. Saw "Buffalo Bill." Beer, 3 bottles "Acme" (West Coast). Lousy.

15 May. Beer 5 bottles, 5 bottles Pepsi-Cola.

K Company, 3rd Battalion, 7th Marine Regiment, trained hard from May through August of 1944. All that we were told was that a "very bad one is coming up." I remember watching a demonstration of a new weapon for use on enemy caves. A volunteer lay down with a 60mm mortar with a large spring attached to it. He fired at a simulated cave from 30 to 40 yards away: great shot, great explosion, *beaucoup* shrapnel (high-explosive fragments), and a dazed gunner. He had been blown back in the dirt, and then, as the spring regathered itself, he was dragged forward. He was a mess, but the weapon was certified to be used, as it later was.

My memories also include the reporting of a madman with a knife, and guards were posted for a while. And as we had no electricity, I recall burning rags in bottles of mosquito repellant for light. I remember that I never missed an outdoor movie, and my buddy and I would sit on coconuts and play Euchre (five-card Bridge) until it became dark enough for the show.

Chapter 2

Peleliu — Hell Island — and Back

INALLY, IN AUGUST of 1944 we boarded an LST and I camped out on the weather deck with my buddy, Private O'Kelly. We shoved off and docked at Banika Island, a large U.S. Navy supply base nearby in the Russell Islands. A large entertainment show was going on, so O'Kelly and I took turns holding one another atop a coconut in order to see over the heads of the massed doggies and swabbies. There was Jack Benny with snow-white hair, and Carol Landis, the most beautiful movie actress you can imagine. At the Red Cross hut I defeated some Army guys at Ping-Pong and then the island champ in two out of three!

When this short interlude was over, we shoved off for the shore of Guadalcanal near a beached Japanese *Maru*, west of the Matanikau River. We boarded the amtracs down on the tank deck, the bow doors were opened, and out we splashed. Our tractor had a rotary airplane engine, and the air had become stifling hot as we had waited. Upon reaching the beach, we exited, holding our rifles with both arms, then collapsed right there, unable to continue for a while. Boy, we thought, the Japs were going to love us!

As I was *hors de combat* — out of action — for a while, with my taped-up badly sprained ankle from my volleyball accident, I was assigned as a runner. While making a "run," I got tangled up in some vines and fell face first onto a punji-like remnant of a sapling. A Japanese soldier in the past had cut it for his *fale* (lean-to), which was still there. He "got me" two years later. I pulled myself up off the impaler and finally located a corpsman who immediately poured sulpha powder in the wound on my lower right chin, applied a bandage from my first-aid pouch, and tagged me as being wounded. Upon making my way back to the beach, I was shunted from group to group as I was unable to talk due to the tightly bound bandage. Marines were running around wearing KIA (killed in action) and WIA (wounded in action) tags, to be placed on the dead and wounded, so no one took me seriously when I motioned to my face.

As I approached the Beach Master, with his flags and bullhorn, he kept looking up and down at me. He was watching the blood, which was now dripping onto the sand. He raised the bandage and had a sailor use the signal flags, calling in an LCVP (Landing Craft Vehicle, Personnel). It deposited me on an LST with a Navy Chief as medical officer. He cussed out the corpsman for using sulpha powder, as he now had to clean it all out with alcohol about three or four inches inside my cheek. After having the wound sewed up, I told him I thought that the corpsman had done fine. But the Chief queried me as to why sulpha tablets had not been used. You know the answer to that: our corpsmen did not have such "advanced" medical technology.

Luckily, I knew the number of my LST (which I now have no record of). A small boat was called alongside with signal flags, and I was safely deposited back aboard my seagoing home.

Before leaving for our next still unknown Japanese island, we pulled into Tulagi Harbor. A beer party had been planned, but naturally the Navy would not allow Marines loose on their island. Small boats were provided, and we poor seasick, pissed-off Marines were motored across Sealark Channel to Guadalcanal for our outing. Beer was doled out to the platoons, one per man, and we had a raffle for the one odd brew — I won.

I felt pretty lucky those days, as back in Australia I had flipped a coin to gauge my chances of getting home. Heads: yes. My first toss was heads, and I had survived "The Island," so heads was the ticket. I then flipped three more times, and the shilling successively came up heads. I had made it from Cape Gloucester, so now I felt lucky going into our next combat. I considered flipping again, but seeing as how I had one successful "heads" left for the next war, I was satisfied.

After twenty or more sickening miles back to Tulagi, we shoved off on September 4, 1944. Goodbye Florida, Tulagi, Gavutu, Tanambogo, and Savo Islands. So long Iron Bottom Sound and Guadalcanal. Others will be back to visit, but never I.

We were soon told that our objective was Peleliu Island in the Palau Islands of the Caroline Group. Few of us had heard of Peleliu, but we had heard much about the Japanese base at Truk Island, and worried about Truk for the 2,000 miles of slow plodding just south of it by our flat-bottomed ships.

The Japanese radio personality Tokyo Rose helped out, however, by playing our favorite music, which was broadcast over the ship's loud-speaker system. But, one day, she really shook us up. She came on the air and commenced to name all the ships in the Task Force transporting the 1st Marine Division, yet all we could see was our own ship in a long col-umn and a few destroyers and cargo ships. All the big ships — battleships, cruisers, and aircraft carriers — stayed over the horizon. We were cheer-ing, as our LSTs did not have names, and thus we thought she would not be able to identify us. Then disaster struck. Tokyo Rose said she did not want to leave out anyone, and proceeded with our LST numbers. Up in the bow, a volunteer was hung over the side by his heels to verify our number and, sure enough, as they say, our number had come up!

Then came the clincher. In a sing-song voice she told us, "We know where you're going." She named Peleliu, and added that some big Japs (she used the same language that we did) were waiting for us with newer and better weapons. Again, sure enough, the big Japs were the Special Naval Landing Force, armed with .32-caliber rifles and the largest caliber mortars that I have ever seen or heard about. Tokyo Rose was often our only entertainment — and we even appreciated her so-called propaganda! (In 1977, President Gerald Ford pardoned Iva Toguri D'Aquino — Tokyo Rose.)

As we sailed across the Equator again into the western Pacific, Private O'Kelly and I had much time on our hands. I thought I had heard men-tioned in demolition school that a new type of hand grenade was to be issued before the landing. In the past, brave Japanese soldiers, upon being the recipients of our hand-thrown grenades, had the presence of mind to throw them back. Well, one day we noticed that a case of supplies, which literally surrounded us on the open deck, was broken open. We investigated and saw the familiar grenade containers. We carefully untaped one and out slid a grenade with a thick cord entangled loosely near the body, attached to a heavy safety pin through the top. We had never seen anything like that; but, having just recently completed a course in demolitions, I realized that this piece of hardware was not safe! We threw it overboard, and it exploded upon hitting the water; then we lay low — "doggo" — until the excitement was over.

We learned later that these were the new grenades to be issued only to right-handed men. When thrown properly — in a spiral hopefully — the heavy cord would unwind, the large safety pin would fly out, and, upon striking anything, the grenade would detonate. But we never saw or heard of them being used.

Four days before "D" day for us, I had signed off a letter to my mother, "Goodbye, Mom!" My morale was low. On September 15, 1944, the usual shore bombardment by the U.S. Navy and aerial assault of Peleliu seemed to have proceeded well, so all boats and tractors were launched. But because the reef was cluttered with coral and man-made obstacles, the 3rd Battalion was pretty well shot up by enemy artillery, mortars, and machine-gun fire. Burning amtracs were everywhere, and the carnage continued. My platoon of Company K, 3rd Battalion, was lucky and came ashore on beach Orange 2, in the 5th Marine Regiment zone of action. We debarked as quickly as possible and charged across the beach to close with the enemy if present and to get under the barrage. My demolition pack was worn on my chest, and so I felt pretty safe from gunfire, as the TNT blocks and composition C-3 and C-4 could not be detonated by bullets or high-explosive fragments. The pack essentially served as a bulletproof vest. However, I believed I would be a goner if I became involved in a bayonet fight, because I was so loaded down.

While aboard the LST, I had stashed my blasting caps in my gas-mask carrier, as the caps were highly explosive and would detonate if struck by anything. Along with the caps was some "pogey" bait (candy); in years past, "pogeys" — ship's cabin boys — were given candy. The carrier bag was slung as low as possible down my left leg, as far as I could get it from my chest.

The vegetation on the island was completely torn to shreds and the smell of gunpowder and cordite was overpowering. Suddenly we came upon a giant tank trap, a deep ditch and embankment. The word was passed to drop our gas masks, lightening our load, as the Japs had not used any gas. We then proceeded to our right, trying to leave the 5th Marine Regiment zone. We soon became bogged down in a swamp, and I had to shit-can — dump — some of my TNT to get out. It was then that I remembered that my blasting caps were with the abandoned gas mask. I retraced my steps, and with all those people on that small island, I met no one on my 100-yard quest. No problems were encountered, so we continued on the attack with me replenishing my supply of TNT from the engineers.

I shall only mention once how terrible the nights are in combat, especially against the Japanese. I have thanked God many times that the Marines believe in and try to maintain all-around security. I have too often seen the results of ignoring this tactic.

Even though we had lost contact with the 5th Marines that first night, the following day we continued with the attack to the far shore of the island. But, tragically, 1st Lieutenant Galbreath was shot through the head, as many were later, and my fellow traveler, Private O'Kelly, was literally shredded by a Japanese Nambu machine gun. He died thrashing around in the sand right in front of our squad, who could do absolutely nothing except go right after the Japs who were responsible.

While on the east beach, our water and food began disappearing at night. The Captain mustered me to seal the caves that were in the nearby cliffs, as footprints were discovered in front of them. I made up some "shock charges" consisting of a half-pound block of TNT and a one-inch fuze with a match head taped in it. These charges were hand-thrown, with no more than a two-second delay to enable you to do your job without interference from the enemy. Two four-block charges were prepared for each cave entrance, and we were ready. I had one of the squad's BAR men fire a magazine or two at each entrance as I ran to the opening and threw the shock charges inside as far as possible. The two main charges, connected together with primacord, were then installed in the caves and the fuze lighters were pulled. We had good results, and no more pilfering or worse by roaming Japanese.

We sacked out in sleeping holes one night just in front of a battery of

155mm Long Tom six-inch guns, our largest artillery pieces, firing direct fire. (If they had fired indirect fire, they would have missed the whole island!) Talk about "bouncing out of bed" — well, we did just that. What a racket and concussion! My ankle felt better, so I removed my leggings, boondockers (high-top field shoes), and bandage. What a smell! I peeled off the quarter-inch of dead white skin that had built up over the previous month.

We fought the Nips in this swampy jungle for a few days. I relieved one of their casualties of his good-luck charm, a .32-caliber pistol bullet and a .25-caliber rifle bullet on a shoelace. I wear the bullets to this day to all of our reunions where we try to fondly remember our buddies who did not make it or were horribly wounded. I hope the Japanese soldier's family and buddies remember him. They never received his last postcard home.

We straggled over to the west side of the island and attacked into the southwest hills for three horrible days, then on to the west road for a day and up into the west hills to "Suicide Ridge," as we called it. One of the replacements, Private Schoonover, and my squad leader were killed there. Sergeant Carter had climbed a blasted tree for a better view and was immediately shot through the head. The film clip of his body being recovered is included in the color motion picture *Fury in the Pacific*, produced on Peleliu. During 1959-1961, I watched this film many times, as it was available for showing to each class of Haitian NCOs that I advised during my postwar tour of duty there. I always closed my eyes at the part showing Sergeant Carter.

On Peleliu, the Japanese had an artillery piece that was periodically rolled out and fired at our left flank. The word was passed to me that Corporal Gaffney, one of my best friends in Australia, had been killed by it. He was blown over a cliff. One particular day, when our company command post, about five yards behind and below our front lines, heard noises coming from below them, I was called. I buried a large charge, which blew away the worries of some cave-dwelling Japanese.

On the way down from this position after three days, we passed a group of black Marines coming up with stretchers. We were proud of them for going forward to the front, scared as we all were most of the time on that Hell-hole island.

As we continued down, we got a little break near the west road and observed some odd reinforcements marching by toward the front. Old,

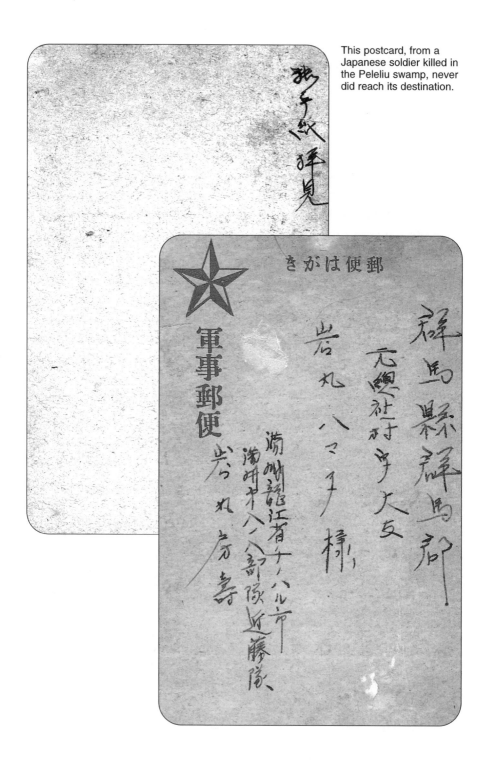

This postcard, from a Japanese soldier killed in the Peleliu swamp, never did reach its destination.

bearded, dirty, and dressed differently — but welcome — these men were part of the 81st "Wildcat" Division of the U.S. Army who had captured Angaur Island, just below Peleliu. They were needed, as our 1st Marine Regiment had been decimated and pulled off the lines. We immediately stopped referring to the 81st as the "Pussycats." I had heard that a boyhood buddy of mine, George Scott, who had lived just a few houses down from me in D.C., was an officer in that division, but I never did run across him.

While on Peleliu we ate anything we could get our hands on, and some of us waded out into the sea for food. One day, while I was heating some crustaceans in my canteen cup, my imagination was racing and I thought I heard a cry. Later I wrote a vignette of this experience, from the viewpoint of those crustaceans, which I shall include here, called "C.Q. '44." C.Q. — "Seek You" — was a short-wave radio signal requesting an answer. The fantasy tale is silly perhaps, but maybe I was becoming "Asiatic."

And meanwhile, as we continued away from our previous position, we marched around to the east road and prepared to attack up a vital ridge.

C.Q. '44

Curséd bodies! Interminable the time it has taken Macro and I to make our way. But now, the sunlight is bright, the sound of softly breaking surf close by. The time is near when we shall make contact, plasm to plasm.

Contact with CalTech, clearance to land, a confrontation with an alien race imminent: all dashéd to bits through incredible chance. A call for help, a feminine voice, had suddenly crashéd into our senses.

"Earhart calling, Earhart calling. Seek you, seek you."

Rrrriipp! — We had been too low, sightseeing while coordinating our 0800 landing at the Salton Sea rendezvous. Now suddenly we had been plungéd into our native environment, but without our metallic appendages of locomotion.

How long ago had that been? But, no matter, we have made it; the breakthrough is near. The squirming and slithering is over. We, Malc and Macro, through silent seas, silent that is until ten time-frames ago. The far-off booming, more vibrant than actual sound, had erupted around us. We had crouchéd together in fear as waves of monsters passed overshell. What was happening? A celebration, a naval review, or simply nature on a rampage? But now, sunlight once again, the blue firmament, soft breezes, peace, calm — and this time, not only mental radio contact, but physical, real coming together.

We heard, *"Hey, J.D., here's some over here. Man, those K-rations are really rotten. Damn Japs got better, I know."*

This is it, dark, putteed legs coming nearer through the shallows. These aliens are large, indeed.

"Macro, your preparéd greeting sounds wonderful." He always is a calm coefficient, as we say.

"Greetings and salutations; we, Malc and Macro, bring felicitations from far-off Neptune . . . and so forth." I never was one for speeches. . . . But, no answer. They passéd by. Can it be? But no, we are expected.

"OK, Macro, I'll handle this. Professor Eichner of Palomar is expecting. . . ." That did it; here they come.

"Quickly now!" . . . Ah, that brief whiff of ozone was exhilarating. The transporter, quite crude, seems to be of aluminum, oblong in shape, stamped with "U.S.," and with a carrying handle. Comfortable though. But why are we among these insentient bivalves? This procedure seems strange; but, on with the business at hand.

"Young man, that was an excellent job, sorry we are late."

"What's that phrase? Oh, yes. . . . Take me to your leader!"

"There, Macro, I said it. You said I wouldn't dare. . . . What is this place? All rocks and coral. And our escort, why the metal helmet? He is filthy with cakéd hands and ragged green fatigues. His face is dirt-streakéd, but his eyes, they are terrible, red and staring."

"Here's some C-3 for yours, J.D. Don't sweat it, you'll love 'em."

"What's this? The water is becoming hot. . . . Macro, my God, Macro, contact them, contact them!"

"Greetings and salutations, we, Malc and . . ."

"OK, you guys, saddle up. Let's move out! Both sides of the road, 2nd, 3rd, and 1st Platoon in the rear. Off the road! Ten paces and keep it! Up ahead's where that stupid Colonel got it the other day. Big game hunt. Yeah, 'cept the 'animals' on Peleliu got guns too!"

"Come on, J.D., they're done now. Hurry, chow down!"

". . . It's hot, my God, it's hot! I'm being torn apart, covered with red sauce . . . *a-a-a-h*, n-o-o, not *THAT!* Seeee Q, Seeeee Q! . . ."

"Gee, J.D., did you hear somethin'?"

Termination.

Postscript

As a Corporal fire-team leader/demolition man serving with K Company, 3rd Battalion, 7th Marine Regiment, 1st Marine Division, on the island of Peleliu, Palau Islands, in October of 1944, I had a very disturbing experience. Now over 58 years later, the foregoing possible explanation has been offered. This unfortunate gourmet regrets to say, however, that the effort has in no way relieved his conscience.

Our Peleliu experience was described in the following vignette I had subsequently written, not long after the events.

Slaughter

October 3, 1944, Peleliu Island, Palau Island Group, Caroline Islands, the Western Pacific during World War II

On the 15th of September, 1944, the 1st Marine Division had assaulted the island of Peleliu and the 81st "Wildcat"

The "fantasy" of the sea is captured in this First Day Cover that submerged with the USS *Sailfish* (formerly the *Squalus*). The submarine sank the Japanese carrier *Chuyo* in December 1942. The *Chuyo* had just days before rescued twenty American sailors from the USS *Sculpin*, which had found the *Squalus* on the sea bottom in 1939.

U. S. S. SAILFISH

(*Ex-Squalus*)

Built at the U. S. Navy Yard, Portsmouth, New Hampshire

Keel Laid: October 18, 1937.   Launched: September 14, 1938
Commissioned: March 1, 1939.   Casualty off Portsmouth: May 23, 1939
Rescue of 33 Men: May 24-25, 1939.   Raised: September 13, 1939
Dry Dock: September 14 to October 16, 1939
By Executive Order of the President of the United States
Named "SAILFISH" - February 10, 1940
Commissioned: May 15, 1940
Lieut. Comdr. M. C. Mumma, Jr., Commanding Officer

Division of the U.S. Army had done the same on the sister island of Angaur, a few miles to the southwest. By October 1944, however, we had lost the 1st Marine Regiment, as it had been relieved by the U.S. Army's 321st Regiment on September 23. The 1st Marines had really been whittled down by the Japanese and would soon ship back to Pavuvu Island in the Solomons. So it was up to the 5th and 7th Marine Regiments, in concert with the 321st, to finish off this island in 115-degree heat.

As a Corporal fire-team leader and platoon demolition man with Company K, 3rd Battalion, 7th Marine Regiment (K-3-7), I was ready with the rest to charge across 100 yards of open area to capture what later became known by us as Hickox's Ridge (for our Lieutenant). (This ridge is listed in the official U.S. Marine Corps Monograph, *The Assault on Peleliu*, as Boyd Ridge.) The open area in front of us was covered by Japanese fire from the ridge to the front and from the hills to the right and left front. This was to be a real "over-the-top" assault.

During the charge, one of our new replacements, Private Rowe, was killed when he jumped into a shell hole unfortunately already occupied by a Japanese soldier. After bayoneting our buddy, the Jap rushed a Sherman tank, which had approached up a dirt road from the right; he was killed as he tried to attach a magnetic mine.

As we assaulted the ridge, I will never forget the horrible tableaux on the path. There, for all to see, was a stretcher with a dead Marine aboard and at each end a dead U.S. Navy corpsman. They looked like wax mannequins. The ridge was taken, and for the rest of the day we had the unfortunate view of Private Rowe's body lying in his shell hole.

Living at a 45-degree angle forces most of us to build foxholes out of available coral chunks, leaving an exit at the bottom rear of the horseshoe for Jap grenades to exit. Unfortunately, some did not do this, and in the ensuing nightly grenade fights, Marines were killed. This occurred right next to my position, when a grenade landed in a machine-gun squad's circular built-up position and did not exit.

The Japanese were just a few feet over the ridge in front of us and in strength on a ridge about 75 yards distant. One morning, to our complete surprise, we saw Marines climbing a brush-and-tree-covered pinnacle to our right front about 75 yards away. Who in the world had ordered this? Were they crazy? The Marines were completely at the mercy of the Japs.

We yelled for them to go back, but to no avail. I yelled to the company command post to rush up as many smoke and white phosphorus grenades as possible. The quiet was eerie. We saw our Marines climbing very slowly by clutching vines, rocks, and small trees. (One of these men, Nuckols, an old 1st Anti-aircraft Machine-Gun Battery (1AA1) man in Cuba, was armed with a rocket-firing bazooka. Battery A of the 1st Special Weapons Battalion had been formed out of 1AA1 in early 1942, and when it had divested itself of many of us Guadalcanal and Cape Gloucester veterans in May of 1944 back on the island of Pavuvu, some of us had volunteered for special duty as demolition men, bazooka men, or flame-thrower men and had been sent to a special school run by our engineer battalion.)

As the troops (later discovered to be members of our own Company L) reached the top, the Japanese opened up on the whole party. It was horrible. We had been furiously tearing into the cases of grenades that somehow had been located and brought up the side of the ridge to our position. We commenced hurling grenades of all types, trying to protect our men, at least from the Japs just in front of us; but we could do nothing about the ones on the far ridge. Just to my left, somebody hit a small tree with a WP (white phosphorous) grenade and with the scream "Grenade!" we all ducked for cover. I saw and heard Abe Podolsky falling down the cliff; he and his mess gear made a God-awful noise. Abe was another original 1AA1 man, and quite a character. He was unhurt.

Nobody was burned by the WP grenade, and the moment of

fear was gone. Through the rifts in the smoke to our front we could see and hear Marines falling and yelling. Later Nuckols told me that he threw his bazooka down from the spire and fell to the bottom, landing right next to it. He is one of the few who made it back safely with his weapon.

What a tragedy! Although it was out of our view, we could hear quite a battle going on at the bottom and in the gully that portions of L Company had invaded. One of my best friends, G. R. Weiland from Wisconsin, was killed there.

A Japanese machine gun also had been bothering us, and after firing a couple anti-tank grenades to no avail, I enlisted Corporal York. We were always hoping he would be promoted so that we could brag that we had served with "Sergeant York," the World War I film hero played by Gary Cooper.

I was going to indicate the location of the enemy machine gun so that York's squad could bring it under fire from the right while I fired some rifle grenades from the shoulder for more accuracy. We crawled up a few feet in front of my position to an old tree branch. I was on Corporal York's right as I pointed out the gun. Suddenly York's head fell forward and the sound of *"puh, puh, puh"* came from the far ridge. The air around us was punctuated, and chunks of coral were flying. Obviously, it was the telltale sound of a Tommy Gun that had been captured from the pinnacle the day before.

As I yelled *"Corpsman! Corpsman!"* at the top of my lungs, I put my arm around York's neck for support. His right cheek had a large blood clot on it. I told him that a bullet had grazed his cheek, but he did not answer. As more .45 slugs peppered our position, I noticed blood streaming down my left arm, then I saw a .45-caliber-size hole in the middle of York's neck. The bullet had entered his right cheek and exited his neck. I yelled again, *"Corpsman! Corpsman!"* and told York not to worry, that nothing important had been hit. I had noticed that there was no red/white bubbling, which neck wounds so often produced.

That was the last I saw or spoke to York, as the corpsman pulled him out of there by his feet. We later heard that he fully recovered in a hospital in the Admiralty Islands. I have always hoped that the information was true.

One day, at some risk, we lassoed and thereby "liberated" a Japanese machine gun from the ridge. It was a World War I Lewis Gun, with a round magazine on top, that had been used aboard Allied aircraft during that war. But before we could put it into action against the Japanese, some idiot field-stripped it and threw the parts down the slope.

My last remembrance of that place was really scary. As the platoon demolition man, I carried on my chest C-3, C-4, and TNT explosives. One afternoon I had just built a stove out of three pebbles and a glob of C-3, at the foot of my U-shaped position. My can of beans was bubbling, and I leaned forward to stir. *"Wham!"* From my position on my stomach, I could see smoke in my hole. I reached over and picked up a smashed red-hot Japanese .32-caliber bullet (which I still keep as a souvenir). We were never surprised to receive incoming fire of all calibers from all points of the compass on Peleliu, and that was one of the reasons some of us spent part of the day spread-eagled on the ground whenever the Japs sent over "air bursts," hoping for that "million dollar" wound that today's Forrest Gump could never understand. Thankfully, for some reason or other, no one ever seemed to get hit.

The left wall of my foxhole was built up a little more after that near miss. We always called our positions "holes," although they could be built up as on Peleliu, dug in as on Guadalcanal, covered in rice paddy dung and pee or built up with ice chunks as in Korea, or surrounded by sandbags as in Vietnam.

I considered October 22, 1944, to be one of the happiest days of my life when the USS *Sea Sturgeon* raised anchor and set sail for good old Pavuvu, Russell Islands. I left Peleliu behind forever. And I hoped that General MacArthur had appreciated our favor of "screening" his landing on Leyte, Philippine Islands, on October 20th.

The remaining men of Company K, 3rd Platoon, 7th Marine Regiment, 1st Marine Division — the author's unit — just before their final foray up into the ridges behind Umurbrogol Mountain on Peleliu Island.

Many more days of fighting ensued on Peleliu, most of them without seeing an enemy soldier. Our K Company got a break, with a few days spent on Ngabad Island off the northeast coast of Peleliu, stopping Jap reinforcements from arriving from the other islands to the north. Every time the tide would come in, it brought bloated dead bodies of Japanese soldiers. It was a terrible thing to see, especially when some Marines would use them as targets for rifle fire and the bodies would explode.

On the way to an island, in a DUKW, the amphibious 4x4 truck that we called a "Duck," in a very rough sea, one of our BAR men was bounced overboard. We informed the driver, who immediately made a very dangerous turn about. No one was in sight. Suddenly up popped the Private treading water, with all his equipment, including his BAR! What a strong guy. As we hauled him in, we believed we had seen a miracle.

We subsequently went back into the hills. One time we were on our way up and I had just liberated a new .32-caliber Jap rifle. I knew I could not keep it, with what was in the offing, so lo and behold as we were crossing the airstrip, I spied a sign in front of a pyramidal tent: "Seabees" — the

"Souvenirs" from the war: A wooden Japanese Dog Tag from the Tenaru River Battle on Guadalcanal, British Solomon Islands, August 21, 1942; and a metal Japanese Dog Tag from Hill 660, Cape Gloucester, New Britain, March 1944.

A Japanese Special Naval Landing Force headband, found on Peleliu; part of a flag belonging to one of Japanese Colonel Ichiki's soldier's, with well-wishes, from Tenaru River; and four aircraft pieces — sea-green camouflage, red graffiti, and the Japanese "meatball."

Corporal Arthur C. Farrington and a PBY Catalina on the airstrip of Peleliu Island, Palau Group, October 1944.

Jack Lartz, the author's boyhood friend (sitting, first row, right) and his buddies, in the 2nd Marine Raider Battalion on New Georgia, with a captured Japanese naval ensign.

Construction Battalion! I broke ranks, went inside, and there they were, sitting on the dirt floor. They had nothing to trade at all, so I gave the rifle to one of the men and told him, "You owe me one!" I collected in Danang, Vietnam, in 1968. The Chief in charge honored the trade.

On October 20th, K Company marched to Purple Beach to help load for our shove-off on October 22nd aboard the *Sea Sturgeon*. We arrived back at Pavuvu on October 30, 1944.

Quite a few old buddies from 1AA1 down in Cuba back in 1941 had been killed or wounded on Peleliu. At the 1st Marine Division reunion each year we remember them all.

In April 1944 we had arrived at Pavuvu Island, Russell Island Group, British Solomon Islands, after the Cape Gloucester Campaign. We left there for the Peleliu Campaign in August 1944, from where we returned to a different atmosphere. We saw a few Red Cross girls, but the rotten coconuts were gone. We had new accommodations, but mainly the island was overrun with replacements. I searched for remaining friends from A Battery of the 1st Special Weapons Battalion, my pre-Peleliu unit, and found that many were dead or wounded — in other words, gone. It was an unreal atmosphere and we "29-monthers" (our overseas time) were very uncomfortable. Fortunately, we soon got the word that we were going home.

Sure enough, it was aboard ship — a long cruise — and we were back in San Diego. We debarked, loaded aboard 6x6 trucks driven by women Marines, and were given a wild and scary ride to the Marine Corps Recruit Depot. Most of us had not traveled over 25 miles per hour in over two years, and few of us had ever seen a woman in the Corps. We were soon issued new clothing, including low-top shoes. Up to this time, we had only the high-top boondockers and high-top dress shoes. We spent most of our time standing in lines of all sorts — but the best was the beer line, where we were able to exchange five-cent tickets for an Aztec or Budweiser.

Most of us had lost contact with all our friends by that time, and thus we were strictly on our own as we boarded trains for the East. With freezing ankles, I debarked at Cincinnati and hiked through deep snow, carrying all I owned in a sea bag many blocks to another train depot. The heavy

Corporal Arthur C. Farrington, Jr., 283222, U.S. Marine Corps Reserve, December 1944. Drawing by Karen (Farrington) Berghorst.

Below: Arthur Farrington's home in Washington, D.C., at 5932 3rd Street, NW, with two "umbrella" (Indian Cigar) trees and the tip of the nose of his mother's blue 1937 Plymouth.

bag was loaded with Japanese souvenirs that I had collected, which were mostly made of iron. I finally arrived at Union Station in Washington, D.C., where my mother was waiting for me.

My first request was for warm socks that would keep my ankles from freezing. My mother drove me home in her blue 1937 Plymouth sedan. I was back, safe and sound!

⬝⟾ ⎯⎯ ⟸⬝

For the next 30 days, I made scrapbooks with all the newspaper and magazine articles that my mother had saved, and I visited friends and attended dances at several hotels in D.C., hosted by the various states. My old girlfriends had moved on, so I found a new one, Loretta Hayes, a Navy WAVE (Women Accepted for Volunteer Emergency Service) Yeomen 1st Class. She was very nice and got along well with my mother, but she was stationed in D.C., and I had to get back to active duty soon.

I was able to borrow a car from Mr. Lartz, the father of Jack, a boyhood friend, who was overseas with the 2nd Marine Raider Battalion. I was very thankful, as Washington was simply snowed- and iced-in at the time. In fact, one night coming home from a dance, I had a difficult time getting off Logan Circle

Flight Officer Robert Farrington, the author's brother (left), and Corporal Arthur C. Farrington, at home in December 1944.

Loretta Hayes, a U.S. Navy WAVE, Yeoman 1st Class, the author's date during December 1944, upon returning home from World War II.

Army Flight Officer Robert Farrington (left) and Marine Corporal Arthur C. Farrington trading uniforms at home in December 1944.

onto 13th Street. Fortunately, parking was not allowed on the edges of the circle; there was so much ice that the only way around was to crawl up against the curb.

My brother, who was a flight officer in the Army Air Corps, came home on leave as well, and we wore each others' uniforms to our church and to visit friends — we really messed with those civilian minds! Then on December 16, 1944, we heard the awful news that band leader Glenn Miller was missing, over the English Channel or over France.

When my leave was over, I went by Greyhound bus to Richmond,

Virginia, where I switched over to a Trailways with the seats along the
sides, just like the front and rear seats on our old D.C. streetcars. The
weather was cold and, naturally, we broke down in Whitakers, North Carolina, and had to wait until the next bus came along about 2½ hours later.
That bus was full, so we had to stand until we reached Rocky Mount. At
Jacksonville, North Carolina, I was happy to find that my sea bag just happened to have been loaded on the very bus I was on.

I reported in to Headquarters at Camp Lejeune, North Carolina, at 11:30
New Year's Eve night, December 31, 1944. This permanent base seemed
to be across New River from our old Tent City and some miles east. The
barracks were nice, with a large recreation room; the mess hall was 50 feet
out the door. My first day there I saw some women Marines playing tennis, so I made plans to play as well, and for a liberty pass. The Major said
we would be at Camp Lejeune for at least eight months before going back
overseas.

Much to my surprise, my MOS (Military Occupational Specialty) had
been changed from Infantry to Engineer. Prior to the September invasion
of Peleliu, I had volunteered for a two-week schooling on flame-throwers,
bazookas, and demolitions, with the 1st Engineer Battalion. The result was
that in addition to being a fire-team leader in my Infantry squad of Company K of the 3rd Battalion, 7th Marine Regiment, I was also the platoon
demolition man. Some clerk had changed my MOS number, so that I was
now assigned to an Engineer outfit called "Demolition Demonstration." It
seemed interesting, however, and when the other Marines decorated my
dungarees with little angels, complete with halos, using black paint and
stencils, I was sold. They really did a job on my jacket, putting Corporal
stripes, a hashmark (for four years of service), and two rows of campaign
ribbons. It was embarrassing. Our outfit was sent way out into the boondocks to a remote place called "The Engineer Stockade," away from
all other troops, recreational facilities, and women Marines for this
training.

Also to my surprise, the schooling was more on demolitions, flame-
throwers, and bazookas. We used explosives, mixed napalm, loaded and
fired flame-throwers, fired bazookas, and put on demonstrations for
all kinds of guests, civilians, women Marines, and Army troops. When
firing the bazookas, we had to wear goggles, as some of the propellant failed to burn due to the cold weather and would blast back into your
face.

I told my mother to forget about me becoming an officer. I did not have two years of college, and the V-12 accelerated college training program for potential officers did not appeal to me. We had four classes of Officer Candidate School OCSs at the base — Officer Candidates Awaiting we called them. They were really something. We demolition men taught about an hour of schooling on the carried 70-pound flame-thrower, and then we each took five OCS men at a time and let them fire it. One fellow could not even squeeze the grip at all; and in other training, one of the boys tried for two minutes to screw a large bolt upside down into a tank! The V-12s were called "America's secret weapon," but all that most of them knew was strictly from books. Four of us could load a 55-gallon petrol drum on a rack, but eight of them could not even move it! We wondered how they could become our future officers.

The demolition course was pretty rugged, and our class had been very lucky for in the other classes ten had been hurt, with three pretty seriously. One officer lost his left hand and two men were blinded. A couple more were hospitalized, but they would recover in a few weeks. The fellow whose hand was blown off had pulled a delay detonator, but it had no delay! He was lucky he did not have a big charge attached. The last week of the schooling we ran the assault course with explosives, flame-throwers, and bazookas.

Altogether I threw 35 short fuzes and only one was a dud. As our class was so small, we combined with an Infantry group to run the assault (on a fortified area), and we had no accidents. The wind was a bit strong, so a few guys were scorched slightly by the flame-throwers, but that could not be helped.

One Army Captain who had watched the assault was simply flabbergasted, for the Army is not allowed to use any fuze shorter than eighteen inches. Well, the Marines didn't use anything over six inches on the pack (satchel) charges, and one or two inches on the shock charges (which were thrown prior to the charge by the flame-thrower men and after the bazookas were fired). Of course, the satchel charges were the last to be deposited on the pillbox. The Army Captain, a technician who worked on flame-throwers, said that this was the first time he had ever seen the flame-thrower used as described "in the book." He was also surprised that we could move so freely with it, as it weighed 72 pounds. The "doggies" — the Army recruits — did not seem to be able to handle them.

Part of our training had included the method of assaulting a fortified position. Some of the steps might be omitted due to the lack of the necessary weapons, the terrain, the nature of the enemy, or other factors. First: rifle, machine-gun, and mortar fire. Second: bazooka or shoulder-fired 60mm mortars (used on Peleliu Island). Third: shock charges (short-fuzed, half-pound TNT blocks hand-thrown). Fourth: napalm if available (usually launched from amtracs or tanks), used against the apertures. If napalm was not available, the flame-thrower men assaulted the position using the regular load, which not only ignited ammunition but exhausted the oxygen within the position. Fifth: shaped-charge demolitions, placed to breach the position and destroy everything inside. (The description "shaped charge" is used to describe how most of the explosive power is directed in one tight direction.)

The men of the 45th Class received their diplomas on a Saturday morning, and I hit Kinston, North Carolina, for the weekend.

At about this time, we started using dynamite regularly for various engineering tasks. The result was headaches! The nitroglycerine was the cause.

Together with the intensely cold weather and no car, I did not make any more liberty runs. I had sold my 1932 Ford V-8 back in 1942 for $65, and never saw it again — nor my best girlfriend, Blanche, over in Dover, North Carolina. The Ford had a rumble seat and Blanche had sent me a picture of herself hitchhiking to see me while I was on Guadalcanal! Talk about a morale booster! Thank you Blanche Cannon! I shall always regret not seeing this lovely little girl again, but I was delaying until warmer weather and until I had finished with the dynamite. Incidentally, subsequently in 1946, in Los Angeles, I paid $500.55 for a 1932 Ford V-8 coupe just like the other one, but it had a turtle back instead of a rumble seat.

The Engineer Stockade in North Carolina (about ten miles outside the main base of Camp Lejeune) was just that. We ate, played Ping-Pong, and listened to "Don't Fence Me In" (which was really apropos), "Rum and Coca-Cola," and other new recordings on the juke box. My hut had two "bomb-happy" cats, and we slept under many blankets.

Then, suddenly everything changed. I wrote to my mother from Portsmouth, Virginia, on March 26, 1945, a Sunday.

I arrived back at camp (from D.C.) on time Monday and we were out in the boondocks really misbehaving, making toothpicks out of trees instead of simply uprooting them. Our mission was blowing gun positions for the artillery when a lieutenant rushed up and said that Watkins and I were supposed to have left at 1000. It was now 1015. But he said that they would wait 'til eleven for us. Well, we rode about four miles back to Courthouse Bay, got the dope, checked our health records out of the sick bay, rode bicycles a half mile to draw [*be issued*] camouflage dungarees, packed our sea bags, got dressed and boarded a truck at 1115. I'm telling you that's the fastest I ever did anything. We drove the 15 miles into the base and caught the 1200 bus to Jacksonville. At J-Ville we caught the Norfolk bus and arrived here at 1000 Monday night. We rate every night liberty here and everything is just fine.

We are waiting for a ship to be repaired so in the meantime it's fun, fun, fun.

They don't put the tennis nets up 'til 1 April here so I've been playing golf with a couple other fellows on the short course just outside the barracks. Yesterday afternoon we played 18 holes, this morning 9, this afternoon 18, and this evening after chow, 9 more!

One day we're riding in an open truck through the base when I see this group of predominately blond men wearing utilities with big P's stenciled on them. It occurs to me that they are German prisoners. I yell *"Was ist los?"* They all straighten up, smile, and one chases the truck for a while yelling: *"Nichts, nichts!"* The Navy chasers just stay relaxed. Where can he go?

A very sad thing occurs the evening of 12 Apr 45. Some of us are at a party in a women's barracks when the news comes over the radio that our Commander in Chief, president Franklin Delano Roosevelt, has died in Warm Springs, Georgia.

My address is now: Cpl. Arthur C. Farrington 283222
                       LST 512 Detachment
                       Marine Barracks, Norfolk Navy Yard
                       Portsmouth, Va.

At my new assignment in Portsmouth, we fifteen Marines, at least one from each of the six Marine divisions in the Pacific, moved aboard LST *512*, a U.S. Navy exhibition ship that would travel the U.S. ports to educate the American public on the role the U.S. Navy and Marines were playing in World War II. LST *512* is described in our shipboard publication, *History of the USS LST 512 United States Navy Traveling Exhibit Ship March 1945-January 1946*, which I have excerpted here:

History of the USS LST *512*

When the LST *512* was launched early in November 1943 at the Chicago Bridge and Iron Company in Seneca, Illinois, the assembled gathering felt certain that this ship would go through many historic campaigns. The turn of current events pointed to an invasion of the continent of Europe as well as accelerated action in the Pacific, yet few of those present realized what an unusual career faced the sturdy vessel. Several weeks after the launching, the officers and men of the combat and ferry crews moved aboard, got the ship underway, and sailed her down the Illinois and Mississippi Rivers to New Orleans where she was commissioned on January 8, 1944. This was followed by a shakedown cruise to Galveston, Texas, two weeks of intensive training, and a trip to New York for the loading of cargo. On March 14, 1944, she sailed for Europe, and arrived in England fourteen days later. Several months of waiting, training, and maneuvers followed. The week preceding June 6, 1944, was one of hard work and anxiety; troops, equipment, and supplies were loaded. When the time came to sail across the Channel, there was a noticeable tenseness aboard, yet the crew performed flawlessly. Upon reaching the Normandy Beachhead, the troops and equipment were unloaded under an amazing protection of support ships and a breathtaking cover of aircraft. Several hours later, she started back to England, reloaded, and subsequently made 20 trips to the Continent. In October a severe storm broached the ship on the beach in Normandy and broke her back. Salvage operations were undertaken, and the ship was towed off the beach and back to England for temporary repairs, before returning to the United States.

In January, 1945, when the USS LST *512* arrived in Norfolk, Virginia, the Secretary of the Navy and the Chief of Naval Operations designated it as a U.S. Navy Traveling Exhibition Ship, which would operate under the incentive division of the Navy Department. Next came many weeks of extensive Navy Yard work, for to transform a twisted, rusted wreck into an Exhibition Ship was a major undertaking. The ship was dry-docked, the warped center section was cut out and replaced with a new one, the engines were overhauled, exhibition bays were built, new superstructure was added, the mast and smoke stacks were made to fold up in order to clear low bridges, and the ship was painted in the green and brown Pacific camouflage. Specially selected new officers and men, all combat veterans, moved aboard. The officers and men of the Marine Detachment, representing every Pacific campaign, reported aboard; all hands worked tirelessly together to outfit the ship. On April 23, 1945, the Navy's first Exhibition Ship left Norfolk, Virginia, on the initial leg of her voyage to the Great Lakes.

The first port of call was Miami, Florida. This gay resort city with its dazzling sunshine, warm sandy beaches, and numerous night clubs was a pleasant change from gray, dingy Norfolk. Here tropical trees and plants were put aboard for the jungle, which was being built on the tank deck. A swimming party, supper, and dance was given for the men by the Miami Blackstone Hotel. When the ship left Miami for New Orleans, everyone was reluctant to leave, for the time had passed so quickly and pleasantly.

Together with the combat-tested sailors, we worked our asses off to ready the ship for public viewing.

I wrote to my mother aboard ship on the following Sunday and Monday nights, a week after we weighed anchor and left Portsmouth.

At Sea — They haven't put out any censorship regulations as yet so I'll just write what I think is OK. This will be mailed at

Miami I guess, where we are to pick up our display "jungle"! We have really been working I mean, to get this ship fixed up, and things are coming right along, strange as it may seem. We have nice sacks and pretty much room to get around in. The food is fine and we get all the fresh water we wish. We just had a few films run off down on the tank deck about Tarawa and the Marianas. I wish I had seen that "Fury in the Pacific." You said that was about Peleliu I believe. I did see a picture of some Corsairs dropping flame bombs on Bloody Nose Ridge and that path right in front sure did look familiar. . . .

30 Apr 45 Monday night — The lights of Miami are getting nearer and so we'll be docking in a few more hours. . . . Mom, Florida sure did look good this afternoon. We passed about ten miles from West Palm Beach and you could see some big hotels and lots of trees. The coast is really alive with lights. . . .
[*I guessed that the U-boats were off duty!*]

We pulled into Miami on Tuesday, May 1st, and began loading our 300+ potted plants and trees, logs, dead trees, eight truckloads of dirt, and Spanish moss. We really worked hard for four days, but miraculously we had four nights of liberty, plus a big party — swimming, supper, and dance — for the ship's company at the Blackstone Hotel out on Miami Beach. After a few Rum and Cokes, I took a dare and attempted to swim underwater the width of the large pool. I succeeded, but the pool had been painted a different color at the water line, and I almost killed myself when I hit the wall with my head!

The uniform of the day was khaki, and we were ordered to wear our division patches (1st Divy, 6th Divy, etc.) and our campaign ribbons, so that people would not mistake us for Army "doggies." But it did not seem to help much, as Marines were a rare and rather unknown commodity in those parts.

Eight or nine of us hung out together, and we usually rendezvoused at the Flagler Gardens restaurant where we went down in history with some photos. Les Brown and his band of renown was playing there with a little blonde singer — Doris Day — doing the honors at the microphone. We adopted one of her songs, "Sentimental Journey," as the theme song for

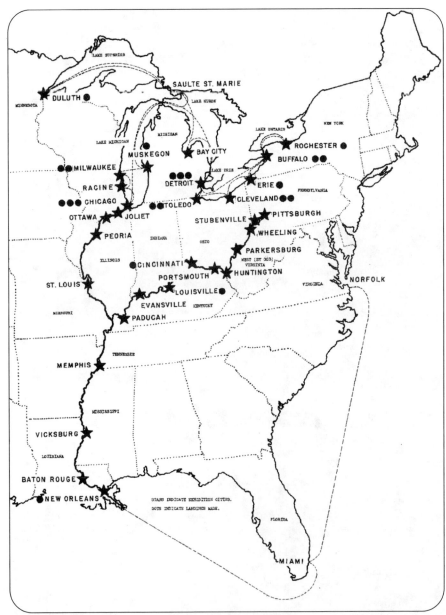

The 1945 route of LST *512*, the U.S. Navy Exhibition Ship, that demonstrated across the eastern third of the country the challenging and dangerous duties of the men of the U.S. Navy and U.S. Marine Corps during World War II.   *U.S. Marine Corps*

A group at the Flagler Gardens restaurant, Miami, Florida, June 1945. From left to right, first row: Staff Sergeant Phillip B. Brown, Brown's civilian friend, Sergeant Garrett Arterburn, and Corporal Henry J. Korkuch. Standing from left to right: Corporal Arthur C. Farrington, Farrington's U.S. Navy WAVE friend, Corporal Charles E. Mitchell, Mitchell's friend, Staff Sergeant William Martin, Corporal Donald W. Royston, a pretty waitress, and Corporal Charles W. Hetrick.

our upcoming adventure. It would be played many times on honky-tonk juke boxes in the next ten months.

We reluctantly shoved off from Miami early Saturday morning, May 5, 1945, and headed around the tip of Florida into the Gulf of Mexico and on to New Orleans. On the radio, we first reached Cuba, then Tampa, St. Petersburg, and finally New Orleans. LST *512* was supposed to be pre- pared to a "T" for its opening in Detroit, Michigan, on the first anniversary of D-Day, June 6th, so we really had a rough go of it between Miami and Chicago. We had to set up the display jungle, and it was really a difficult task. Some of the trees weighed 1½ to 2 tons, so we really counted on the U.S. Navy guys to rig the block-and-tackle. The jungle floor was formed with webbing made of very thick and tough metal, and we had to prepare circular cut-out sections for the hundreds of potted plants.

I wrote home to my mother:

> There are spiders, ants, bugs, chameleons, grasshoppers, and three birds even appeared yesterday and today. It has really been a smooth run from Miami but since five o'clock it has been getting rougher and rougher. [*But it was nothing compared to my next ride on LST 611 from Kobe, Japan, to Inchon, Korea, in the teeth of a typhoon.*] . . . Well, here I am all sweated up again. The gulf water is so rough, and they say it is liable to get worse, that we just went up on the weather deck and brought down, via the elevator, the rest of the plants. . . . While up there a pretty little bird that was among the plants flew to the forward end of the ship by the 40mm guns. I went up after him and caught him when the wind upset him. I took the bird below and let him go in the jungle and so now there's a total of five birds down there.

We arrived in the old French city of New Orleans on V-E Day — Victory-in-Europe Day — May 8, 1945, the day the Germans had sur- rendered. However, due to Navy Department restrictions, we were not allowed ashore to celebrate. Only some of the officers were permitted to leave the ship. I wondered if we would get any liberty when Japan was licked.

On May 9, we began our trip up the rivers. I wrote a letter home when we were above Natchez, Mississippi:

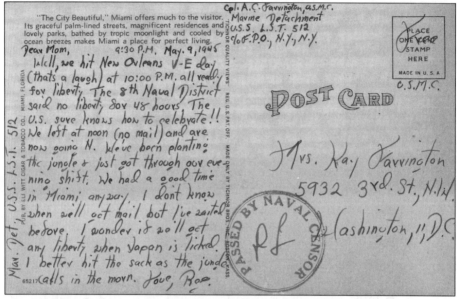

On V-E Day — Victory in Europe Day — May 8, 1945, the Germans were *kaput*.

The jungle is coming right along. We now have all of the dirt off the weather deck and half of it spread around down below. The native hut is finished and looks pretty good. Natchez was really a pretty little town perched up on high cliffs. The Mississippi is nineteen feet above normal so we just cruise all over the place. We've been running at night but it seems an order came through that we aren't to any more so I guess that's why we aren't working tonight.

P.S. The anchor's going down. It looks as though we're anchored out here in the woods again like last night. We pull right up (to the shore) like a show boat.

Our 1st Sergeant, Roper Henry, USMC, was from Hickman, Kentucky, which we would pass as we wound around up toward Illinois. We were prepared as we approached Hickman, and as LST *512* pulled in close to the shore we unfurled a banner reading:

A NATIVE SON OF HICKMAN.

Roper spoke to his relatives and friends way up on a bluff with the aid of a loud speaker system we had rigged up. We sang "My Old Kentucky Home" and "The Marine Corps Hymn" for them, led by 1st Lieutenant Paul E. Cramer. And 1st Sergeant Henry, using field glasses, identified and waved to everyone. We were one happy bunch of shipmates.

Meanwhile, Staff Sergeant Phillip B. Brown and I, the demolition men aboard, had helped to set up the barbed wire on the beach leading into the jungle, and we planned to actually blow up some wire and coconut logs for realism. This was not going to be some rinky-dink show. Our guests were going to enter the jungle from the tank deck over a sandy beach through a blown breach in the Japanese barbed wire.

LST *512* moved on up the Mississippi and we had a liberty in St. Louis, Missouri, then entered the Illinois River in the beautiful scenic southwestern part of the state. We eventually preceded north/northwest and then east past Peoria, Ottawa, and Joliet. Going through Joliet, we sailed through drawbridges or under six or seven bridge spans, hitting most of them. We lined up and made a run at them, but because our ship was flat-bottomed, it was very difficult to steer in a current. At times we had experienced pilots at the wheel, but they had no better luck. We Marines and the U.S. Navy sailors were frequently on duty with ship bumpers and old tires to prevent serious damage, and we cheered and booed as we hit and missed. At Peoria, the 328-foot ship had been raised by four or so locks, each one lifting us 30 to 50 feet. As we had moved between the towns of Ottawa and Joliet, we passed the shipyard at Seneca, Illinois, where LST *512* was built; it became the first LST to travel up the Mississippi and to return to its birthplace in inland waters. Our mailman and the Captain of the ship had traveled on ahead to Chicago from Joliet one morning to bring back the mail.

From Joliet, we moved on to Chicago. We spent two weeks there working on the jungle and the exhibits, placing the display onto the main deck, and preparing LST *512* for the opening exhibition in Detroit. We then had over 600 growing plants. We were progressing well with the jungle down

Most of the original U.S. Marines aboard the USS LST *512* serenading the family, relatives, and friends of 1st Sergeant Roper Henry, from the Mississippi River, below Roper's hometown of Hickman, Kentucky. From left to right: Corporal Donald W. Royston (Red Lion, PA); 1st Sergeant Roper Henry, with field glasses (Hickman, KY); 1st Lieutenant Paul E. Cramer (Columbus, OH); Sailor (name not remembered); Marine (name not remembered); Corporal Henry J. Korkuch (Irvington, NJ); Corporal Daniel M. Duncan (Whiteville, NC); Private 1st Class Bert Hensick (Deroit, MI); Corporal Clarence L. Jay, Jr. (Hollywood, CA); Corporal Arthur C. Farrington (Washington, D.C.); Corporal Charles E. Mitchell (St. Louis, MO); Corporal Charles W. Hetrick (Blackwell, OK); Sergeant Byron A. Hanks, Jr. (Duncan, OK); Technical Sergeant Edward J. Driscoll, Jr. (Elmhurst, IL). Those missing and those unrecognizable in the rear: Quartermaster Sergeant Charles H. Hale (Meadowview, VA); Staff Sergeant William C. Martin (Eugene, OR); Staff Sergeant Phillip B. Brown (Media, PA); Staff Sergeant Garrett Arterburn (Dallas, TX).

Installing the barbed wire on the "beach" leading to the "jungle" abcard LST *512*, from left to right: Corporal Charles W. Hetrick and Sergeant ("Nce and Good") Garrett Arterburn, and demolition men Corporal Arthur C. Farrington and Staff Sergeant Phillip B. Brown.

below, but it was getting very dense and gloomy there. We knew we would be done by the time we hit Detroit all right, but it was really a grind.

For the previous three days we also had been chipping rust and old paint off of the tank deck, forward of the jungle. We had worked all day long, and they even worked us on shifts throughout the preceding night, painting the major part of LST *512*. We also put ant poison around the jungle, as the little birds had given up the ghost and died. The smell of their dead bodies was going to add another dimension to the scene!

We had docked at the Calumet Shipyard & Drydock Company in South Chicago on May 21, 1945. There, over a hundred new Marines, all veterans, including some from Iwo Jima and Okinawa, were piped aboard, as were fifteen Coast Guardsmen to man the landing boats. Staff Sergeant Brown and I received two additional men for our demolition team, Sergeant R. J. Wurtzel and Private 1st Class W. R. Orr. Sergeant Wurtzel had been with me in Demolition Demonstration back at Camp Lejeune. When we had finished in the jungle and with the round-the-clock painting and chipping, we reported directly to Captain John E. Sivec, of Detroit, Michigan.

Sergeants Brown and Wurtzel, Private 1st Class Orr, and I set up shop in a large lot in South Chicago amid factory buildings. We put together 100-yard-long bunches of electric wires by taping them with tire tape. We had already constructed a map of where the explosives were to be located on the landing beach so that at certain intervals we could make sure that charges of TNT could be wired in. We prepared ignition boards with metal buttons that could be touched with a metal bar on a swivel to detonate the charges at precisely the right time. Three normal cables were made, and two for special effects as needed.

This "Demo Ship" assignment was really a racket by then. We "Jeeped" around, all over Chicago, like "BTOs" — Big Time Operators — and our "working greens" were actually our liberty uniforms. South Chicago was about ten miles from Chicago, so we took the Illinois Central Electric Railroad. But we really put in an effort there in Chicago, and we were ready to set up any beach they wanted!

At a little bar called the Town Club nearby, one night I met the most beautiful girl in the world by anyone's standards. In fact, we spent hours sitting on the same bar stool, and my whole side was paralyzed! Eileen Binns agreed to be my date when we would return to Chicago in September.

It was obvious that a celebratory D-Day landing in Detroit was not going to be made, as we left the cold Windy City on the 7th of June. A much-delayed letter to my mother read:

> Here's a letter at last from your son. We left Chicago yesterday morning and are now in Lake Huron heading towards Detroit. We passed the Straits (Straits of Mackinac) around noon today. We really had a long stay there in South Chicago and we all had a good time. The jungle is practically completed, most of the exhibits are in, and we have the deck loaded with guns, trucks, tanks, etc. Down below on the tank deck we have three amphibious tractors (Water Buffaloes), one Buffalo mounting a 75mm gun, and an amphibious "Duck."
>
> P.S. We have Siwash and her owner, Corporal Francis J. Fagan of Chicago, Illinois, aboard. Remember the duck in *Life* who was the mascot of the 2nd Marine Division? After being won in a raffle in New Zealand by Fagan she went ashore at Tarawa and "beat the feathered pants off a Japanese rooster." She was wounded at Tarawa, made Sergeant, and went in with the assault waves at Saipan and Tinian. She is really tame and goes all over the ship. One egg already.
>
> Right now they are doubtful whether we are going to make any landings on Belle Isle off Detroit as they don't wish the grass messed up! [*We would mess it up all right!*]

Anyway, we traversed Lake Michigan and Lake Huron and came into Detroit, smashing into the dock and sideswiping the *Bob-Lo*, a sightseeing riverboat, as we docked at the foot of Woodward Avenue for a ten-day stay. An article in the *Detroit Free Press* by Norman Kenyon, a staff writer, dated June 16, 1945, stated:

Realistic Enemy Jungle on View for Detroiters
Navy's LST 512 Brings City Graphic Section of Pacific War

Detroit awoke Sunday to find a Jap-infested jungle floating

Part of the crew of LST *512* test the amphibious tank for the demonstration, on the Detroit River, June 16, 1945.

U.S. Coast Guard

LST *512* in Detroit, Michigan.   *Detroit Free Press*

at the foot of Woodward. . . . 200 battle-scarred Navy, Coast
Guard and Marine fighters will demonstrate how the Allies are
staging amphibious warfare against the Nipponese.

The article described the entire exhibit, as well as the ship's mess hall and
crew quarters, which were seen on the 1½-hour tour.

Our demonstration would consist of three amphibious landings on a
150-yard stretch of beach between the yacht club and bathhouse. According to the newspapers, the spectators surrounding "Red Beach," the bridge,
and Memorial Park amounted to 75,000, 150,000, and 450,000 for the
three "invasions."

One of the *Detroit Free Press* reporters, Elmer W. Gaede, wrote:

If I were Hirohito I'd call this whole mess off right now.
And if Hirohito would visit the next point our Marines, Coast

Guard and Navy invade and watch from such a vantage point as
I enjoyed Friday night on "Bello Jima" (Belle Isle), he'd certainly call it quits.

Free Press staff writer Clyde Bates wrote:

> Noise sounds different on your belly.
> It's right next to your ear. The ground shakes. You wonder
> why you're here, in this Marine show at Belle Isle. . . . The
> 1,500 degree heat backwashes on your sweaty face. As you
> scuttle back like a crawfish, a machine gun singes you.
> Take it from me, no spot for a 4-F.

One day at Detroit, Odis W. Elder, Navy Chief Motor Machinist
(CMoMM), and I (a lowly Corporal) decided to find a couple girls, so we
left the ship and walked to near the end of the four-abreast line waiting
to go aboard. We spotted two pretty ones, and invited them to be our
guests. We four charged up the bow ramp, toured the displays and jungle,
then eventually ended up downtown in a cafe. In the cafe, the Chief's
choice, a very beautiful young lady was sitting directly across from me. As
the conversation concerning the LST slowed down she said, "My brother
was a Marine." I learned that her name was Muszynski, and I immediately asked if his name was "Thaddeus." She just stared at me, so I quickly
said, "Thaddeus Muszynski?" Although in the Marines we very rarely
knew a guy's first name, this one everybody knew. The young lady
acknowledged that Thaddeus was her brother. He lived at home in Hamtramck, a part of Detroit. But she told me to "Never tell my family how we
met!"

Muzzy had been in my outfit, the 1st Antiaircraft Machine-Gun Battery, and later in A Battery, 1st Special Weapons Battalion, 1st Marine
Division, from Cuba in 1941 to Pavuvu Island, Russell Islands, in 1944.
After that, as an infantryman, he had been guarding an M-4 Sherman
tank on Peleliu Island, Palau Islands, when a Japanese soldier had
emerged from the scrub with a magnetic anti-tank mine. When the Jap
pulled the safety pin, the mine detonated, with no delay, killing him and
seriously wounding Muzzy. All we ever heard was that the doctors had

taken strips of skin from his upper leg and grafted them onto his right arm.

Chief Elder dated Claire Muszynski for months after this chance meeting. I saw Muzzy at his home later, and was invited to be his second best man at his wedding in September of 1945.

We four demolition men — myself, Staff Sergeant Brown, Sergeant Wurtzel ("The Zombie"), and Private First Class Bill Orr — had a Ford reconnaissance truck at our disposal. One day we were tooling through Detroit with our "EXPLOSIVE" signs displayed when we sighted a Brinks armored car. I think it was Brownie who said, "Let's get 'em!"

We pulled up along the vehicle's left side at a red light and Zombie, sitting in the passenger seat, subtly aimed a bazooka at the driver. You should have seen the man's face — nonplused to say the least. Brownie pulled ahead from the light, and as we crossed over in front of them, I was cradling a flame-thrower gun out the back. I'm sure that this was the last of a youthful "good thing," as a few years later the famous Brinks robbery occurred in New England. You must take into account that we did a little drinking on this tour, especially after successful and safe periods of handling explosives and napalm.

Claire Muszynski, sister of the author's wartime friend Thaddeus Muszynski, and Arthur Farrington, "Skippy," on board the LST *512* in Detroit, Michigan.

Meanwhile, LST *512* was enjoying great popularity. The ship's history book noted concerning Detroit:

> Admiral Woodward, Chief of the Industrial Incentive Division, with overall charge of the vessel, opened the exhibition in Detroit. Soon afterward mounted police were called to control the large crowds of people who were fighting to get aboard. Detroit also brings to mind the "bobby soxers," the Bob-Lo steamboats, the daily parade of the burlesque queens, and the dramatic first invasion which was supported by spectacular dive bombers and fighters from Gross Isle.

But soon it was time to move on, traverse Lake Erie, and take on Buffalo, New York. On our way, we ordered three strong pillboxes from one of the foundries in Pennsylvania near Erie. Two landings were scheduled for Buffalo, but due to the restricted areas, they were not made at full strength as we would have preferred. The demolition team supported the landings, and we were also asked to put on an explosive demonstration in a large garbage dump right next to the ship, which was anchored at the foot of Main Street. We had to be very careful to locate each charge on or under harmless sand, so that there would be no dangerous projectiles launched.

The large mortar tubes that I operated against the exhibition aircraft were a safe feature. We loaded them with large explosive fireworks made by the same company the whole trip. When I touched a button on the firing board, a squib ignited the fuze. I was always very careful and got in trouble only a few times. I tried to lead the planes by a good distance or right at them.

At that time, my father lived in Woodlawn Beach, just south of Buffalo, and he visited the ship several times, bringing frogs for the demo team. He cooked the frogs whole, except for the heads, as they were so large. After a few beers, all the various parts were excellent!

LST *512* was back on schedule, staying in Buffalo from June 26 to

July 1, 1945. I recall one day when I was sitting in a bar drinking, and something strange was taking place. Everything was revolving — passersby outside on the sidewalk, tables and chairs, and restroom signs! The beer seemed to have more effect than I had expected. This was a first for me.

Meanwhile, an old civilian sitting next to me, with whom I had been conversing, asked me to watch his beer while he went to the head. As he left, he dropped his glass eye into his glass. The effervescence of the brew kept the eyeball bouncing around in the bottom of the brew until he returned, retrieved it, and popped it back into its socket. I concluded that some civilians are nuts also!

We were told that our next stop was to be Rochester, New York, on the shore of Lake Ontario. We, of course, wondered how in the world the ship was going to get over Niagara Falls, which is about 325 feet high. Meanwhile, we happily sailed westward about 25 miles to Port Colborne, Ontario, Canada, and entered the Welland Ship Canal, which parallels the Niagara River to Lake Ontario. The canal was 27.6 miles long and had eight locks, which lowered the ship a total of 325 feet. The first lock at Lake Erie was 1,350 feet long and 80 feet wide. The others averaged 862 feet long and 80 feet wide. The canal itself was 25 feet deep and over all the sills, 30 feet. It could handle all the sea-going ore ships, and others to and from the Atlantic Ocean. We dutifully lowered our tall, hinged main mast, and stood by to man the ship's bumpers.

Most of the railroad and highway bridges we had encountered, however, had to be opened, swiveled, or lifted for us to move through unhindered. It was an uneventful passage, however, and we were soon in Lake Ontario (245 feet above sea level). Before we knew it, we were moored in the Genesee River, in Rochester.

LST *512* moored at the Municipal Docks and opened for visitors as soon as possible. The crowds were headline news in the Rochester *Times-Union* and in the *Democrat* and *Chronicle*. The *Times-Union* called the July 4th day "a Glorious Fourth for thousands of the city's war workers, many of whom were permitted a holiday for the first time since 1941."

The demolition team had to work around the clock to set up the beach for just one gigantic landing. The new pillboxes had arrived, and we incorporated them in the assault, which basically proceeded like this:

The corps of Marines aboard LST *512*, June 1945.   *U.S. Marine Corps*

(1) Offshore bombardment — TNT blasts on shore and three or four cases, of 50 pounds each, in the lake, river, or whatever.

(2) Dive-bombers and fighters (if available) make bombing and strafing attacks — TNT blasts and machine-gun strings of small explosions.

(3) Japanese antiaircraft fire — large aerial explosive fireworks from mortar tubes.

(4) Armored amtrac "Belching Bertha" leads two LVTs (Landing Vehicle, Tracked) in toward the beach firing its 75mm cannon — black powder charge explodes in cannon's breech followed by TNT detonation on the beach.

(5) Japanese shells detonate around LVTs — TNT blocks secured to wooden blocks thrown overboard by squad leaders in LVTs.

Marines and sailors, all combat veterans, aboard LST *512*, 1945.   *U.S. Marine Corps*

(6) LVTs disgorge troops and withdraw to load reinforcements from LCVPs (Landing Craft Vehicle, Personnel).

(7) Japanese mortar shells land among the advancing, crawling troops — TNT charges connected to three or four 100+-yard-long wire bundles.

(8) Second Wave lands, including a 37mm anti-tank gun and an amphibious truck "Duck."

(9) Bazookas fire at pillboxes — practice anti-tank (AT) rounds are fired. As the rocket enters the pillbox embrasure (opening), I detonate two TNT charges, one each side of the pillbox. The AT rocket impacts inside against the back of the pillbox steel wall, which we have reinforced with railroad ties, as the four pounds of TNT explode.

(10) Napalm is fired at the pillboxes by flame-throwers from a distance, both by an amtrac and a Marine infantryman.

A photo montage of the "Lake Erie Landing" demonstration by the crew of LST *512*, at Erie, Pennsylvania.   *Erie Times*

(11) Bangalore torpedoes (empty of explosives) are placed under the concertina barbed wire in three places and detonated. We have previously cut the wire and reattached it with tire tape. Primacord (detonating cord) is wrapped around the tape and primed. If it fails to detonate properly, the Marines lie on the wire and the squad advances over them. This is a big hit with the crowd, but we never deliberately have duds!

(12) The flame-thrower teams advance and fire liquid fuel bursts onto the emplacements.

(13) The troops charge with fixed bayonets, and the green signal flares signify that the "Marines have landed and that the situation is well in hand."

The landing at Charlotte in Ontario Beach Park (it seems to be called Durand-Eastman today) on the west side of Irondequoit Bay went very well, with only one thing going wrong. A charge near the pillbox must have blown one of my charges inside, and when it detonated, the whole pillbox jumped straight up in the air. The welded seams did not hold, and it landed flat as a pancake on the sidewalk just in front of its position. It scared the Hell out of us, and we made sure that nothing of the sort would happen again.

One of the local newspaper writers, Jean Walrath, had this to say:

Land, Trees Quake as Marines Hit Beach; Scribe 'Invades' Charlotte by Eating Sand Girl News Writer Finds Herself Praying

> I sat five feet behind the captain in the command post when the Marines hit the beach at Charlotte last night, and I know what they mean about hell. . . .

The next stop was Cleveland, Ohio, where two landings were to be made. The *Cleveland Plain Dealer* observed:

> . . . Near record breaking crowds jammed the East Ninth street pier yesterday and wandered through the LST 512, first armed combat vessel to sail into Cleveland harbor during the war. The official attendance figure was 19,381.

My mother, Kittabel Farrington, visited me from Washington, D.C., and enjoyed the show. The invasion beach was just east of the Cleveland Indians' baseball stadium, and we received air support from the U.S. Navy for the second landing, as it took place in the lighted early evening.

We then left for Toledo, and the demo team kept busy mixing napalm and liquid fuel and loading the thickened fuel (napalm) and liquid fuel (diesel oil and gasoline) into the flame-throwers. We also had to charge the pressure tanks to 2,100 psi and the fuel tanks to 390 psi to propel the flame to the target. We had this equipment and gear stowed on the starboard afterdeck.

We pulled into Toledo on Thursday, July 26, 1945, and moored at the foot of Madison Avenue in the Maumee River. The *Toledo Blade* and the *Toledo Times* covered the LST *512* and the two landings thoroughly, having reporters and photographers landing with the troops and getting "all shook up."

Forty planes from Grosse Ile covered the landings with crowd-scaring low-level passes — Helldivers, Avengers, and Corsairs (dive-bombers, torpedo-bombers, and fighters). We literally burned, blew apart, and destroyed a portion of Riverside Park. The crowds around the landing area were estimated at 85,000 and 100,000, with East Toledoans looking on from across the river.

Our time in Rochester through our stop in Toledo was covered in the ship's history book:

> Rochester is to be remembered for its bathing beach and the Fourth of July. First Lieutenant Cramer took Erie by storm when he spanked two girls. The heat in Cleveland necessitated a stretcher detail which brought ladies who had fainted out of the jungle. The penny puncher, who would put the Lord's Prayer or the "LST Boat" on a penny for a dime, was following the ship from port to port. Toledo brought the episode of the baby being born while its mother watched the invasion; the Marines assisting in both operations at the same time.

Then on July 28, 1945, a newspaper photo showed a B-25 Mitchell bomber impacted into the Empire State building's 79th floor, with fourteen people killed! The power and danger of our aircraft and armament were evident.

We left Lake Erie (570 feet above sea level), cruised up the Detroit River, crossed Lake St. Claire (573 feet), maneuvered up the St. Claire River, entered Lake Huron (579 feet), made a turn to the port, entered Saginaw Bay, went up the Saginaw River, and moored at Wenonah Park at the foot of Sixth Street in Bay City, Michigan.

We remained in Bay City for two days, had no landings, and enjoyed liberty. I remember one night we visited Art Narlock's Broadway Show Bar, and I personally vowed never to go to another topless bar. The only "clothing" the female entertainer wore was three white cockatoos or parrots, which flew all around the room in the lowered lights and returned to her private areas at the appropriate time. Very interesting.

I wrote home to my mother from Michigan:

Saginaw Bay, Sat., Aug 4

We're on our way to Duluth at last. We left Bay City this morning at nine-thirty. It seems that there is a little city we passed this afternoon that Congress wished us to make a landing at as there is some Congressman from there or something. Well, as it only has about seven thousand (people) we couldn't so they called on the demo men (Orr is at Great Lakes Hospital) to put on a little show for the people on the beach and aboard some boats. We set up some tubes on the deck and let them have about fifteen ack-acks and threw some TNT overboard. We threw two block charges (1 lb.) and it woke everyone on the ship. They felt like depth charges! . . .

As no landing was scheduled for Bay City, Brown and Wurtzel took 72s [*72-hour leave*] to Saginaw, Orr went to the hospital and is to rejoin us in Duluth, so only I was left aboard. . . .

We had planes at both landings in Toledo and they were both good shows. It seems that we are really going to have good ones at Chicago as we're making two more switchboards (to accommodate more detonations). . . .

⋅⊷═◉═⊶⋅

Lake Superior, 11:00 p.m. Sunday

. . . As we are not going to use the pontoons [*for boarding the LST through the bow doors*] at Duluth we stopped at Sault Ste. Marie for three hours this afternoon to drop them off and also to buy some Sunday papers. A sailor caught four seagulls off the fan-tail with string and a piece of food on the end. They would catch it, get tangled up in the string, and fall in the water. One took a great big bite out of Siwash [*the pet duck that had*

*come through the Tarawa, Tinian, and Saipan campaigns with
the Marines*]! . . . Love, Reggie

The history of LST *512* described events at Bay City:

Bay City started the swing song "Who Threw the Eggs at the
Shore Patrol?" [— *involving Sergeant Sherman Loudermilk,
who had literally camouflaged Hollywood at the beginning
of our war with Japan and would be "Cowboy Slim" on early
TV in Los Angeles (he would later become an art director in
Hollywood)*] and modernized the old story of "Babes in the
Wood," while postwar uses of the rubber boat were demonstrated. Wild Man O'Rourke, who set the world's record for
changing from full ahead to full astern more times in one
minute than any other man in a lifetime, did nothing more serious than knock down the bridge tenders outhouse as he hit the
bridge [*in the Saginaw River; O'Rourke was our pilot at the
time*].

For 2½ days we had steamed northwest in Lake Huron, gently lifted 21
feet by the Soo Locks at Sault Ste. Marie. We entered Lake Superior and
finally docked safely at the foot of 6th Avenue West in Duluth, Minnesota. The date was August 7, 1945, three years to the day after I had
landed on Guadalcanal, British Solomon Islands, in the Southwest
Pacific.

We were welcomed with open arms, and our four days in Duluth were
great, with mine the best. The ship was open every day. The first landing
was canceled, however, as reported in this article from the *Duluth
News-Tribune*:

Capt. David Zeitlin, USMCR, commanding officer of the
Marine detachment of the invasion ship, said today's heavy rain
has flooded the beach to the extent that spectators will be
unable to get to the area.

Further, the rain has eliminated . . . pyrotechnics used in the
invasion and army planes . . . have been grounded.

The "invasion," however, was to proceed as scheduled on Sunday, and the *Duluth Herald* had an article, noting that:

> . . . four [*B-24s*] Liberators [*would be*] flown here from St. Paul. The planes will "soften up" the beach for the invaders by flying over at 3 p.m. Sunday. To assure precision in hitting the beach installations they will fly over at less than 500-foot altitude.

The B-24s did just that, and I sure enjoyed firing my projectiles at four-engined bombers. They made one Hell of a noise, and many of the people actually thought the planes were dropping bombs on the beach!

It was really chilly in Duluth in August, as I remember going on a garbage run behind the city up on an escarpment and having a cold wind hit us in the face. How terrible it must be in the winter.

The Duluth Marine Club at 222-24 West 1st Street attracted me for three liberties, as I was so naive as to think that the club was for Marines. A girl I met there, Lorayne, was my companion for three fantastic nights. I would never look at life the same way again! Enough said. And meanwhile, at this time in the real world of war, atomic bombs were being dropped on two Japanese cities. We were obviously taking Duluth by storm to such an extent that the bombings were not totally understood by us and did not seem to affect our future, which would be the upcoming invasion of Japan.

Anyway, while we were tied up in Duluth, more egg throwing at the Shore Patrol (and police) went on, which we demolition men were completely unaware of, as all our time was either at Park Point or in the sack.

The Navy had finished up a new fence all around the weather deck of LST *512* and as we were leaving port a very, very large ore boat, with overhanging bulwarks, brushed our whole starboard side. It was traveling at about a half-mile per hour, and as the new fence was laid down by the boat, all the Navy and Marine personnel tried to protect the Navy project with bumpers, beginning at the bow. We were laughing hard, but were trying to help at the same time, believe me. What a disaster! The whole fence and all the bumpers were destroyed, from stem to stern.

Our next stop was Muskegan, Michigan, on Lake Michigan, but we were in for a surprise. I wrote home about this time:

Aug. 14, 1945
8:30 P.M.
Sault Ste. Marie

Dear Mom & Bob,

Well, we heard the news [*that Japan has surrendered*] just as we were approaching the lock here at Sault Ste. Marie. All the big ore boats, factories, and cars blew [*their*] whistles and horns for about an hour. . . . I guess we won't do much celebrating this time either as we don't get to Muskegan until Thursday morning. . . . I hear you get tomorrow and Thursday off. That is pretty nice and you surely deserve it. . . .

Aug. 15, 1945

Just after I finished writing you last night we ran aground on a sandbar just this side of Sault Ste. Marie and huffed and puffed there all night with the aid of a tug. This morning at about six one of the most powerful tugs on the lakes latched on to us but still we didn't move until ten-fifteen when we slid clear. The cost of the tug was $125 an hour! We've been going through the Straits all day and it is really beautiful country. We passed close to Mackinac Isle and saw huge mansions, hotels, yachts, beaches, bicycles, and horses and buggies. It looked as if they don't have any automobiles. . . . Love, Reggie

After we had been lowered by the Soo Locks, we had passed through a fairly narrow waterway between Canada and the United States on our way to Lake Huron. But we did not make this passage. Have you ever heard the expression "rocks and shoals"? Well, I learned what it is like. We got hung up on the sandbar I mentioned in my letter home and spent all night and day of August 14th there, the day Japan surrendered. Emperor Hirohito broadcast to his people the *Imperial Rescript* that ordered the acceptance of the unconditional capitulation demanded by the Allied

The crew from LST *512* prepare 300 pounds of TNT for a "mock invasion" at Duluth, Minnesota. From left to right: Sergeant Roger J. Wurtzel, Staff Sergeant Phillip B. Brown, and Corporal Arthur C. "Skip" Farrington. *Duluth Herald*

Powers. We had also missed celebrating V-E Day, Victory in Europe Day, May 8, in New Orleans.

We could hear automobile horns, factory whistles, train whistles, ship blasts and bells, explosions, and other sounds of celebration as we marked time, waiting for the powerful Great Lakes' tug to arrive and push, pull, or shove us off our sandbar.

The history of LST *512* also described the events:

In Duluth the Marine Corps mothers gave the best parties of

LST *512* arriving in Milwaukee, Wisconsin, via Lake Michigan. The *Milwaukee Sentinel* noted "The LST is a veritable floating museum of captured Jap war materials."

Milwaukee Sentinel

the trip. [*The Japanese surrender*] was celebrated by securing the ship in three feet of water at Sault Ste. Marie. It was only set free by having the morning exercise squad of Germaine, Mills, Fagan, Henry, Schiff [*Seaman 1st Class Irwin J. Schiff of Chicago, one of my good Navy buddies, who had been shot with three or four wooden bullets by a German machine gunner at Anzio, Italy*], Almeida, and its colorful leader "Foghorn" move to the port side instead of working out amidships.

After being freed from the sandbar, we headed for the Straits of Mackinac, passing offshore of Mackinac Island. We subsequently pulled into the bay made by the Muskegon River and docked in downtown Muskegon for two days of exhibition and one landing. What made this city memorable was that in the pockets of our clean clothing, done at a city laundry, were notes with the numbers of the girl workers. How many rendezvous that occurred in Muskegon is anyone's guess.

Our next stop was Milwaukee, Wisconsin, west-southwest across the 579-foot depth of Lake Michigan. At about this time I was appreciating the fact that our address was c/o FPO, NY, New York, for we were considered "at sea" and received "overseas pay." As a Corporal of Marines, I received $82.50 per month, though it was barely getting me along. Every now and then I had to send a telegram for my mother to wire me money via Western Union. I had been able to save some overseas, as only 10 of the 29 months had been near liberty.

We arrived in Milwaukee the evening of August 26, 1945, and docked at the Wisconsin Avenue bridge. Upon opening for view at 12:30 p.m., the people got a view immediately of our newest attraction — a captured *Baka* bomb from Okinawa. *Baka* means "stupid" or "dumb" in Japanese. The small, rocket-propelled manned plane was dropped from underneath a bomber, the rocket would ignite, and the pilot would guide it with a small "joy stick" to its target, a U.S. ship. The forward part of the rocket was loaded with 1,135 pounds of high-explosive, which was enough to make the pilot's end a spectacular suicide.

In the *Milwaukee Sentinel* and the *Journal,* the first mention was made of this tour as a "thank you gesture" for America's support, now that the war was over. And after the crowd got over its initial wonder about us, the inevitable question came up: "Where's Siwash?" It seems that the

Marines from LST *512* "invaded" Milwaukee's South Shore Beach, demonstrating the action used in the Pacific Campaign.   *Milwaukee Journal*

Marines of the LST *512* Exhibition Ship landing and advancing on the beach at Milwaukee, Wisconsin.
Milwaukee Sentinel

Crew members of LST *512* demonstrate hand-held flame-throwers for the crowd at Milwaukee, Wisconsin.
Milwaukee Sentinel

The headline of the *Milwaukee Sentinel* stated: "Marines Show City How Wars Are Won." The accompanying photo showed bombers and strafing planes "zooming" overhead and simulated Japanese artillery shells sending water many feet into the air, with an armored tank approaching the Milwaukee beach area for the waiting crowd.   *Milwaukee Sentinel*

Milwaukee citizens had, in the near past, a celebrity duck of their own that lived and bred on a piling of the Wisconsin Avenue bridge. The *Milwaukee Sentinel* had a full page of Siwash and Corporal Francis Fagan, Siwash's owner, visiting Mrs. Drake's piling, with three pictures. While in Milwaukee I dated Jane Van der Zander, who worked for the *Sentinel*, and she kept me supplied with articles on the LST. She was even kind enough to send me some after we had left the area. She was really a nice young lady.

Milwaukee Journal "combat photographers" Charles Huston (left) and Robert Boyd take part in the LST *512* demonstration. *U.S. Navy*

Just after we had left the ship for liberty one day, we made a right turn, walked a few blocks, and found the imposing Schlitz Brewery. The company had declared "open house" for the ship's complement, and we all took full advantage of that. Free beer was provided and all we could eat, in the hospitality room. The main course came from a giant ball of "raw hamburger" into which was mixed all kinds of spices, fruits (including cantaloupe), and other goodies. You could not ask for a better start to a glorious liberty.

We put on two great shows at Milwaukee's South Shore Beach. A lot of preparation was needed, and a great many kids visited the area. We had some small demonstrations for them and for many months to come I received letters from three little girls who were just thrilled with the whole thing. Little Alice Turner had a brother and an uncle in the service somewhere, and even sent me a picture of herself in her Brownie uniform. And Dolly Wiken sent a letter from herself and Charlene Olson the day we left.

Hi Skippy [*my nickname on the tour, as someone caught me wearing my engineer cap sideways à la Skippy in the movies*]. I suppose you won't remember us, but you signed our parachutes [*from the flares*] so we are writing you this letter hoping you gave us the right address.

If you remember the show you fellows put on at South Shore Beach in Milwaukee you will know who we are. Our names are Dolly Wiken and Charlene Olson. We are the pests that kept bothering you when you were working and also when you were sleeping. [*The demo team had to sleep at the site in order to guard the explosives and all our gear.*] . . . I hope you don't think we're silly doing this because we just wanted to thank you for the parachute and shells. And also for the experience of meeting a swell Marine.

How is Brownie and the guy you all call Zombie? OK I hope. . . . Oh!!!!!! before I forget do you remember little Alice Turner? The sweet little child. Ha Ha. How I love that girl. . . . All this time you've been gone the kids have been playing "Here Come the Marines." They all miss you fellows a lot especially you. The one that misses you the most is that little boy that didn't have any teeth in the front of his mouth.

All the adults just love you for ruining our beautiful park, anyway the park that used to be there.

If you can figure out what this letter means and says I shall class you as one of the most intelligent persons we know. (We had to look up the word intelligent before we could write it.)

Loads of Luck to you and the other guys.

Signed Dolly and Charlene Olson
Boy, what you see us Norwegians do.

It was a joy meeting all those little people and being looked up to. None of us had had any experience to speak of interacting with youngsters, and these little Milwaukeans were so respectful and full of fun.

Records were set as to numbers coming aboard LST *512*, and according to the papers we had 75,000 and 150,000 at the landings. Both

Alice Turner, of Milwaukee, in her Brownie uniform. Alice had a brother and an uncle in the armed services and had visited the LST *512* demonstration in Milwaukee.

Milwaukee city newspapers provided full coverage of the ship and the landings, including a boat overturning, a large pike killed by the underwater charges, large pictures of the flame-throwers in action, some of the 40 low-flying U.S. Navy planes (including for the first time the F6F Grumman Hellcats), cringing spectators, and the crowds.

After a subsequent one-day stop at Racine, Wisconsin, the ship pulled into the Chicago River and heaved to in the Windy City between Wabash and Michigan Avenues. We had planned three amphibious landings during our long stay in Chicago, up the Gold Coast at Foster Beach, right next to the Edgewater Beach Hotel. As we worked, we really got an eyeful of the young ladies who appeared in the hotel's stage shows, for they insisted upon sunbathing on the beach in the skimpiest things.

I got together with Eileen Binns, who I had met previously in May, and we took in the town. We visited a nightclub decorated in medieval trappings of armor, and we went backstage at a show and met Ted Lewis, who had just finished his act singing his popular "Me and My Shadow." He was pretty well inebriated, but I forever enjoyed meeting famous people. Eileen and I were really hitting it off; she even loved bowling, as did I, but at this juncture I received a letter from Detroit and had to take a train to Hamtramck, Michigan, for Muzzy's wedding.

His bride was beautiful. The wedding was just great, and the three-day Polish celebration was exhausting. As of 2002, Muzzy and his wife live in Florida, and I still frequently look at the wedding picture they gave me.

My last memories of Chicago are seeing Russ Morgan and his band; a Redskin-Bears football game; and helping a pretty girl named Laura celebrate her birthday in a nightclub called the Band Box down on West Randolph Street in downtown Chicago, to the tune of the new song "Laura," played over and over. Eileen and I also made plans to meet again in the future.

The LST *512* history summed up our Milwaukee and Chicago visits:

> In Milwaukee some hoodlums stole some TNT from the invasion beach and the Schlitz Brewery gave a beer party. Sgt. Brown and a few Marines still think they bought a bar in Chicago, where the six Coast Guard men of the small boat crews were on leave for a change and where the millionth visitor was entertained royally.

To begin the so-called second half of our tour, LST *512* went south on the South Branch of the Chicago River, which soon turned into the Illinois Drainage Canal, opened for just one day each at Joliet and Ottawa. We arrived safe and sound back at Peoria, Illinois, on September 21, 1945. We anchored in the Illinois River at the foot of Main Street.

The *Peoria Morning Star* had the following to say on the morning of September 22:

> . . . A composite of the shores of Saipan, Tinian, Leyte, Iwo Jima and Okinawa where the famous amphibious landings of World War II scored such remarkable successes, the floating "jungle" reproduces a grimly-realistic atmosphere, of which not the least striking feature is a 102 degree temperature.

Twenty thousand Peorians toured the ship the second day of our visit.

The fireworks company that had been supplying us threw a party at Jack Adams' "The Sportsmens' Club." It was some bash. Intoxicated as usual, my demolition buddies volunteered me for a nightclub act! A couple on rollerskates held me under my arms as they skated wildly around and around on top of a cocktail table! I was lucky I didn't get sick; I sure was unable to navigate for a while. The man that punched the pennies was at the party as well.

And I finally wrote a letter to my mother:

Peoria, Ill.

I'm really sorry I haven't written since we were on our way to Muskegon. . . .

We had a good landing . . . . Then Milwaukee and two good ones. From there the ship went to Racine and six of us drove straight to Chicago, where we stayed at the Sherman Hotel and The Towers. At Chicago we had three super landings using 10-12 cases of TNT instead of 4-5 as usual per landing. . . . From there the ship left for Joliet, Ill. and I left for Detroit, Michigan. I had a five day leave. . . . Muzzy wore his Marine uniform for the last time. . . . I wired to Joliet for an extension [*of my leave*] and got it. What a seven days! I joined the ship at 0300 yesterday morning just as it was ready to leave Ottawa, Ill.

And here we are at Peoria.

Fifteen fellows are getting discharged in St. Louis. I would be in that group if I had not shipped over on Gloucester [*Cape Gloucester, New Britain Island*] in 1944.

That's OK Mom. I'm enclosing a schedule so you see what kind of a trip I have ahead.

I saw "Pride of the Marines" in Milwaukee (with Van der Zander naturally). "Anchors Aweigh" with Frankie is a good show too.

Ole "Siwash" got discharged in Chicago. I'm sure going to miss drinking beer with her and Fagan all over the Great Lakes. Fagan is getting out in Saint Louis. . . .

P.S. I saw the Washington Redskins play the Chicago Bears at Soldier Field. D.C. won 14-7. Love, Reggie

We were next in St. Louis for a week, and had some great liberties. The Mississippi was not suitable for any amphibious landings, so we just put on some fireworks and loud explosions.

A letter to my mother from St. Louis reads:

26 Sep 45 Well, they didn't pay me and aren't 'til the fifth and we leave for Pittsburgh the fourth. I'll get paid seventy dollars and then have ten days with no spending. . . . I only had fifty-five cents so that's why I had to send the telegram collect. I've started bowling again and so far my average is 139. All they have out here is ten pins though.

The letter was on USO stationery and, of course, required no stamp.

From this point in my LST *512* travels, my newspaper-article collecting suffers, and thus I hope that my memory serves me well.

I received a nice letter written to me on October 20, 1945, from East St. Louis, simply addressed "SKIP," U.S. Marine, Attached Personnel, L.S.T. 512, Riverfront, Foot Market St., St. Louis, Missouri."

Dear Skip: You will recall the incident that occasioned this note when you took it easy on the front bumper of the radio equipped Jeep, as you suggested you would answer any questions visitors might ask.

One visitor, myself, took up your offer and asked about the duck, amtracks, buffalo, and other amphibious equipment. Perhaps you will remember the fellow in dark gray suit, brown hat, black shoes, and eyeglasses.

You answered several more of my questions about the L.S.T. itself and how its light draught enabled it to navigate the Illinois River.

After some discussion about the long line of visitors, and my mention of the fact that time and the number of people would

An "Official Visitor" pass for USS LST *512*.

OFFICIAL VISITOR

USS LST-512

The Navy's "HIT THE BEACH" Exhibit

Present this card at the Bow door entrance and you and your guest will be admitted ahead of the line.

The ship ready for a show

LST *512* at night, preparing for a demonstration.

prevent our seeing the display aboard the vessel, you were very kind and presented us with the official admission card.

Well Skip, the first question the wife asked when we left you was, "Do you think this will work?" My answer was, "Skip knew what he was doing when he gave it to us and I'm going to present it."

We saw a big, sailor at the opening of the roped off lane and I gave it to him, telling him what you told me to say. He said "Certainly, two of you? Right in here."

My missus' eyes were large as saucers, you should have seen her strut; I hope I didn't, but I sure felt like it.

. . . All this is by way of saying many, many thanks for the kindness and courtesy you showed in giving us the card, Thanks again. . . . Quite a few of my young nephews and cousins are in the service, all branches. The wife has a young cousin serving with the Third Marine Division, and I myself have about 15 or 20 good friends in the Marines.

I've always hoped if Uncle Sam reached for me (which he didn't) that I'd be able to make the Marine Corps or the Navy. . . . Sincerely, Alfred H. Kueneth

I did not go to Pittsburgh with LST *512*. After sailing down the Mississippi for 150 miles, making a left turn at Cairo, Illinois, and traveling up the Ohio River for hundreds more, they dumped me off in Louisville, Kentucky, where I was admitted into the Veterans Hospital with a severe case of gingivitis, obviously caused by a dirty beer glass in St. Louis.

I was in Louisville for a week in the ward with World War I veterans! Can you imagine all the hacking and coughing going on from the effects of phosgene, chloropicrin, mustard, and other gases? But we spent our time exchanging war stories, and they told me that every once in a while some of them were allowed to go home, though soon they were back at the hospital as their families could not stand their hacking. It is unbelievable to me that they had been there since 1918! Thank God the Japs never used gas. We always carried gas masks but dropped them after we had crossed the beach. Veterans' hospitals after war are worse than the ones brought into play soon after combat. These people never get well.

When I finally arrived in Pittsburgh, via Pullman car, I requested a 72-hour leave, got it, and went by Greyhound bus to Washington, D.C., to visit my mother and to recuperate a little more. It took me four rides hitch-hiking to get back to the ship. I wrote to my mother:

> The crew . . . surely has changed since I left [*in Louisville*] and a lot of good guys have gone. . . . Yesterday about twenty of us rode the Duck and saw Notre Dame beat Pitt 39-9. There are really big long lines here I tell you. We are not scheduled to make any landings until we reach Cincinnati so we demo men have it easy. We are practicing for a parade in Steubenville for Navy Day and we are really good, no kidding. . . . The Doc says he'll try to get me a tooth in Memphis. [*I lost a front tooth somewhere, and I looked salty without it. I finally got a replacement in New Orleans and had a gold border put around it.*] I think I'll stay on board here for a while longer, Mom. Love, Reggie

LST *512* was moored at the Monongahela wharf and the *Pittsburgh Post-Gazette* of October 22, 1945, stated that "the long lines waiting to enter the ship created a colorful scene, stretching from Market Street to Smithfield Street bridge." My memories of Pittsburgh are solely of the Hotel Fort Pitt, the "Members Only" bars, and walking up Mount Washington on wooden steps with a girl. And one more recollection: debris from the smokestacks of the mills would fall at times like rain, and our dress uniforms, especially the collars of our khaki shirts, were black at the end of a liberty on the town.

On the morning of October 23, 1945, we left "Steeler Town" and headed down the Ohio River. We had our parade in Steubenville on our second day there, and I wondered who all the scantily clad girls were. I was informed that they were all the town whores! We then made two-day stops in Wheeling and Parkersburg, West Virginia, and three days were spent in Huntington. At each of these short visits we demo men put on antiaircraft and TNT shows that rocked the cities. The *Huntington Adver-tiser* described the scene:

> Last night a rocket display, simulating an antiaircraft barrage, and TNT demolition charges, set off on the river bank, jarred the area and sent echoes rolling from hill to hill on both sides of the Ohio.

Incidentally, the paper also had the following to say about LST *512*, which we Marines did not realize:

> The 512, however, requires special handling because with her heavy load of equipment she draws 10 feet of water instead of the regular nine-foot draft. Since the Ohio is only cleared for a nine-foot channel, the 512 has had to travel on her present cruise by the "splashing" method whereby the locks and dams throw their wickets down and create a deeper pool for the passing of the ship.

The Associate Editor of the *Huntington Herald-Dispatch*, James E. Casto, wrote me in August 2002 the following regarding LST *512*:

> Let the record show I still recall the 1945 visit of LST 512 to Huntington. Its recreated Japanese-held jungle was so real and so vivid that I wet my pants. Of course, I was only four years old at the time.

We celebrated the 170th birthday of the U.S. Marine Corps on November 10th, in Huntington, West Virginia; and we acknowledged my 23rd birthday and Armistice Day on November 11th. I was recommended for promotion to Sergeant, which I finally made in 1948.

The Marines took precedence in the Huntington showing of LST *512*; collectively representing veterans of more than 40 major Pacific invasions and wore the shoulder patches of every Marine division in existence. These patches told the story of fighting men and divisions.

The star-studded blue diamond with the red "1" of the 1st Marine

Division was worn by men who fought at Guadalcanal, Cape Gloucester, Peleliu — as I did — and Okinawa.

Marines of the 2nd Division who fought at Guadalcanal, Tarawa, Saipan, and Tinian displayed their unit insigne, which consisted of a golden torch on a red spearhead. The five stars that surround the torch represent the Southern Cross, the same constellation displayed on the 1st Marine Division's patch.

The 3rd Marine Division wore a three-pointed star of black and gold on a yellow-bordered red shield. The 3rd Division had won fame at Bougainville and then at Guam; and landing as reinforcement, it broke the back of Japanese resistance in the northern part of Iwo Jima.

A large gold figure on a red diamond is the insigne of the 4th Marine Division, which took Roi-Namur Island and Eniwetok in the Marshall Islands, participated in the Saipan and Tinian campaigns, as well as the Iwo Jima operation. What looks like an unusual-looking number "4" on the patch is actually the Japanese airfield on Roi-Namur, from an aerial photograph taken by a U.S. flier.

The shoulder patch identification of the 5th Marine Division is in the shape of a Crusader shield. The gold "V" symbolizes both the number of the division and victory; the blue spearhead signifies the part taken by the Marines in an offensive. The background of the insigne is red. Although the 5th Division participated only in the Iwo Jima Campaign, many of its members had fought in one or more of the other Pacific campaigns.

The 6th Marine Division, along with the 1st, was engaged in the bitter fighting on Okinawa, which was its first engagement as a division. However, as the 1st Provisional Marine Brigade, it fought with the 3rd Division at Guam. The 6th Division patch is a red-bordered circle bearing the words "Melanesia, Micronesia, Orient." On the blue field in the center of the circle is a silver dagger, surmounted by the figure six in yellow. The 6th Division is comprised, in part, of the 4th Marine Regiment, which fought at Corregidor, and the Raider and Paramarine Regiments, which participated in the Solomons campaigns.

Our next two-day stop was at Portsmouth, Ohio, and on or about November 17, 1945, we pulled into Cincinnati for a week stay at the foot of Broadway. A Cincinnati paper had the following headline

Shoulder patches of the U.S. Marine Corps divisions. *Top left:* 1st Marine Division (Guadalcanal, Cape Gloucester, Peleliu, Okinawa). *Top right:* 2nd Marine Division (Guadalcanal, Tarawa, Saipan, Tinian). *Center left:* 3rd Marine Division (Bougainville, Guam, Iwo Jima). *Center right:* 4th Marine Division (Marshall Islands, Saipan, Tinian, Iwo Jima). *Bottom left:* 5th Marine Division (Iwo Jima). *Bottom right:* 6th Marine Division (Okinawa, Guam, Corregidor, Solomon Islands).

The December 2, 1945, edition of the *Roto Magazine*, of the *Louisville Courrier-Journal* (Kentucky), described the visit of LST *512* and the "jungle warfare methods" the crew had demonstrated. In photo, Private 1st Class Carl Craig, Iwo Jima veteran.   *Louisville Courier-Journal*

about our amphibious landing on Tacoma Beach in nearby Dayton, Kentucky:

Reporter Wades in River to See
How Marines "Invade" Dayton, Ky.
Enormous Crowds Witness Thrill
and Spectacular Demonstration.

On liberty in Cincinnati, I remember just one big four-sided block devoted entirely to bars, restaurants, and the like.

From the city of the Cincinnati Reds baseball team we floated down-river to Louisville, Kentucky, for an exhibition and our last landing on the Ohio. On some of these relatively short hauls we did not on-load the wheeled vehicles, and I got to drive a Ford Jeep a couple of times between cities.

LST *512* was tied up at the foot of Fourth Street in Louisville for about a week during the first week of December 1945, and was open for the public as ever from noon to 9:30 at night. The weather was cold in Louisville, and the beach was really a field abutting the river. We worked hard, and the day before the landing we had visitors. Captain Sivec, our Command-ing Officer, came to the "beach" with some "hot-shot" aviators. Spotless in their flying jackets, crushed caps, and dark glasses, they were black Tuskegee airmen who had served in the U.S. Army Air Forces in North Africa, Sicily, and Italy flying P-40 Warhawks, P-39 Airacobras, P-47 Thunderbolts (in lieu of P-63 Kingcobras), and P-51 Mustangs.

It seemed that the U.S. Navy was indisposed or over-extended at the time, and thus these pilots were going to be our air cover. They looked over the terrain thoroughly, as some Navy and Marine Corps pilots had in the past, and seemed especially interested in one very large tree in the middle of the field. The men were based at Godman Field, which serves Fort Knox, Kentucky. There were supposed to be sixteen P-47 Thunder-bolts, but when four planes later buzzed the field, we realized that they were P-51 Mustangs!

The following day was really exciting. We set off the pre-bombardment explosions in the river and the Tuskegee aviators came through the spray in their Mustangs, flying low over the river and right around that big tree, with white vapors coming off their wingtips and vertical stabilizers. Everyone was just amazed at the performance, but I did not see anything in the newspapers later about the men who were flying those planes. What a show they put on! No wonder they downed so many German Messer-schmitts, Focke-Wulfs, Me-262 jets, and bombers. My hat was off to them.

Bill Orr, our PFC demolition man, had been discharged and Wurtzel, "The Zombie," was leaving after this landing.

This seems to be a good place to explain just how we prepared the TNT shots. The half-pound blocks came in yellow cardboard TNT-labeled jackets. The jacket ends were a lightweight metal. One end of the explo-sive had a hole the size of a pencil drilled in it, and this hole was covered with a heavy paper; the drilled-out area was provided to accept a blasting cap. One of our most tedious tasks was to remove the metal ends from all the TNT used near the Marines and spectators. We had to pry them off with our side-cutters (pliers) so that there would be no danger to anyone from the flying pieces. Then an electric detonating cap was inserted into the end of one of the blocks (some charges included more than one of the half-pound blocks), and we tied the cap's wire securely around the charge before attaching it to the master cable (the wire bundle totaling over 100+ yards). Our firing boards were hooked up to some powerful batteries just before the show, as we had previously checked and re-checked the circuits with our galvanometers. My antiaircraft charges had quick-burning fuzes that were ignited by hissing, spurting squibs attached to a special wire bundle.

A letter I had written home described some of my Cincinnati and Louisville experiences:

> Did I tell you that at the landing in Cincinnati I finally managed to hit a plane with the ack-ack? I sure did. A little one hit his wing, bounced off and burst.
>
> Did I tell you that in Cincinatti Bill Orr and I were invited to a chicken dinner on Thanksgiving and had a Jeep for the night? Last night I went out and ate at a fellow's house who I had met here in Louisville when I was in the hospital. . .
>
> A Navy officer and I drove to Cincinnati day before yesterday on business and had a $2½ steak dinner on the way back. . . .

I had also asked my mother to look at my Jap covers (the First-Day mailing covers) for Karl Lewis's address in Yokohama. I had wanted to write him to see how he had fared. I never did hear of his fate; however, in the 1980s I won an award at the Del Mar (California) Fair exhibiting the hand-painted covers he had sent me during the 1930s and early 1940s.

The LST *512* history describes this start of the second part of the tour:

> The second half of the tour was given much applause by the cities of Joliet, Ottawa and Peoria. Al Mills, the first man eligible for discharge on points, left the ship in Ottawa. The

Chicago River, with its delightful color and smell proved tempting to Maviglia who went for a swim wearing his 45 just for the reward of a shot of brandy. The rain in St. Louis will long be remembered. When it finally subsided and the swollen river dropped, "Belching Bertha," the armored amtrack, with all her campaign stars and ribbons, was called upon to push the ship off the levee. The eight day trip up the Ohio River to Pittsburgh, without liberty, seemed endless. Lieutenant Stevens relieved Lieutenant Brock as Commanding Officer in Pittsburgh. The Recruiting and Induction Division of the Bureau of Naval Personnel took over the operation of the tour to assist in the intensive drive to procure men for the post-war Navy. Lieutenant (Junior Grade) Glenn's Navy platoon successfully competed with Sgt. Hill's well-drilled Marines in the annual Navy Day parade in Steubenville. Captain Sivec's ambitious demolition squad caused more excitement in Portsmouth than did the mysterious disappearance of the DUKW in Cincinnati.

Our next two stops before hitting the Mississippi River were at Evansville, Indiana, and Paducah, Kentucky. While the ship was in Evansville, I took a four-day leave to Chicago, where I saw Eileen Binns again. The visit started off great, as the Dearborn Plaza hotel had reserved a great room for a Colonel instead of a Corporal. My telegram clearly reads Corporal and not Colonel, so there was no problem with "misrepresentation." Eileen and I "painted the town" as it should be painted.

Paducah was our next stop and following is a portion of a letter I wrote home aboard ship in Evansville:

10 Dec Dear Mom & Bob, I just arrived back from Chicago this morning after a very good time visiting a girl and her mother and father. [*Right!*] . . . Among other things I saw the operetta "The Desert Song" with Walter Cassel at the Chicago Opera House. I bought three dollar box seats and it's the first time I knew that box seats weren't on the sides. They were right in the middle and just perfect. The music was very good and so were the colors. I hardly expected it to be humorous but it surely

USS LST *512* at its stops throughout America's heartland.   U.S. Navy, *History of the USS LST 512*

turned out to be. Eileen and I enjoyed it immensely. . . . It was 17 degrees when I left Chicago last night. . . . After I get off this ship I'll try to get the scoop on some trucks somewhere. [*My mother had alerted me that she was planning on our moving to either Florida or California upon my brother's and my own discharge. The following May we bought a 1935 four-door Cadillac and a covered luggage trailer and drove to Hollywood.*]

The first day in Evansville I put up a good ack-ack barrage as a come-on for the people. It went off perfectly. I wish this ship would hurry and get down south. The boilers blew out and it has been cold as fury all day. [*They're*] fixed now but the compartments are miserable.

The first night in Evansville three Marines were beat up by plain clothes men with clubs and pistols on the street, in the wagon, and in the station and were refused medical attention.

They were really cut up. It was released by A.P. yesterday and today as it was in the D.C. papers. The cops were reported to Navy Hdqts. . . .

What articles of furniture do you intend to take to California? I just want my F.D.C.'s [*First-Day Covers*], tennis racquet, and war souvenirs. [*What a mistake this was. Can you imagine the value today of all my* **Big Little Books** *and baseball and foot-ball cards that I left behind?*] . . . . In the meantime I can always get a job as a powder monkey [*in demolition work*] to earn a little money. See you, . . . Love, Reggie

Paducah was history, and we reached the Big River and headed south to Memphis, 273 miles down-river. It was really, really cold in Memphis. The *Memphis Press-Scimitar* of December 19, 1945, a Wednesday, had the following to say:

> LST 512 laid down the welcome mat to Memphis today. By the time the first day of its five-day exhibition ends at 9:30 tonight, thousands are expected to have boarded the big invasion ship at the foot of Beale.

The newspaper added: "The flag-bedecked vessel [*was*] painted in weird Pacific camouflage. . . ."

The demolition squad had three days off, and we took advantage of it. The Peabody Hotel got to know us, and we spent quite some time and money in the "WAVE CAVE" at the Claridge. There were a number of WAVES stationed around there.

We went back to work on Saturday, transporting all our gear to Mud Island. The amtrac carrying us at first could not get up the steep sides out of the Mississippi due to the extremely slippery mud, but our driver was an expert and we finally made it. We were greeted by howling wind-blown snow and frozen ground.

It was impossible to dig holes for the explosives and to properly prepare for a decent, safe landing exhibition. Captain Sivec then made the decision that due to the weather, the difficulty in getting a landing party ashore, the swift river water, and many other reasons that I was not privy to, no landings would be attempted Sunday on Mud Island. An alternate plan was formulated. A giant Japanese flag was made and we flew it over a large Jap emplacement we built out of material we found on Mud Island. We were asked to expend most of our old explosives and fireworks, as we were only scheduled for one more beach assault, in New Orleans.

We had a great show at Memphis, with the Jap bunker and flag disappearing in a horrific blast at the very end. On Monday, the newspaper headline said:

Many Broken Windows In
Wake Of Navy TNT Show

Many years later, on August 7, 1998, a museum opened on Mud Island and the famous B-17 Flying Fortress *Memphis Belle* was on display. The island is now connected to the city by a beautiful bridge. In fact, part of the movie *The Firm*, with Tom Cruise, was filmed on the island and bridge.

But that December of 1945, with as much damage done as we were able to get away with, we up-anchored and headed down-river on Christmas Day, after the Red Cross brought aboard some holiday cheer. I do not remember just what the "cheer" was, but they brought it as the ship was closed that day.

Our schedule had us stopping in Vicksburg, Mississippi, for four days. I do not recall the details of the stops, but I do remember looking up at the palisades and being glad that I was not at the siege of Vicksburg during the Civil War — on either side.

We subsequently had a New Year's party in Natchez, Mississippi, and proceeded south to Baton Rouge, Louisiana, where we spent two days. A buddy and I visited the Statehouse, upon whose steps "Kingfish" Huey Long had been assassinated. It was night, but the building was open and we were able to get to its very top for a great view of the Mississippi River and Baton Rouge. My barracks hat (a heavy hat with a bill) blew off, and we spent a long time finding it on one of the roofs of the Capitol. I am afraid that my buddy and I had been drinking Old Crow whiskey on this liberty, and I decided to stick to beer in the future, until my family and I were stationed in Haiti in 1959.

Crew members of LST *512* on shore leave in Miami, Florida.

Our last stop was New Orleans. LST *512* tied up at the foot of Canal Street downtown in the city on January 5, 1946. The liberty in the French Quarter was fantastic, and because only one landing was scheduled for about January 14, we overdosed on the great variety of drinks, foods, and girls. My liberty buddy was Private 1st Class Workman, from San Diego.

We had a close call soon after LST *512* tied up. A couple of large barges broke loose up-river and came really close to the ship; we were fortunate, however, as the barges could carry everything they hit with them and Ole Man River was really swift and dangerous at this time.

The landing went well out the Airline Hiway, as a prelude to the Moisant International Airport dedication. The only casualty was Belching Bertha. She went to the bottom of the Mississippi after being overcome by the rough water. But all hands were saved! Twenty-four U.S. Navy planes, probably from the New Orleans Naval Air Station, supported the invasion.

Meanwhile, I was in love, and intended never to leave New Orleans. With Regulars getting discharged with only 65 points, my 135 allowed me to request a discharge from the Marine Corps Reserve whenever I desired to do so. And at that time, at age 23, in that great city, I desired. I saw

The New Orleans newspaper covered the visit of LST *512*. From left to right, standing: Corporal Arthur C. Farrington, Private 1st Class Bert Hensick, and Corporal Donald Royston; seated: Corporal Edwin J. McMahon, Specialist 1st Class Louis R. Church, Ships Cook 3rd Class Carl H. Adkins, and Specialist 1st Class Irwin James Schiff.   *New Orleans Picayune*

Corporal Royston, our clerk, and he arranged for me to be transferred down-river to the Post Farm, where vegetables were raised for the base at the Naval Ammunition Depot. I stood guard out on the levee for some nights awaiting my discharge. I had not had to stand guard duty in a long time, and four hours out there alone with the coughing alligators was the worst I had ever experienced.

Finally, I was discharged from the Marine Corps Reserve on February 18, 1946. I sewed on my "Ruptured Duck," the World War II patch issued upon honorable discharge, and was permitted to wear my uniform for three months. I also qualified to receive a paycheck every two weeks for three months. I remained in New Orleans with Annette Williams.

The last entry in the history of LST *512* described the last days of December 1945 and early 1946:

The cold wave in Memphis, which dropped the attendance to as low as 428 for a day, did not chill the spirit of the Red Cross, which brought us all a very merry Christmas. The Navy mothers in Natchez gave a party that welcomed in the New Year and all men were treated to a taste of Southern hospitality. In New Orleans the two millionth visitor was welcomed aboard and the eight months tour of 31 cities came to an end.

The parting of good friends and shipmates brings to mind incidents that will be remembered for a long time, yet it is certain that the experience and confidence gained on the tour of the USS LST *512* has better fitted us for success in life, no matter what career we may choose.

The *Leatherneck* magazine subsequently noted LST *512*'s tour stops after New Orleans:

Battle vets enjoy 100,000
miles of Stateside seagoing

The last exposition of landing party tactics was given in New Orleans. The craft then opened its publicity layout for Tampa and St. Petersburg, swung around the Florida Peninsula, and visited Miami and Port Everglades. After Norfolk, Va. the LST 512 entered the Washington, D.C. channel for a show in the national capital. Here its 300 exhibits were inspected by Secretary of the Navy Forrestal.

From Washington the crew could look forward to liberty in Baltimore. Then would come other seacoast cities until Bath, Maine. After that display, the ship will tour the Gulf of Mexico for more of the most colorful duty and varied liberty in the American services. By the end of her itinerary she will have well over 100,000 water miles under her lowslung waist.

Inasmuch as no more amphibious landing demonstrations were put on for the public, it seems that my decision to get out of the Marines at this time was appropriate. After arriving in New Orleans on January 5, 1946,

The author's beautiful French girlfriend, Annette Williams, at Lake Ponchartrain, Louisiana.

Corporal Arthur C. Farrington, a "free man," just discharged, at Lake Ponchartrain, Louisiana, 1946.

Mrs. Kittabel Farrington, the author's mother, in her Nutria fur, *ca.* 1946.

Corporal Arthur C. Farrington, a four-year veteran, home from World War II.

The Farrington family's 1935 Cadillac in front of the author's home in Washington, D.C., June 1946, ready for their move to California.

my diary lists my itinerary as follows until I went on active duty with the 1st Marine Division for duty in Korea on July 29, 1950:

18 Feb 46	Discharged from the U.S. Marine Corps Reserve at the Post Farm, Naval Ammunition Depot, New Orleans, Louisiana.
18-23 Feb 46	New Orleans, Louisiana. 1033 Dauphine, on the "Streetcar Named Desire" trolley line.
24 Feb-1 Mar 46	Daytona Beach, Florida (my father's winter home).

LST 512 *"FIGHTS ON"* IN RECRUIT DRIVE

Its guns silent but its part in a peace-time Navy just starting, the veteran man-of-war LST-512 docked in New Orleans Jan. 9-14, spurred on recruiting for the Navy and Marine Corps.

The 4,000-ton LST, largest landing craft and workhorse of invasion, appeared all to calm as it rested in the Mississippi.

Here on exhibition under cognizance of the Bureau of Personnel, its cavernous doors and displays were open to the public.

Upon entering visitors were able to cross over specially rigged causeways, across a steel ramp and then into the tank deck, which is more than a block long and normally appears to be a nautical warehouse.

At the entrance of three exhibit halls has been placed a Jap Baka suicide plane, captured at Okinawa. To its left flank is assembled the paraphernalia which the average Jap foot soldier carried, including the assorted medals of Jap General Nishida , killed on Saipan. Directly across the deck a bay contains an American fighting man's equipment.

Highlight of the exhibit aboard ship is a realistic jungle, 80 feet long and 40 feet wide, with growing tropical plants and actual sound recordings made overseas of jungle noise and sporadic gunfire.

On the main deck of the ship heavy ordnance both Japanese and American is assembled, all the way from the smallest anti-tank guns up to the powerful 155 mm Marine Howitzer, which throws a 100-pound shell for thousands of yards.

While docked at the foot of Canal Street, The LST-512 became host to its two-millionth visitor on its present tour of 30 cities.

Publicity sheet for LST *512.*

U.S. Marine Corps

Foreword

THIS BOOKLET IS AN EFFORT OF A FEW INDIVIDUALS OF THE USS LST 512 TO COMPILE PHOTOGRAPHS AND NOTES OF INTEREST FOR ALL WHO HAVE SERVED ABOARD. IT IS MORE THAN A MEMENTO, IT IS THE STORY OF THE MOST UNIQUE DUTY IN THE ANNALS OF THE UNITED STATES NAVY. THIS SHIP HAS GIVEN THE PUBLIC LIVING ALONG THE INLAND WATERWAYS OF AMERICA A FIRST HAND GLIMPSE OF OUR AMPHIBIOUS FORCES. THESE PEOPLE, LEAST FAMILIAR WITH OUR NAVY, WERE GIVEN THEIR FIRST OPPORTUNITY TO BECOME ACQUAINTED WITH LANDING SHIPS AND THE PART THEY PLAYED IN WORLD WAR II. TO THOSE UNFAMILIAR WITH THIS ASSIGN-MENT, IT MAY HAVE APPEARED TO BE A PLEASURE TOUR. WE KNOW DIFFERENTLY! WE HAVE HAD GOOD LIBER-TIES AND GOOD TIMES TOGETHER. BUT BY THE SAME TOKEN OUR JOB HAS DEMANDED HARD WORK AND PLENTY OF IT. EVERY MAN, AN AMBASSADOR OF GOOD WILL, HAS DUTIFULLY EXPLAINED THE COMMONPLACE, ANSWERED INNUMERABLE QUESTIONS, AND EFFICIENTLY HANDLED MORE THAN TWO MILLION VISITORS. WE HAVE SUCCESSFULLY STIMULATED INTEREST IN THE NAVY; WE HAVE NOT LET AMERICANS FORGET ITS ACHIEVEMENTS IN WAR NOR ITS ROLE IN MAINTAINING PEACE

ALL HANDS ARE COMMENDED FOR A JOB WELL DONE.

John Calvin Stevens 2nd.

The Foreword to the USS LST *512* history.

Officer-in-Charge Officers

LT. COMDR. LOUIS H. BRENDEL, USNR	OFFICER-IN-CHARGE	APR. 1945 - JULY 1945
LT. HARVEY A. SEIFERT, USNR	OFFICER-IN-CHARGE	JULY 1945 - SEPT 1945
LT. RUSSELL Q. FACCHINI, USNR	OFFICER-IN-CHARGE	OCT. 1945 - NOV. 1945
LT. WILLIAM L. MAY, USNR	OFFICER-IN-CHARGE	NOV. 1945 - JAN. 1946
LT. NELSON G. WETTLING, USNR	OPERATIONS OFFICER	APR. 1945 - JAN. 1946
LT. W. B. BOOTH, USNR	OPERATIONS OFFICER	APR. 1945 - SEPT 1945
LT. DON E. DELONE, USNR	PUBLIC INFORMATION OFFICER	APR. 1945 - NOV. 1945
LT. (JG) STIRLING D. SILLIPHANT, USNR	PUBLIC INFORMATION OFFICER	APR. 1945 - JAN. 1946
LT. JUSTIN MAHON, USNR	BUSHIPS TECHNICAL ADVISOR	FEB. 1945 - JAN. 1946
LT. E. J. BECKER, USNR	AIR LIAISON OFFICER	NOV. 1945 - JAN. 1946
LT. (JG) JOHN F. PIVAL, USCGR	PUBLIC INFORMATION OFFICER	MAY 1945 - SEPT 1945
ENSIGN SAMUEL B. WHITE, USNR	PUBLIC INFORMATION OFFICER	DEC. 1945 - JAN. 1946
C. W. O. JOSEPH L. MC KEE, USCGR	OPERATIONS OFFICER	DEC. 1945 - JAN. 1946

Marine Detachment Officers

LT. COL. G. MC GUIRE PIERCE, USMCR	EXHIBIT ENGINEER	FEB. 1945 - JUNE 1945
CAPT. DAVID I. ZEITLIN, USMCR	COMMANDING OFFICER	MAY 1945 - NOV. 1945
CAPT. JOHN E. SIVEC, USMCR	EXECUTIVE OFFICER	APR. 1945 - NOV. 1945
	COMMANDING OFFICER	NOV. 1945 - JAN. 1946
CAPT. EDWARD F. TAYLOR, USMC	QUARTERMASTER OFFICER	APR. 1945 - JULY 1945
1ST. LT. PAUL E. CRAMER, USMCR	PLATOON LEADER	APR. 1945 - NOV. 1945
1ST. LT. PAUL D. STROHKIRCH, USMCR	AMPHIB OFFICER	MAY 1945 - NOV. 1945
	EXECUTIVE OFFICER	NOV. 1945 - JAN. 1946
2ND. LT. GEORGE I. HAMPTON, USMCR	QUARTERMASTER OFFICER	JULY 1945 - JAN. 1946
W. O. ALBERT A. NOVATNEY, USMC	ORDNANCE OFFICER	MAY 1945 - AUG. 1945
W. O. MARVIN D. BUSCHOW, USMC	ORDNANCE OFFICER	SEPT 1945 - JAN. 1946
W. O. JOHN F. LEOPOLD, USMC	PHOTOGRAPHIC OFFICER	APR. 1945 - MAY 1945

10

Page from the USS LST *512* history.

U.S.S. L.S.T. 512 Officers

LT. JEROME BROCK, USNR	COMMANDING OFFICER	APR. 1945 - OCT. 1945
LT. JOHN CALVIN STEVENS, II, USNR	COMMANDING OFFICER	OCT. 1945 - JAN. 1946
LT. DONALD S. LACEY, USNR	EXECUTIVE OFFICER	APR. 1945 - OCT. 1945
LT. DOUGLAS SEAMAN, USNR	ENGINEERING OFFICER	MAR. 1945 - NOV. 1945
	EXECUTIVE OFFICER	OCT. 1945 - JAN. 1946
LT. JAMES G. BUSICK, USNR	NAVIGATOR	APR. 1945 - OCT. 1945
LT. (JG) LEO SILVERSTEIN, USNR	FIRST LIEUTENANT	FEB. 1945 - NOV. 1945
LT. (JG) CHARLES R. TIPPIN, JR., USNR	FIRST LIEUTENANT	OCT. 1945 - JAN. 1946
LT. (JG) BARTHOLOMEW J. D'ELIA, USNR	COMMUNICATIONS OFFICER	FEB. 1945 - JAN. 1946

LT. (JG) HARDY GLENN, USNR	GUNNERY OFFICER	FEB. 1945 - DEC. 1945
LT. (JG) EDWARD M. LEPPARD, USNR	COMMUNICATIONS OFFICER	OCT. 1945 - JAN. 1946
ENSIGN PETER V. SIRA, USN	SUPPLY AND DISBURSING OFFICER	APR. 1945 - JAN. 1946
ENSIGN JEROME J. YOFFIE, USNR	ASS'T. COMMUNICATIONS OFFICER	OCT. 1945 - JAN. 1946
ENSIGN FREDERICK J. SCHMIEDER, USNR	ASS'T. FIRST LIEUTENANT	OCT. 1945 - JAN. 1946
ENSIGN GEORGE P. PASSABET, USNR	GUNNERY OFFICER	OCT. 1945 - JAN. 1946
ENSIGN EDWIN R. RUBICK, USNR	NAVIGATOR	OCT. 1945 - JAN. 1946
ENSIGN JOHN H. WHITE, USN	ENGINEERING OFFICER	NOV. 1945 - JAN. 1946

11

Page from the USS LST *512* history.

Naval Personnel

ADKINS, Carl H.	SC3c	16 Shopping Court, Harshman Homes, Dayton, Ohio
ALDERMAN, Lawrence A., Jr.	S2c	703 North Main St., Kissimmee, Fla.
ALMEIDA, Elizeu (n)	SM2c	324 Winsor St., Ludlow, Mass.
ARMSTRONG, Jacob V.	Csp(R)	Recruiting Station, Milwaukee, Wisc.
BALDWIN, Melvin A.	BM1c	Staples, Minn.
BENEDICT, Howard L.	SC1c	1749 Hayden Ave., Cleveland, Ohio
BENNETT, Arnold T.	F1c	1625 No. Mobile Ave., Chicago, Ill.
BERGE, Olaf W.	PhoM3c	206 13th St., Hoboken, N. J.
BINIAK, Eugene J.	SC1c	3078 Elston Ave., Chicago, Ill.
BISHOP, Robert E.	S1c	Kenbridge, Va.
BLESSENT, John (n)	SC3c	Spokane, Wash.
BOGDAN, Cyril (n)	S2c	915 2nd St., Monessen, Pa.
BOGOVIC, Stephen J.	S1c	263 Union St., Luzerne, Pa.
BOMBASH, Andrew J., Jr.	S1c	375 West Luke Road, Erie, Pa.
BONDI, Joseph B.	MoMM1c	915 West 68th St., Chicago, Ill.
BOOSER, Chalres E.	S2c	1322 Walters Ave., Millvale, Pittsburgh, Pa.
BOWE, Kenneth T.	S2c	29 Montgomery Ave., Meriden, Conn.
BOWSER, Roland V.	BM2c	U.S. Naval Hospital, Philadelphia, Pa.
BRADFIELD, Joseph B.	WT2c	Catlin, Illinois
BRERETON, John F.	S1c	USS SNYDER, c/o Fleet Post Office, N. Y.
BRUNO, Elmer A.	SC3c	1123 West 7th St., Chester, Pa.
BUSCH, Edward P., Jr.	RM3c	195 Northfield Rd., Bedford, Ohio
BUTLER, Sam E.	StM1c	724 Court-E, Jacksonville, Fla.
BUYSSE, Cyril (n), Jr.	CMoMM	681 E. 31st. St., Paterson, N. J.
CAMPBELL, Charles A., Jr.	StM1c	417 N. Wolfe St., Baltimore, Md.
CANAVAN, Robert J.	Cox	4514 Lake Park Ave., Chicago, Ill.
CANNADY, Marsdon (n), Jr.	S2c	R. R. #5, Clinton, N. C.
CAREY, Raymond Z.	S1c	139 Willowbank St., Bellefonte, Pa.
CASSIS, Peter J.	EM3c	144 Marine Rd., Boston, Mass.
CATERINO, Samuel J.	CMoMM	159 Orient Way, Lyndhurst, N. J.
CATTANACH, Paul C.	GM2c	650 McClellan St., Long Branch, N. J.
CAUSEY, Paul S.	CM3c	2918 W. Wishart St., Philadelphia, Pa.
CHAMBERS, Raymond M.	MoMM2c	Calhoun, Tenn.
CHAMPER, Orren S.	CPhM	5439 Elowe St., Pittsburgh, Pa.
CHURCH, Lewis R.	S1c	909 Lee St., Connersville, Ind.
COFFILL, Albert D.	Cox	1901 N. Kedzie Ave., Chicago, Ill.
COKER, Billy L.	BM2c	1407 East Randolph St., Enid, Okla.
COLA, Peter J.	GM2c	204 Sisson St., Providence, R. I.
COLEY, James H.	MoMM1c	3412 Simmes Ave., Richmond, Va.
COOPER, Earl (n)	MoMM3c	223 2nd St., Spencer, W. Va.
COOPER, William F.	EM2c	329 Princess Anne Rd., Norfolk, Va.
COPLIN, George E.	S1c	Payne, Ohio
CORDNER, Carter E.	Sp(X)3c	Hotel St. Regis, New York, N. Y.
COX, Gerald D.	QM1c	819 McArthur Ave., San Francisco, Calif.
COX, Robert A.	GM1c	Spring St., Spartansburg, S. C.
CULVER, Vivian W.	SF1c	Quinhippa Ave., North Haven, Conn.
CUMMINGS, Reuben W.	SC2c	9 New St., Glassboro, N. J.
DAILEY, Prince (n)	Ck3c	Tunnel Springs, Ala.
DAVIS, Kenneth L.	SC1c	S. Fair St., Marion, Ill.
DAVIS, Leo D.	St3c	2929 Taylor St., Dallas, Texas
DEHART, Robert E.	MoMM1c	118 8th St., Salem, N. J.
DERDZINSKE, Robert F.	S1c	R.R. #2, Box 31, Kingstree, S. C.
DICKERSON, Albert C.	S2c	Armed Guard Center, Brooklyn, N. Y.
DIMALANTA, Ramon A.	Ck1c	1408 Imogene St., Philadelphia, Pa.
DOWNEY, Richard L.	GM1c	653 So. Joliet St., Joliet, Ill.
DRAPER, Clarence W.	Cox	939 Geo. Washington Highway, Portsmouth, Va.
DUFFIELD, Louis L.	GM2c	Armed Guard Center, Brooklyn, N. Y.
EBERLE, Edward L.	EM3c	423 East Utica St., Buffalo, N. Y.
EHRLICH, Dale H.	WT3c	106 Park St., Beatrice, Nebraska
ELDER, Odis W.	CMoMM	68 Felice St., Salinas, Calif.
EMCH, Leo (n)	MoMM1c	3633 Ludgate Rd., Shaker Heights, Cleveland, Ohio
EVENINGRED, Russell H.	EM2c	624 Erie St., Port Huron, Mich.
EWERTZ, William (n)	GM1c	1612 Greenwood St., Toledo, Ohio

12

Page from the USS LST *512* history.

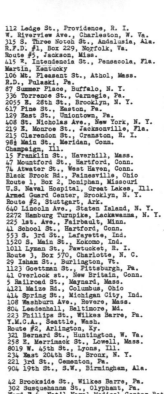

FAMIGLIETTI, Eugene A.	S1c	112 Ledge St., Providence, R. I.
FLETCHER, Charles B.	Y1c	W. Riverview Ave., Charleston, W. Va.
FOREMAN, Max M.	QM2c	315 S. Three Notch St., Andalusia, Ala.
FOREMAN, Neil (n)	StM2c	R.F.D. #1, Box 229, Norfolk, Va.
FORTENBERRY, Daniel W., Jr.	SK1c	Route #5, Jackson, Miss.
FRANKLIN, George W.	Bkr1c	415 E. Intendencia St., Pensacola, Fla.
FRAZIER, Paul (n)	S1c	Martin, Kentucky
FULLER, Arnold L.	RM3c	106 Mt. Pleasant St., Athol, Mass.
GARRETT, Jack R.	S2c	R.D., Pulaski, Pa.
GAWRONSKI, Edmund S.	MoMM2c	87 Summer Place, Buffalo, N. Y.
GEOROJC, Chester C.	MoMM2c	336 Torrence St., Carnegie, Pa.
GERMAINE, Francis F.	CCS	2055 E. 28th St., Brooklyn, N. Y.
GERMANO, Salvatore T.	Cox	617 Pine St., Easton, Pa.
GOGLIN, William M.	S2c	129 East St., Uniontown, Pa.
GREEN, William H.	St3c	408 St. Nicholas Ave., New York, N. Y.
GREENWELL, Warren (n)	Bkr1c	219 E. Monroe St., Jacksonville, Fla.
GREN, John S.	CPhM	215 Clarendon St., Cranston, R. I.
GUASTELLA, Antony R.	S1c	98½ Main St., Meridan, Conn.
HARKNESS, Donald W.	EM1c	Champaign, Ill.
HARRIGAN, Richard F.	SC3c	15 Franklin St., Haverhill, Mass.
HAVEY, David H.	Y1c	47 Mountford St., Hartford, Conn.
HAWLEY, William R.	EM2c	74 Atwater St., West Haven, Conn.
HAYWARD, Perry W., Jr.	F1c	Black Brook Rd., Painesville, Ohio
HEADLEY, Billy E.	F2c	Route 1, Box 2, Doniphan, Missouri
HEAVENER, Charles F.	S1c	U.S. Naval Hospital, Great Lakes, Ill.
HENRY, George T.	S1c	Armed Guard Center, Brooklyn, N. Y.
HESSE, Calvin A.	WT2c	Route #2, Stuttgart, Ark.
HESSE, Roy J.	RM3c	640 Lincoln Ave., Staten Island, N. Y.
HETEY, Steve P.	S1c	2272 Hamburg Turnpike, Lackawanna, N. Y.
HOHENHAUS, William E.	EM1c	225 1st. Ave., Fairbault, Minn.
HOLEWA, Edward S.	S1c	41 School St., Hartford, Conn.
HOLLADAY, Paul D.	S1c	553 S. 3rd St., Lafayette, Ind.
HOST, Raymond A.	S1c	1520 S. Main St., Kokomo, Ind.
HURST, Robert D.	F1c	1011 Lyman St., Pawtucket, R. I.
HUSKEY, Dewey D.	F1c	Route 3, Box 570, Charlotte, N. C.
IVERSEN, Robert D.	S1c	29 Isham St., Burlington, Vt.
JANCZAK, Raphael A.	S2c	1123 Goettman St., Pittsburgh, Pa.
JASZ, Walter H.	S2c	41 Overlook st., New Britain, Conn.
JOHNSTON, Richard E.	F1c	5 Railroad St., Maynard, Mass.
JOHNSTON, Robert D.	MoMM1c	4121 Maize Rd., Columbus, Ohio
KEENEY, Eugene J.	SC2c	414 Spring St., Michigan City, Ind.
KELLY, Daniel A.	S1c	108 Washburn Ave., Revere, Mass.
KELSON, Leonard N.	GM3c	804 Leadenhall, Baltimore, Md.
KERDOCK, Joseph (n)	CBM	223 Phillips St., Wilkes Barre, Pa.
KILPATRICK, Robert W.	GM2c	Y.M.C.A., Seattle, Wash.
KING, Richard (n), Jr.	Cox	Route #2, Arlington, Ky.
KITCHEN, Elmer A.	MoMM3c	321 Bernard St., Huntington, W. Va.
KLKPACZ, Karol S.	F1c	258 E. Merrimack St., Lowell, Mass.
KUPKA, John (n)	F1c	8019 W. 45th St., Lyons, Ill.
LAFONZINA, William N.	F1c	234 East 204th St., Bronx, N. Y.
LAUFIK, Frederick B.	S1c	221 3rd St., Cementon, Pa.
LEGGETT, William H.	Ck2c	904 19th St., S.W., Birmingham, Ala.
LESLIE, Ernest F.	S1c	
LISOSKI, Edward F.	S2c	42 Brookside St., Wilkes Barre, Pa.
MACKRELL, Paul M.	Cox	302 Susquehanna St., Olyphant, Pa.
MAGUIRE, Paul J.	MoMM3c	Ward E-6, Nat'l Naval Medical Center,Bethesda, Md.
MAVIGLIA, Herbert J.	Cox	423 Nortrem Parkway, Ridgewood, N. J.
MAXIAN, Paul G.	Cox	Binghampton, New York
MAYNARD, Benjamin D.	MoMM2c	Council, N. C.
McBRIDE, Frederick T.	F2c	Receiving Station, Norfolk, Va.
McKEE, Lewis C.	SF1c	Box 103, South Point, Ohio
MEHALKO, Andrew (n), Jr.	S2c	1401 Penn St., Nanty-Glo, Pa.
MILFEIT, Joseph P, Jr.	Y1c	610 Edmond St., Pittsburgh, 24, Pa.

13

Page from the USS LST *512* history.

MILLIMAN, Robert L.	S2c	R.R. 1, Butlerville, Ind.
MILLS, Alfred L.	MoMM2c	North Olmstead, Ohio
MOORE, John R.	MoMM2c	764 8th St., Allentown, Pa.
MOSLEY, Lee R.	S2c	Allisona, Tenn.
MOSS, James C.	S1c	Hayesville, N. C.
MULLEN, Joseph T.	Y2c	914 Buenzli Court, Scranton, Pa.
NASHLON, James (n)	F1c	6891 Bulwer Ave., Detroit, Mich.
NEELY, William L.	SKD1c	17208 Tarrymore Rd., Cleveland, Ohio
NELSON, Robert N.	S1c	2165 No. Wallace St., Indianapolis, Ind.
O'BOYLE, Joseph C.	MoMM3c	902 69th Ave., Philadelphia, Pa.
O'BRIEN, William P.	SF1c	107 Edgehill Court, Peoria, Ill.
O'DELL, James F.	CPhM	Mrs. Irene D. Baker, RFD #3, Waterbury, Conn.
O'MALLEY, Richard F.	BM1c	1123 George St., Chicago, Ill.
OPPENHEIM, Max (n)	MoMM2c	Chicago, Ill.
OSWALT, James E.	SC2c	
PATROU, George T.	SC3c	840 Division St., Webster City, Iowa
PATTON, Joseph C.	F1c	107 N. 58th St., Birmingham, Ala.
PEGGS, Robert J.	Csp(R)	Chicago, Ill.
PERCY, Gilbert T.	S1c	2717 Orthodox St., Philadelphia, Pa.
PEREZ, Jose L.	S2c	1119 43rd St., Chicago, Ill.
PERRY, Robert J.	Y2c	P. O. Box 4691, Jacksonville, Fla.
PIERCE, Robert (n)	S2c	3 Dock St., DuBois, Pa.
PUCHOWSKI, Theodore (n)	S1c(QM)	2846 Dehalb St., Gary, Ind.
PULNIK, Joseph J.	CBM	64 Wegman Parkway, Jersey City, N. J.
RAGER, Richard L.	RM2c	Broad St., Milroy, Pa.
RAINONE, Anthony (n)	CY	176 Lynch St., Providence, R. I.
REASONOVER, Sherril T.	StM1c	47 Post Lawrence Home, Toledo, Ohio
RISGER, Louis R.	SM1c	5801 Bergenline Ave., West New York, N. J.
ROUMAINE, Calvin M.	CM3c	4911 N. Leavitt St., Chicago, Ill.
RUEHL, Arthur R.	BM2c	17 Alpha Place, New Rochelle, N. Y.
SCHIFF, Irwin J.	S1c	1234 Columbia Ave., Chicago, Ill.
SCHULMAN, Ivan (n)	S2c	
SHENEMAN, Henry W.	F1c	5 Huntington Pike, Philadelphia, 11, Pa.
SIMONSON, John D.	CY	168-06 Linden Blvd., Jamaica, L. I., N. Y.
SKELLY, Daniel P.	CM3c	14 Beacon St., Hyde Park, Mass.
SLOOP, Brady O.	S1c (Bkr)	429 E. Lafayette St., Salisbury, N. C
SMITH, Ray A.	SC3c	118 Terrence St., Lenoir, N. C.
SOLBERG, Thomas M.	SF1c	Daugherty, Iowa
SPICER, Harold S.	PhoM1c	4103 Ridgewood Ave., Baltimore, Md.
SPOFFORD, Peter P.	F1c	170 Winthrop Road, Brookline, Mass.
SPURLING, Jesse A., Jr.	F1c	510 E. 11th St., Indianapolis, Ind.
STROHL, Harry (n), Jr.	CCS	Route 1, Pelham, N. C.
SULLENBERGER, Samuel D.	CBM	Box 58, Casstown, Ohio
TERRY, Willie (n)	Ck2c	Post Office, Mason, Tenn.
THOMAS, Louis W.	S1c	Chesapeake Ave., Crisfield, Md.
THOMPSON, Fred H.	StM1c	1063 Delmar St., Memphis, Tenn.
TINSTMAN, Charles R.	MoMM2c	Route 2, Box 163, Concord, Calif.
TODD, William F.	QM2c	405 Washington Ave., Sandersville, Ga.
TOKARSKY, Harry J.	Bkr3c	524 Fountain #9, Youngstown, Ohio
TUCKER, Julian G.	RM3c	Danville, Va.
TURNER, Eunice H.	Cox	205 Crosset St., Memphis, Tenn.
UNDERFANGER, John E., Jr.	F1c	108 McArthur Blvd., Springfield, Ill.
VAN DEUSEN, Milo C.	SK1c	R.F.D. 1, Brunswick, Ohio
WALLEY, Robert L.	S1c (SC)	410 Summer St., Lynn, Mass.
WALQUIST, Jack D.	S1c	Marine-on-St. Croix, Minn.
WASSER, Edward L.	PhM1c	805 N. New St., Bethlehem, Pa.
WHITE, Bernie L.	F1c	1410 W. College Ave., Independence, Mo.
WILKES, David (n)	Ck2c	West 114th St., New York, N. Y.
WILLIAMS, Hudson L.	StM2c	904 "B" Hinmon St., Muskegon Heights, Mich.
WRIGHT, Edward P.	MoMM3c	Apt. 612, 350 E. Armour Blvd., Kansas City, Mo.
YOUNG, James O.	CQM	207 N. 21st St., Corvalis, Ore.
ZACHARY, Thomas O.	GM2c	Greenwood, Ark.

14

Page from the USS LST *512* history.

39

Marine Personnel

40

41

ADAMS, Othello R.	PlSgt.	R. #1, Snyder, Texas.
ALPER, Simon	PFC	4212 W. Thompson St., Philadelphia, Pa.
ALTMAN, James H.	PFC	539 3rd St., Huntington, Ind.
ARCHON, William M.	GySgt.	53 Towsend Ave., Girard, Ohio.
ARTERBURN, Garrett	Sgt.	4012 S. Fitzhugh St., Dallas, Texas.
ASHBY, Edward C. Jr.	PlSgt.	2719 W. 32nd Ave., Denver, Colo.
AYERS, Tony T.	Corp.	Tapoco, N. C.
BAKER, Walter J.	Corp.	Elihu, Ky.
BARKER, Joseph R. Jr.	PFC	1201 Grand Ave., Joplin, Mo.
BAXTER, Theodore C.	Corp.	R. #1, Box 137-A, Henderson, Texas.
BEALER, Bernerd C. Jr.	PlSgt.	824 15th St., Moline, Ill.
BEDARD, Roland J.	Pvt.	36 Maumkeag St., Salem, Mass.
BLASS, Walter F.	PFC	135 W. Main St., Waterbury, Mass.
BLONDEEL, Alphonse C.	PFC	Star Route, Brunswick, Mich.
BLUMENTHAL, Eugene A.	PFC	3026 N. Robinston St., Sioux City, Iowa.
BOOKER, Donald E.	PFC	804 Amity St., Homestead, Pa.
BOYD, Johnny W.	PFC	Brookside, Ky.
BRINEGAR, Edouard W.	PFC	2501 St. Joseph Ave., St. Joseph, Mo.
BROOKS, Charles D.	PFC	R. #2, Kilmichael, Miss.
BROWN, Phillip B.	StfSgt.	300 E. Baltimore Ave., Media, Pa.
BUCKWALTER, John K.	Sgt.	217 E. New St., Lititz, Pa.
BUSCHOW, Marvin D.	C.W.O.	Woodward, La.
CAMMACK, George T.	GySgt.	224 E. 18th St., New York, N. Y.
CARTWRIGHT, John W.	PFC	318 30th St., Huntington, W. Va.
CATHEY, Frank W.	PFC	303 N. "B" St., Fairfield, Iowa.
CHANDLER, Hershel M.	Sgt.	R. #3, Box 687, Jacksonville, Fla.
COCHARIC, Carmen A.	PFC	3 South St., Summit, N. J.
COFFIN, Zacharias T.	Corp.	R. #5, Shawnee, Okla.
COKEN, John J.	PFC	1401 Loraine Ave., Bethlehem, Pa.
COLLINS, Ellis D.	PFC	R. #2, Lawrenceburg, Ky.
COLUCCI, Louis C.	PFC	23 Wesley Ave., Youngstown, Ohio.
CORNWELL, Bob R.	PFC	513 17th St., Sioux City, Iowa.
CRADDOCK, James T.	StfSgt.	119 Thomas St., Reidsville, N. C.
CRAIG, Carl E.	PFC	R. #1, Sellersburg, Ind.
CRAMER, Paul E.	1stLt.	3008 Niel Ave., Columbus, Ohio.
CROOK, David Jr.	PFC	1107 7th Ave., Nashville, Tenn.
CURRY, Frank A. Jr.	Sgt.	3864 Royal Palm Ave., Miami, Fla.
DABROWSKI, Walter	PFC	114 Milton Ave., Syracuse, N. Y.
DAVIS, Bellmar H.	PFC	R. #2, Purvis, Miss.
DE BORD, Ralph F.	Corp.	Maud, Ohio.
DE MOISEY, Truett R.	PFC	156 N. Main St., Walton, Ky.
DIEHL, Joseph J.	StfSgt.	37-20 81st St., Jackson Heights, N. Y.
DIVELEY, Gerald R.	Corp.	Peoria, Ill.
DOWNS, Francis E. N.	Sgt.	R. #1, Lake Elmo, Minn.
DRISCOLL, Edward J. Jr.	TSgt.	599 Prospect St., Elmhurst, Ill.
DUBOVICH, Edward J.	PFC	75 Main St., Franklin, N. J.
DUNCAN, Daniel M.	Corp.	R. #4, Whiteville, N. C.
EDWARDS, William C.	PFC	Box 312 Horse Cave, Ky.
EGBERT, Edmund W.	PFC	Annapolis, Md.
ENGLING, Everett L.	PFC	General Delivery, Luray, Kans.
EVANS, Ralph C.	Sgt.	1723 Sidney St., Pittsburgh, Pa.
FAGAN, Francis J.	Corp.	1661 E. 79th St., Chicago, Ill.
FARRINGTON, Arthur C.	Corp.	5932 3rd St., N. W., Washington, D. C.
FELTMEYER, Donald L.	PFC	Pickneyville, Ill.
FERRY, Harry E.	PFC	Philadelphia, Pa.
FOSBRE, James F.	Corp.	415 Grant Ave., Plainfield, N. J.
GIBSON, Mathew B.	PFC	Centenary, S. C.
GIFFEAR, Joseph A.	Pvt.	2420 S. 2nd St., Philadelphia, Pa.

42

15

Page from the USS LST *512* history.

GILBERT, John E. Jr.   PFC   R. #1, Fredericksburg, Pa.
GOFF, Albert S.   PFC   907 Walnut St., Atlantic, Iowa.
GOREET, Kenneth L.   PFC   Carlisle, Ark.
HALE, Charles H.   QMSgt.   Meadowview, Va.
HALFORD, John L.   PFC   60 William St., Cauverneur, N. Y.
HAMPTON, George I.   2dLt.   833 Eastern Ave., Connersville, Ind.
HANKS, Byron A. Jr.   Sgt.   702 Willow St., Duncan, Okla.
HARGADON, James F.   Corp.   Camden, N. J.
HAUPTMAN, Joseph   Corp.   R. #1, La Salle, Ill.
HAWES, William R.   Pvt.   733 Edwards St., Daytona Beach, Fla.
HAYES, William J.   Corp.   2367 Newland Ave., Chicago, Ill.
HAYS, Herbert J.   Corp.   762 A. St., Ashland, Oreg.
HENRY, Howard R.   PFC   R. #2, Blue Ridge, Geo.
HENRY, Roper   1stSgt.   R. #4, Hickman, Ky.
HENSICK, Bert M.   PFC   13709 Wadsworth Ave., Detroit, Mich.
HERSEY, Cheever L. Jr. PFC   45 Beacon St., Gloucester, Mass.
HETRICK, Charles W.   Corp.   521 W. Okla. St., Blackwell, Okla.
HILL, Richard C.   PlSgt.   1807 Melrose Ave., Roanoke, Va.
HOLLEY, Richard J.   PFC   8 N. 2nd St., Alabama City, Ala.
HUDSON, Robert M.   Corp.   2114 Acqueduct Ave., New York, N. Y.
HUFFMAN, Clair C.   PFC   R. #1, South Fork, Pa.
HUGHES, Leonard R.   PFC   Station "B", Charleston, W. Va.
HUNTER, Le Roy B.   PFC   Pleasant St., Oxford, New York.
HURLEY, Earl J.   PFC   Mc Carr, Ky.
HURST, William E.   Pvt.   R. #5, Greensburg, Pa.
JAY, Clarence L. Jr.   Corp.   Hollywood, Calif.
JETTER, Harry Jr.   PFC   Quincey, Mass.
JOHNSTON, John C.   Corp.   315 E. Tremont St., Hillsboro, Ill.
JOHNSON, George G.   PFC   133 Church St., Marion, Va.
JONES, "C" "H"   Pvt.   Killer, Ala.
JONES, John T. Jr.   PFC   Pittsburgh, Pa.
KARST, Albert L.   Corp.   80 Bay St., Charleston, S. C.
KEPLER, Robert R.   Corp.   16917 Inverness St., Detroit, Mich.
KIRK, James F.   PFC   Gold Hill, N. C.
KITCHENS, Leroy   PFC   R. #1, Covington, Tenn.
KORKUCH, Henry J.   Corp.   352 S. 21st St., Irvington, N. J.
KNELL, Charles A.   PFC   Washington, D. C.
KRAYNIEWSKI, Stanley   Pvt.   206 Jarvie St., Aliquippa, Pa.
LA CROIX, Leo J.   PFC   56 May St., Putnam, Conn.
LA FLAMME, Norman E.   PFC   6 Drummer St., Brattleboro, Vt.
LAFLIN, David G.   PFC   803 W. North St., Lebanon, Ind.
LAWRENCE, Robert L.   PFC   1504 George St., Sandusky, Ohio.
LEONARD, William P.   PFC   109 N. Caldwell, Salisbury, N. C.
LOHFINK, Louis E.   Corp.   Boyceville, Wis.
LOUDERMILK, Sherman C. Sgt.   Abiline, Texas.
LOVE, Raymond C.   Corp.   902 Florida St., San Antonio, Texas.
LYNCH, Paul E.   Pvt.   Falleton, Md.
MALINE, Vernard A.   PFC   Stuart, Iowa.
MALONEY, De Wayne W.   PFC   400 Marshall Ave., St. Paul, Minn.
MARTIN, William C.   StfSgt.   207 Auburn Apts., Eugene, Ore.
MATHENY, Glen E.   Corp.   97 E. Washington St., Pittsburg, Kan.
MEHARRY, Cecil R.   Sgt.   74 Oakwood Ave., Newark, Ohio.
MIESZKUO, Karzymiesz P. PFC   56 Levinson Ave., South River, N. J
MITCHELL, Charles E.   Corp.   4320 Forest Park Blv'd, St. Louis, Mo.
MITCHELL, Keith E.   PFC   R. #1, Packwood, Iowa.
MOORE, Wallace B.   PFC   General Delivery, Somerville, Texas.
MC GARRY, William J.   PFC   Bloomfield, Ind.
MC INTOSH, Robert D.   Pvt.   740 E. 78th St., Chicago, Ill.
MC MAHON, Edwin J.   Corp.   11631 W. Bluemond Rd, Wauwatosa, Wis.
NEAL, Edward L.   PFC   1217 W. North St., Kalamazoo, Mich.

16

Page from the USS LST *512* history.

NOGGLE, Leslie E.	PFC	1409 E. Center St., Warsaw, Ind.
NAVATNEY, Albert A.	C.W.O.	49 3rd St., Navy Yard, Charleston, S. C.
ORR, William R.	PFC	443 W. Central Ave., St. Paul, Minn.
ORTON, Jim R.	StfSgt.	Stratford, Calif.
PARKER, James W.	GySgt.	Upper Malboro, Me.
PARKER, Roy W.	Pvt.	R. #1, Stevenson, Ala.
PARKER, Vernon,	PFC	R. #3, Muskegon, Mich.
PARTLAK, Michael	PFC	Dilles Bottom, Ohio.
PASCOE, William M.	Sgt.	1901 S. Grant St., Amarillo, Texas.
PENNOCK, John J.	Corp.	Box 132, Emeigh, Pa.
PETERSEN, Robert E.	Sgt.	885 E. Grand Blv'd, Detroit, Mich.
PETERSON, George A.	PFC	28 Aston St., Lynn, Mass.
PHILLIPS, Alvin O.	PFC	6557 LaFayette Ave., Chicago, Ill.
PHIPPS, Herbert L.	Pvt.	4306 Evans Chapel Road, Baltimore, Md.
PHILLIPS, Stanley C.	PFC	Big Timber, Mont.
PIETRUSEWICZ, Walter V.	Corp.	Washington, D. C.
PIGOTT, Robert A.	PFC	Meridian, Miss.
PRADZINSKI, Raymond L.	PFC	1537 W. Chestnut St., Chicago, Ill.
RADFORD, John L.	PFC	Alturas, Fla.
RANDALL, Edwin R.	PFC	Detroit, Mich.
RICHEY, Virgil M.	PlSgt.	Dayton, Iowa.
RIEF, Collins H.	PFC	119 W. 2nd St., Chaska, Minn.
ROSE, Lewis E.	Corp.	Corpus Christi, Texas.
ROYSTON, Donald W.	Corp.	653 W. Broadway, Red Lion, Pa.
RUFFNER, Richard M.	PFC	717 S. Illinois St., Decatur, Ill.
SANDLEY, Russell D.	PFC	Browntown, Wis.
SASSE, Herman J.	Sgt.	533 S. New York Ave., Evansville, Ind.
SCHNOOR, Richard F.	PFC	2672 Coventy Road, Columbus, Ohio.
SCOTT, Landon F.	PFC	R. #2, Box 510, Jacksonville, Fla.
SERVON, Edward G.	Corp.	Ryder's Lane, Milltown, N. J.
SHADD, Daniel	PFC	2360 11th St., Milwaukee, Wis.
SHANAHAN, Robert E.	PFC	8823 Bennett Ave., Chicago, Ill.
SIVEC, John E.	Capt.	17844 Gruley Ave., Detroit, Mich.
SOTTILE, Edward	PFC	11 Franklin St., Poughkeepsie, N. Y.
SMITH, Aron	Pvt.	1004 Gate City Highway, Kingsport, Tenn.
STEELMAN, Pettus R.	Corp.	R. #7, Fayetteville, Tenn.
STOSIC, Anthony R.	Sgt.	406 E. Willock Road, Pittsburgh, Pa.
STRAZISAR, Joseph H.	PFC	R. #2, Box 239, Johnstown, Pa.
STROHKIRCH, Paul D.	1stLt.	485 Wilcox Road, Rochester, Mich.
TATUM, Santiago H.	Pvt.	7510 Avenue "P", Houston, Texas.
TAYLOR, Edward F.	Capt.	15906 Fielding Ave., Detroit, Mich.
THISSEN, Edward A.	Corp.	304 N. Ridgley St., Algona, Iowa.
TODD, Ira G. Jr.	Corp.	Bradner, Ohio.
THOMAS, Frank J.	PFC	Fredericksburg, Va.
TRUDEAU, Henry A.	Sgt.	333 Broad St., Valley Falls, R. I.
TULLY, John	PFC	Boston, Mass.
TURNER, James A.	Corp.	400 N. Main St., Anna, Ill.
VIVARDO, Vincent J.	PFC	838 Garabaldi Place, Chicago, Ill.
WALSH, Joseph F.	PFC	804 N. Rebecca Ave., Scranton, Pa.
WATTS, George R.	PFC	600 S. Orange St., LaFayette, La.
WELLS, Marvin	Pvt.	132 Mechanic St., Cape May Court House, N.J.
WILSON, Clayton L.	Pvt.	St. Paul, Minn.
WITTE, Alvin H.	Corp.	806 N. East Ave., Oak Park, Ill.
WOODS, Victor L.	Corp.	R. #5, E. Wenatchee, Wash.
WOODS, Walter B.	Pvt.	P. O. Box 895, Dumas, Texas.
WORKMAN, Ross F. Jr.	PFC	3429 Browning St., San Diego, Calif.
WURTZEL, Roger J.	Sgt.	7021 Elmwood Ave., Harrisburg, Pa.
YELVERTON, James L.	PFC	R. #1, Enterprise, Miss.
ZEITLIN, David I.	Capt.	4th Thames Ave., Stratford, Conn.

17

Page from the USS LST *512* history.

2-7 Mar 46	New Orleans, Louisiana.
7-18 Mar 46	Golden Meadow, Louisiana, on bayou La Fourche.
18-29 Mar 46	New Orleans, Louisiana.
31 Mar-5 Apr 46	Daytona Beach, Florida.
7 Apr-15 May 46	Washington, D.C., 5932 3rd Street, NW.
17-19 May 46	New Orleans, Louisiana.
19-25 May 46	Lafitte, Louisiana, on Lake Barataria.
25-27 May 46	New Orleans, Louisiana.
29 May-Jun 46	Washington, D.C. Mom bought the black 1935 Cadillac four-door sedan and luggage trailer. She had sold the house to a school teacher, and we shipped a little and loaded the trailer with everything we could, then took off for California. Mom probably regrets to this day leaving many memories behind. Incidentally, we avoided New Orleans, as Mom thought I would defect.
6-15 Jun 46	Arlington, Texas. We visited Mom's relatives.
18-24 Jun 46	Motel, Ventura Boulevard, Los Angeles, California.
25 Jun-30 Sep 46	2120 Fairfield Avenue, Hollywood, California. We moved into a duplex, which we shared with Richard Basehart (Captain Nelson on the TV series *Voyage to the Bottom of the Sea*) and his beautiful wife. Bette Davis, the owner, had just taken up with Gary Merrill and moved to Laguna Beach. I bought a 1932 Ford V-8 coupe, with hatchback, attended the University of Southern California summer session, and worked my

butt off as a result of an ad in the *Hollywood Citizen-News* stating, "Ex-Marine will do anything for 75¢ an hour."

1 Oct 46-29 Jul 50   2515 Tilden Avenue, Los Angeles, California (near the intersection of Pico and Sepulveda Boulevards.

Sep 46   Matriculated at UCLA under the GI Bill.

10 Oct 46   First enlisted man to join the 13th Infantry Battalion, United States Marine Corps Reserve, at Lilac Terrace, Chavez Ravine, Los Angeles, California (the present-day location of the Los Angeles Dodgers). I was a Corporal.

Feb 47   Hitchhiked to and from New Orleans — for Mardi Gras?

Jul 48   To Mexico City via New Orleans.

Jul 49   To Mexico City via New Orleans to attend my second summer session at *La Escuela de Verano* (summer school), the University of Mexico.

18 Jun 50   Graduated from UCLA in the Hollywood Bowl with a B.A. degree in Latin American Studies. My mother and my girlfriend, Erlinda L. Treviño, attended. Assured by the Marine Corps since 1946 that upon graduation I would be eligible for a commission, HQ Marine Corps responded to the necessary qualifying papers with a message that I was six months too old, having become 27 in November 1949! Luckily I had been promoted to Staff Sergeant on May 1 so I was ready for what was to come. Instead of going to New York

for an interview concerning a job with the Macmillan Publishing Co. in Brazil, the Korean War broke out on June 25, 1950, and I was on my way to Korea for the "winter sports."

Semper Fidelis

Chapter 3

A UCLA Bruin

*M*Y FOUR YEARS AT UCLA, from 1946 to 1950, thanks to the GI Bill, were very rewarding. I joined the CALVETS organization for veterans and became best friends with George Saperstein, who had been in the Coast Guard, and Jerry Fields, who had been a destroyer sailor. (George had to drop out in his senior year at UCLA as his father was dying of cancer, but Jerry graduated and went on to the University of Southern California to become a dental surgeon.)

I had a three-year platonic relationship with Vera Sutter, a Ph.D. in bacteriology, attending Marine Corps birthday balls, CALVET trips to Lake Arrowhead, parties, dances, and frequently providing companionship during her lab work. The year that the Marine Ball was held at the Ambassador Hotel. Vera and I were introduced to the movie star Maureen O'Hara by her sister's husband, Colonel Gorman, who had been a passenger in my Ford V-8's rumble seat back in North Carolina in 1942. In 1946, he was the Executive Officer of the 13th Infantry Battalion, U.S. Marine Corps Reserve (Organized), headquartered in Chavez Ravine, today the home of Dodger Stadium. ("Organized" Reserve units, by the way, held regularly scheduled meetings;

"Unorganized" units held no regular meetings.)

I attended all summer camps with the USMCR(O), and was promoted two ranks to Staff Sergeant. I joined the Kappa Alpha Order fraternity in 1949. I learned that they had lost their house on fraternity row when, during their regular Monday night meeting the day after Pearl Harbor, most of them had opted to join one of the services. In 1946, the Kappa Alpha members that had survived the war were back. Our brother fraternity at USC was one of the largest and included many of their top athletes. Needless to say, the subsequent yearly combined parties were something else. I was lucky enough to take the first "Sheena, Queen of the Jungle," the beautiful, blonde Irish McCalla, to a fraternity party. My brothers couldn't stand it!

Much of my CALVET time was spent at the beaches. Zuma, out near Point Dume, was our favorite — both for parties and for fishing from our two-man rubber boats, with girls aboard. It really got exciting when we would pull in a huge sheep's-head fish with those large protruding incisors. Either the fish or the girls would bail.

And the UCLA riding club

The late Vera Sutter, Ph.D., *ca.* 1946. Vera was a member of the Bacteriology Department at UCLA. She later worked for the Center for Disease Control. Many years later, Vera attended the weddings of the authors' two daughters, Karen and Lynn, in Escondido, California.

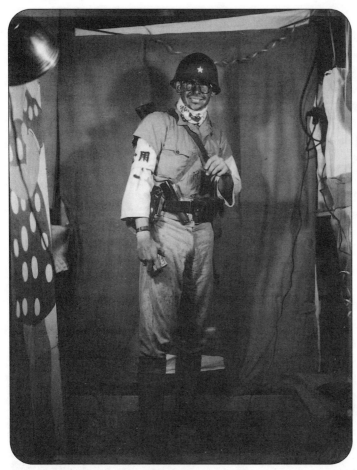

Halloween, 1946, at UCLA — in "uniform" — the author's complete Japanese soldier's uniform from helmet to two-toed rubber jungle shoes (a separate compartment for the big toe, and one for the others), including a .25-caliber rifle, bayonet, canteen, "potato-masher" hand grenade, ammo pouch, and wrap leggings *à la* World War I.

also was great. We rode on Will Roger's State Park off Sunset Boulevard near the polo grounds. One day a pretty blonde had been unhorsed and had broken her arm. I rode back to the stables and drove my Ford up the fire breaks. The group had put a long branch on her arm as a splint, so we had to take it off, break it, and reattach it before she could fit in the coupe. Blondes don't necessarily have more fun.

As my major was Latin American Studies, I attended the summer school of the University of Mexico during 1948 and 1949. I missed a big party that the CALVETS threw in 1948, and upon returning the guys told me that a girl had been there who they had wanted to set me up with. The scheduling was better in 1949, and the party was just after I returned from Mexico. It was then that I was introduced to Erlinda Lopez Treviño, a fellow GI Bill attendee from Texas, who had been stationed in my home-town, Washington, D.C., during the war. I remember Erlinda drilling a squad of Kappa Alphas in the parking lot out at La Cañada Country Club. She had been a WAVE. And we are still together.

While in Mexico in 1948, my two roommates at 22 Etla, *Colonia Hip-pódromo,* and I decided to check out one of Ernest Hemingway's great descriptions of the macho sport of bull fighting. One Sunday afternoon José, Rogelio, and I hiked over to the *Plaza de Toros*, which was nearby. It was absolutely horrible, sickening, and all in all the worse exhibition that I had ever seen in my life. I took some photos at a distance, and we finally just walked out, to some pretty nasty booing. Briefly, this is what occurred. The great-looking bull came out and raced around the arena. Then some horses appeared with riders armed with long spears. (I'm not sorry that I don't know the names of the weapons used or of their pic-turesque bearers.) The horses wore large rectangles on each side, which appeared to be mattresses. The bull then charged and the riders sank their spears into the bull's neck or as close to the neck as they could. While they were mangling the *toro*, he was coming up from below and literally tore the innards, viscera, and entrails out of the horses! *Olé! Olé!* My God!

Vera Sutter and Arthur Farrington at Turner's German beer garden — probably celebrating a UCLA victory.

A brace of mules then appeared and one by one the dead and dying horses were dragged off the sand, leaving trails of blood and guts. Next appeared *hombres* on foot, armed with two short daggers. Of all the gentlemen involved in this massacre, these were the bravest. They antagonized the animal to charge and then sank the two daggers into his neck, after deftly dodging his horns. When several of the men had completed their task, the bull was left alone, shaking the daggers loose and covered in blood, while the band struck up and the brave *toreador* appeared strutting and posturing. What a sick spectacle. The sword and capework then commenced, with the sword missing the mark, being withdrawn, and in some cases seeming to be plunged into the previous holes. Hemingway sure knew good things when he saw them, but I guess the talent finally caught up with him.

Los Pirámides de Teotihuacán y Pulque
July 1948, Mexico City

As Roger (Rogelio), Joseph (José), and I (Arturo) boarded the bus of the *Estrella de Oro* (Gold Star), I felt proud that we were up to "some good" for a change. We were from the Los Angeles area, attending summer school in Mexico City, I at the University of Mexico on San Cosme Street and they at City College. We were staying with a Mexican family at 22 Etla, *Colonia Hippódromo*, near Chapultepec Castle. I had talked Roger and Joseph into "storming the castle," just the way the U.S. Marines had back in 1847 in the Mexican-American War.

The climb had been almost straight up, made by clinging onto vines, rocks, and whatever. We had come upon some cannonballs embedded in the rock, and I had kept my friends from claiming them as souvenirs, as I knew that if they were indeed high-explosive, they would be more dangerous than 100 years earlier.

After a very long, hot, and dirty climb, we had reached the base of the castle walls. I wondered how the Americans had ever taken this bastion. I had seen re-creations of the battle on

Los Pirámides de Teotihuacán y Pulque — The Pyramids of the Sun.

level ground, but what a travesty it was. *Los jóvenes heróicas* (young heroes) of the Mexican Military College, who were among the defenders, did their duty to the bitter end and were remembered for their bravery. The Marines also would be remembered in the "Marine Corps Hymn": "From the halls of Montezuma to the shores of Tripoli. . . ."

We were on our way to *Los Pirámides de Teotihuacán*, about 40 miles northeast of the capital. We always traveled "last class" — economy — as I was on the GI Bill ($92 per month) and the other students were not much better off. We had noticed that our treatment improved if we introduced ourselves as students rather than as tourists, and sporting mustaches!

As we entered a wide valley, there ahead was the largest pyramid in the world — the Pyramid of the Sun — surrounded by the Pyramid of the Moon and other less imposing but highly decorated structures.

As beer drinkers we were in heaven in Mexico, for some of

the best brews in the world were made there. We also knew that the fermented juice of the maguey, the century-plant cactus, was the most consumed alcoholic beverage in all of Mexico. It was called *pulque*, and we were on its trail, for there was practically none in the cities, as it required nominal refrigeration.

Upon debarking from the bus, we headed into the maguey fields, which covered the landscape, and we approached a farmer. He described the process of cutting out the center of the cactus to gather the liquid used in making the *pulque*, then invited us to his home. He asked if we would like to buy some "good-luck charms" that the Aztecs had scattered in their fields to encourage better crops. We entered a small shed and he showed us a pile of dirt with items that he had uncovered. I purchased three of the charms. One was an exquisite head and neck of very fine features; the second was the head of an animal (dog?) with a harelip and fantastic eyes; and the third was an Aztec warrior's feathered head made of light, porous, volcanic pumice.

The *campesino* had told us that there was a *pulquería* near the base of the Pyramid of the Sun, and we wisely decided to do our duty before imbibing. We thus clambered up the large stones — and sometime steps — to the very top. There, to our surprise, was a group of about ten or eleven young ladies in long white dresses, and each had a Red Cross pin on her blouse.

A gentleman dressed "to the nines" was photographing them. The view was breathtaking; it was probably at an altitude of over 7,000 feet. I walked over to the seemingly "tourist" gentleman and ask him if he was a *padre*. He looked all around, and seeing that we were the only ones up there he admitted that, indeed, he was, and that the women were really nuns from Spain. I knew it! In 1926, the president of Mexico, Plutarco Calles, in line with the anti-Roman Catholic, anti-clericalism provisions of the Constitutions of 1857 and 1917, had issued a decree prohibiting the clergy from wearing religious garments or insignia outside the churches of Mexico, and thus they were "incognito." It seemed to me that conflicting religious beliefs, both with others and with non-religious governing bodies, always have been, are, and forever will be the greatest source of upheavals and conflicts on this planet!

We bid *adiós* to our fellow "pyramid climbers," descended from the heights, and commenced our search for the objective. There, over what appeared to be a cave in some very large boulders, we espied a weathered board with the word *PUL- QUERÍA* barely visible. We entered. Knowing that in Mexico most high-class bars (those without domino and pool tables) were pitch dark, made more so by the pupil-shrinking Mexican sun, we were not surprised by the complete lack of light in this particular place. I felt out and selected a stool at the bar; Roger sat to my right, and Joe to his right. I ordered *tres pulques*, and we heard glasses tinkle and liquid pouring. Then three glasses of fresh *pulque* were in front of us. I felt and heard heavy breathing just to my left, but saw no one. We tried our *pulque*, which was served in water glasses; it had a very strange and slightly bitter taste. Today I am reminded of it when I down a Zima, a malt beverage brewed in Memphis, Tennessee.

Suddenly from my left, I heard in a deep, guttural voice that could only be emulated by a Japanese Samurai: "*Somos Mexicanos puros!*" (We are pure Mexicans!) I turned to my right — we could see a little better by this time — and observed Roger looking at Joseph. They were noncommittal. I swiveled around and announced: "*Y, nosotros somos puros Gringos!*" (And we are pure Gringos!) — in not exactly good Spanish. Magically, to our left appeared four sets of gleaming white teeth in the faces of four "pure," smiling Mexicans. International relations were secure for the time being, and we confidently put away a couple glasses of their "national drink" in the small, seven-seater bar.

And, thus, in answer to the pleas of the summer school staffers to "get out and see our country," we had, and we completely enjoyed it — except for the upset stomachs on the bus ride back to Mexico City.

⋯≡◉⊂≡⋯

One day I walked down San Cosme Street to the huge, then 480-year-old tree under which Hernando Cortez had wept on "*El Noche Triste*," June 20, 1520, the day his army was routed from the Aztec capital. In their retreat over the causeways of Tenochtitlán, the Spanish conquistadors had lost 450 of their own, 4,000 Tlaxcalan Indians, 46 horses, and most of their looted treasure. The famous tree is an Ahuehuete, a Moctezuma Cypress, and has many trunks among which you may make your way.

On another weekend we decided to take a trip to see Paricutín, a volcano that had recently, in 1943, arisen from a corn field near the town of Uruapan in the state of Michoacán. We traveled west by train to Morelia, and then on to the town of Pátzcuaro where we went by native boat to the island in the middle of a grand lake and investigated the giant statue of José María Morelos, a hero of Mexico's war of independence from Spain. We returned to the train, and we were taken on to Uruapan, discovering that the volcano was miles outside the town and thus horses would be needed. As the hour was late in the afternoon, the trip could not take place until the next morning, so we got a room. A *Club de Noche* was next on our list, and to our surprise, we found a group of girls from the summer school. I introduced my friends from Mexico City College, the *cerveza* flowed, the band was really good, and we had a great time. The prettiest of the girls, a blonde from East L.A., had been my partner in the dance program that we had put on for the summer school.

A *viejo*, a really old Mexican gentleman, sailed his sombrero out on the dance floor with a flourish, and the crowd called for *los Gringos* to show them something. Each state in Mexico has its own style of sombrero, and Michoacán's is large, heavy, and

The author's dance group at the *Escuela de Verano*, University of Mexico. Top row, fifth and sixth from left, Arthur Farrington and his partner.

Two "Gringas" and one "Gringo" — the author — adrift at the Floating Gardens of Xochimilco, appreciating Mexican culture.

has a wide brim. With a little *machismo* I dared my blonde friend, and to the lively tune *"La Jarabe Tapatío"* we danced the Mexican hat dance. As you may know, the *señorita* progresses to dancing on the brim of the sombrero. Well, my girl was somewhat *borracha* (tipsy), could not stay on the brim, and simply stomped the señor's cover to bits. I thought we were in trouble, but when we looked over, the *viejo* and the whole cabaret were cheering and clapping. *Viva los Gringos!* There are good sports in Uruapan.

We three *amigos* were now broke, and as the young ladies rode off into the sunrise, we utilized our round-trip tickets to return to Mexico City. We always bought round-trip tickets, so that even when we had spent everything by the end of the summer in Acapulco, we could at least return home. I had to travel all the way to Los Angeles with no food money. Meanwhile, the girls were good enough to describe *Paricutín* for me, and I noticed that they didn't seem to be walking so well either.

You may be wondering why we take no umbrage at the use of Gringo. The following information, true nor not, was given me by my Spanish professors at UCLA. Before the Mexican War began in 1846, there was a "cold" war. In Texas, between 30 and 100 miles east of the Rio Grande, is the Nueces River. At the time, Mexico claimed that parcel, and thus for three months elements of its army were encamped on one side of the Rio Grande and our army on the other. A popular tune of the day, sung by the American troops, had the phrase "and green grow the lilacs. . . ." The Mexicans across the water picked up the refrain as it wafted over the river, and thus, it is said, we have become "Gringos" ever since. I wish I could remember what the professor had said was the name of the tune, but my memory has deserted me.

Following is an age-old Mexican conundrum — a good one, I am sure you will agree.

Tres señores llegaron al hotel Cortez a pasar la noche. Vinieron tres cuartos y el botones les cobró treinta pesos. Al entregar el dinero al administrador éste le dijó al botones que solamente cobrada veinticinco pesos. Entonces el muchacho dió a cada uno de los señores un peso y los otros dos pesos se los enbolsó. Entonces el resultado fué que cada uno de los señores pagó nueve pesos por su cuarto, o sean veintisiete pesos por los tres. Dos pesos que tomó el botones hacen vientinueve peso.

Qué pasó con el otro peso?

The only answer I can give you is the following spelled backward for secrecy: *¡aniporp anu arE*

The translation, if you really need it:

Three men arrived at the Hotel Cortez to spend the night. Three rooms were produced, and the bellboy charged them 30 pesos. Upon handing over the money to the manager, the bellboy was told that the cost was only 25 pesos. Then the boy gave to each one of the gentlemen one peso and he pocketed the other two pesos. The result was that each one of the *señores* paid nine pesos for his room, or 27 pesos for the three. Two pesos that the bellboy took makes a total of 29 pesos.

What became of the other peso? The only answer that I can give you is the following spelled backward: *¡pit a saw tl*

Back at UCLA, the after-game parties at Turner's (a German beer garden down on Vermont near the Coliseum), at Pico Pete's (on Pico near Sepulveda) and at The Glen (the nearest allowable bar to the campus up on Beverly Glen Boulevard) were great. One night at The Glen we met Jane Russell and her new husband, Bob Waterfield, the quarterback of the Los Angeles Rams — talk about two large and great-looking people! Another time at Turner's in the fall of 1946, one of the waiters had on a black turtleneck sweater, and I kid you not, a German submariner's pin!

Right: José (Joseph) and *Rogelio* (Roger), the author's friends, at Vera Cruz, Mexico, 1948.

Below: *América Salas,* the author's *señorita,* from Cuernavaca, Mexico, 1948.

Some football players in the next room sure straightened him out, and we saw no more Nazi gear. The floor at Pico Pete's was allowed to fill up with peanut shells so the dancing was always "different."

My prettiest sorority date at UCLA was Miss Dolfer, from Van Nuys, but in my last year at UCLA, Linda and I went everywhere and did everything, including the wrestling matches out on Pico Boulevard in Santa Monica. Our favorite was Baron Leone, and I enjoyed the Becker brothers, who I had seen as a kid with my father back in D.C. at Turner's Arena, along with "The Golden Greek," Jim Londos. (Incidentally, Londos lived in Escondido for many years. I should have paid him a visit, but I didn't want to bother him; he has since passed away.)

A large black wrestler named Woody Strode was one of our favorites

Three Kappa Alpha fraternity brothers with their dates: Arthur Farrington, center, and Miss Dolfer.

also. He had been a UCLA Bruin, and later appeared in many movies. In fact, his last was *The Quick and the Dead* with Sharon Stone. Linda and I went out into the San Fernando Valley one time after I had read that Medal of Honor winner Colonel Pappy Boyington was to be there. He had flown with the Flying Tigers before the war and had commanded the Black Sheep Squadron in the New Georgia area just above Guadalcanal. He also had been shot down over Rabaul, New Britain Island, had been rescued by the Japanese, and then had been a POW for some time. Later, in the 1970s, there was a great television series about Pappy and his Marines and their F4U Corsairs.

Pappy Boyington was the referee for the wrestling matches. In one tag-team match the wrestlers stripped him to his skivie drawers. Many times I have been asked if I had been embarrassed for him. I still say, not in the least. He took the bad behavior in the spirit of the night, and I was proud of his coming back into his own after a divorce and a problem with drinking. He got his life back together and became involved as an adviser to many military aircraft businesses, one of which was situated in San Marcos, California.

I would be remiss if I forgot to mention all of the dances I attended while at UCLA, all Western. I took an ex-Army WAC, Ilona Mardiga, who was a CALVET and smoked, to a dance down on Glendale Boulevard. One day in the co-op, where you could buy your lunch or bring it, I had mentioned that I knew the cowboy who had written "Smoke, Smoke, Smoke That Cigarette," and Ilona wanted to meet him. After a set of dances, the bands always took a break and signed autographs at a kiosk selling their records. Ilona was thrilled, and so was I, to meet the famous "Tex" Williams. Others I met through the years were Ernest Tubb and Spade Cooley out on the Santa Monica Pier, "T" Texas Tyler down on Riverside Drive, the Maddox Brothers and Rose (sometimes I drove all the way to Stockton to see them at George's Playhouse out on the river with my girl Annette from New Orleans), and "Cliffie" Stone, Merle Travis, "Tennessee" Ernie Ford, and Tex Ritter down near Sunset and Vine. But my favorite was Rose Maddox, who was the first in my mind to really "get down" with country music in her colorful western costumes. When she sang "Whoa, Sailor," with one of her brothers peering through a pair of Coke bottles taped together, it was really great. She passed away on April 15, 1998, at age 71.

Because the work at school was so difficult, I didn't have much time for athletics. I had been out of tennis completely for six years, and the idea of making the UCLA team was ridiculous. I played some in Rancho Park and down in Hollywood, however. But when playing flag football for my fraternity, I did intercept a pass and ran it back for a 103-yard touchdown, and I had scored the only run for my USMC Reserve softball team one time down in Culver City against a fast pitcher, when I luckily connected for a home run. You just don't forget things like that!

I mentioned earlier that I was unable to receive a commission upon graduation. When I had first joined the Marine Reserves, I had asked the I&I (instructor/inspector) whether I should join the Naval ROTC. But he advised me to stick to my studies, telling me that six months before graduating they would supply the necessary papers and with my professors' recommendations I would receive a commission in the Marines. Well, in the spring of 1950, all the papers were returned with the remark that "I was six months too old." I had turned 27 on November 11, 1949.

The author's "two loves" in California: his girlfriend Erlinda Treviño, with him at his graduation from UCLA in the Hollywood Bowl, June 18, 1950; and his 1932 Ford V-8 in his back yard.

Company A of the U.S. Marine Corps, 13th Infantry Battalion, based at Clover Field in Santa Monica, California, left for summer camp on Saturday morning, June 17, 1950, bound for Camp Joseph H. Pendleton. The next morning, my mother and Erlinda came down early and picked me up as I had special liberty to return to L.A. to graduate with my class in the Hollywood Bowl. Ralph Bunche, a UCLA graduate and Nobel Peace Prize winner in 1950, was our guest speaker.

Our training went well. One of our Master Sergeants was George Temple, a professional wrestler and a brother of the famous Shirley Temple. We had spent liberties with him and his buddy, "The Bomber," many times in Santa Monica. "The Bomber" went on to make many television shows and movies, including *Voyage to the Bottom of the Sea*. Master Sergeant Temple was not able to qualify for our call-up to active duty, and later was diagnosed with Multiple Sclerosis. He was a great Marine who will never be forgotten by me.

Left and below: A "dress re-hearsal" before the Korean War. Linda and the author at their en-campment on Lake Tahoe in northern California, July 1950.

The field work also went well. I even got to set TNT and primacord charges to make the maneuvers more realistic. Then on Tuesday, June 28, as we were set up on the stream at Tent Camp #1 (Las Pulgas), a report came over the radio that in response to the North Korean attack across the 38th Parallel on June 25th, President Harry Truman had authorized our Armed Forces to intercede, along with the United Nations. I knew a little bit about the situation over there as my brother, by then a 1st "Looey" in the Air Force, had been in South Korea during the last few years serving as one of President Syngman Rhee's personal pilots. We were told that active duty was possible in the near future for service in the "Hermit

VALLEY EDITION

Zen - News

HOLLYWOOD, CALIFORNIA, FRIDAY, JULY 21, 1950

Newly Landed
Captures Red R

TIMETABLE CHANGE

Korea Detour Halts Trip to South America

He was planning to go to South America to work.

Now he's going into a long-familiar Marine uniform and on to destinations unknown.

He is S/Sgt. Arthur C. Farrington, 27, West Los Angeles, of the area Marine Reserve 13th Infantry Bn., which has been called to active duty.

The Korean crisis has changed the timetable of his plans and hopes just as it has topsyturvied life for the battalion's part-time Leathernecks.

Farrington, in the Marines from 1940 to 1946, has been in the reserve battalion longer than any other member. He has charge of the First Platoon of A Company.

A Purple Heart vet of Marine First Division fighting at Guadalcanal and Pileliu, he was graduated in June from the University of California at Los Angeles, where he majored in Latin-American studies—Portuguese among them.

Next on his program was a South American job. But today he began packing to go back to Camp Pendleton about July 31— the battalion wound up to weeks training there July 1.

"I shouldn't, but I feel pretty good," he said. "We've been expecting it. It's exciting. We've got a good outfit. Now that you ask me, I'm not sure how I feel."

He thought a bit. "But I'm lucky I'm single. Some of the other guys have wives, children, and other responsibilities."

His brother, Robert, an Air Force second lieutenant and P-51 pilot, made headlines recently when Tokyo dispatches said Robert wanted to give up his U.S. citizenship to become a "world citizen."

"Robert wrote us he was misquoted," said Arthur. "He likes it out there, and wanted to be discharged there so he could go to art school.

"We haven't heard from him since the fighting began."

The Marine sergeant and his mother, Mrs. Kay Farrington, a Veterans Administration employe, reside at 2515 Tilden Ave.

S/SGT. ARTHUR
. . . change in plans

Staff Sergeant Arthur C. Farrington appeared on his local newspaper's front page, the *Hollywood Citizen-News*, on July 21, 1950, just before he was sent to Korea. *Hollywood Citizen-News*

Kingdom" — the country of Korea, so-called because they did not want anything to do with outsiders.

The 5th Marine Regiment left almost immediately for Korea and served with distinction as a "fire brigade" in the beleaguered Pusan Perimeter. My girl Linda and I took off for Reno and Lake Tahoe in my '32 Ford V-8 and had a wonderful vacation.

Then the FBI showed up at my door and wanted to know why my younger brother, Robert, wanted to defect, become a Communist, or whatever. My Mom and I were shattered. My brother was at Misawa, Japan, with the U.S. Air Force, and as he explained in a letter that we received after this incident, he had simply requested to stay in Japan to study art rather than be transferred back to the States! Unfortunately, he had also supported Gary Davis in his "One World" project. He was denied his request. Of course, the media had gone wild with this, and I was afraid it would prevent me from going off to war. Robert has been a successful artist for 50 years now.

Leaving behind Linda, my mother, my car, and my desert tortoise, Ozone, was sad; but at least I would not have to go to New York City for an interview with the Macmillan Publishing Company about working for them in Brazil. If I had, I would probably be dead now from some mysterious tropical disease, and there would be no Farrington family. Fate surely takes a hand every now and then.

Chapter 4

A Marine Infantryman in Korea

*I*NCLUDED IN THIS chapter are four vignettes covering the mobilization of A Company, 13th Infantry Battalion, USMCR (O); our shipboard movement to Otsu, Japan; the Inchon landings; the recapture of Seoul; the Wonsan operation; fighting in North Korea; the Chosin Reservoir; and finally our jump-off from Wonju for Operation Killer, to drive the hoards of Chinese out of Seoul and back across the 38th Parallel.

The North Koreans had invaded South Korea in June 1950, and our 5th Marine Regiment there was helping the United States and the Republic of Korea armies defend what was left of South Korea on the so-called Pusan Perimeter.

The Private
On July 29, the U.S. Marine Corps 13th Infantry Battalion, 1st Marine Regiment, was called up for active duty. The first stop was a World War II building on the west side

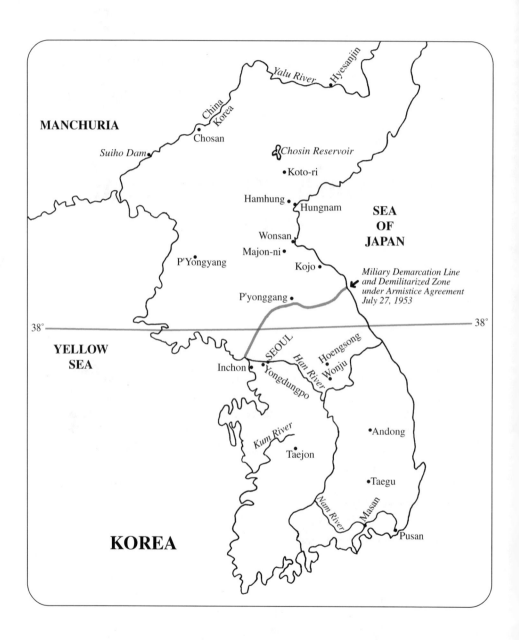

of the main area overlooking the Camp Pendleton rodeo grounds at Oceanside, California. By this time I had gotten rid of my Engineer MOS (Military Occupational Specialty) and regained 0302, Infantry. When interviewed, I requested a line company. We L.A. Reservists and others from the West were needed to bring the 1st Marine Regiment up to strength; we had to get to Korea as soon as we bloody-well could before a possible disaster occurred.

A division has three Infantry regiments, and thus the 7th Marine Regiment was hurriedly forming back East. It joined us as part of the 1st Marine Division, soon after the landings at Inchon; the third regiment of the division, the 5th Marine Regiment, was already at Pusan.

As a recent graduate of UCLA and a newly promoted Staff Sergeant in A Company, 13th Infantry Battalion, Marine Corps Reserve, I found myself in front of and in charge of the 2nd Platoon, F "Fox" Company, 2nd Battalion, of the 1st Marine Regiment (the 1st Marines), of the 1st Marine Division, Fleet Marine Force. We were thrilled to be assigned a 2nd Lieutenant named Waller. His grandfather, L.W.T. Waller, had served on the island of Samar, Philippine Islands, during the Philippine Insurrection at the beginning of the 20th century. I informed the platoon of this and that it was tradition that whenever a man who had served on Samar entered a room, everyone stood up. We thus stood in honor of his grandfather. This man, Lieutenant Waller, had not only the traditions of the Marine Corps to uphold, but also his own. But our morale was soon dashed when he was transferred elsewhere in the battalion. We were issued another Lieutenant named Maiden. He told me to call him "Go Go," and our enthusiasm soon soared again when we discovered that he had received that nickname on the island of Iwo Jima during World War II where, as a Sergeant, he would yell *"Go! Go!"* to his troops.

The 2nd Platoon consisted of 44 men: one Lieutenant, one platoon Sergeant, one platoon guide, three squads of thirteen men each, and two Navy corpsmen, Doyer and Carsanaro. Of these, only four had seen combat in World War II: Lieutenant Maiden, myself, Sergeant Jennings, and Corporal Baxter, who had been in the Los Angeles Marine Reserves with me.

We also had "The Private." One day he was dispatched to draw (be issued) fifteen sets of eating utensils. He returned with five forks, eight knives, thirteen spoons, and three canteen cups! This kid was going to be trouble. We had problems with him during the two weeks of training before embarking aboard ship in San Diego for overseas duty; and trouble he remained. While aboard ship on our way to Japan, the Lieutenant became aware of The Private's insubordinations and had him dry shaving for various infractions.

Then, in Otsu, near Kyoto, the ancient capital of Japan, we were in a barracks one fine day when the 1st Sergeant called in the NCOs and gave permission to the platoon Sergeants to forgo the morning formation. Thus the next morning, as I sat on my bunk in the squad room (the staff NCOs at this time did not have separate quarters), The Private was still sitting on his, staring at me. I could not believe the golden opportunity that presented itself. We ("Go Go" and the platoon) had been looking for just such a chance to get rid of this unreliable person. I could hear the reports of the formation outside, as to who was present and who was absent, and I immediately went to the company office and reported The Private missing from the formation. Unfortunately, however, my buck Sergeant platoon guide had already reported "All present, Sir" at the formation! Well, The Private "skated" (escaped punishment) that time, but the Sergeant was transferred. This was fortunate for the 2nd Platoon, however, as the Sergeant was very intelligent and educated but not efficient as a platoon guide. His replacement, about a month later, was an excellent Marine, Sergeant Joe Goggins, who had received a Silver Star on Okinawa in World War II. I must mention that he was a black man, a rarity at this time in the Marine Corps line (Infantry) companies.

From Otsu we went to Kobe, boarded LST *611*, set sail in a typhoon across the Sea of Japan, and passed near Pusan,

South Korea, where we were joined by our brother regiment, the 5th Marines. We entered the Yellow Sea and ended up off the western Korean city of Inchon. There, because of the 50-foot tides covering and uncovering the mud flats, we spent all day ship-bound watching the bombardment, the air attacks, and the taking of Wolmi Do Island. We at last launched out the bow doors of the LST in our LVTs, or amtracs, as we called them.

It was very late in the afternoon of September 15, 1950. I had refused to allow the steel covers to be deployed over our heads in the tractor, as I believed that the danger of a mortar hit was a lot less likely to occur than it was for the loaded amphibian to just take a dive off the ramp of the LST to the bottom of the drink. "Go Go" was with half of the platoon in one tractor, and I had the other half in mine. We headed for Blue Beach on the right flank and entered smoke that was so thick we got lost. Finally, the tractor stopped, we heard gears meshing, a lot of rocking went on, and the amtrac driver eventually told me that he could not get loose from the mud. I yelled something like, "Okay, let's get out of here and hit the beach!" This is not a direct quote, as I have no recollection of what I said; but I'll tell you one thing, I'm sure glad that I did not allow the steel covers to be locked over our heads!

Anyway, the two Marines in the rear started to do their duty and crank down the rear ramp. "*No, no, no!*" I yelled, "*Over the sides!*"

Can't you just see the ramp going down, the sea rushing in, and the men swimming for their lives inside the tractor? I was faced with a whole amtrac load of incredulous stares, so I climbed up and over, dropped into the water, and pointed in the direction of the beach, which I hoped was at the bottom of the cliffs that were visible periodically in the distance through the smoke. I saw two men disappear under the sea then a few seconds later reappear as they headed for the shore. They obviously had plodded through the gouges in the mud made by the tractor.

Suddenly I heard a voice from the top of the tractor. "Hey, Sarge, hold this!" I could not believe my eyes. It was The Private, handing me his M-1 rifle! I grabbed it as he daintily made his way down into the water, thinking to myself, "This kid's got to go!"

At three o'clock in the morning of the third day ashore, some of the troops were called down to the road, and they soon returned with cases of C-rations. Having been in the Reserves for the past four years, I had never seen these rations before. As we were fumbling around with them in the dark, I decided I would just settle for something to drink. I do not particularly care for plain water, so when I found something that said "lemon" on it, I asked someone next to me if that was lemonade. Guess who said "Yeah, Sarge, that's lemonade!"? I spent the time left, before we had to move out, trying to dissolve lemon-flavored candy in a canteen cup of water — an impossible task! The guy was a menace.

We subsequently killed some T-34 Russian tanks, and watched the first South Korean Marines charge past us down the road at double time, at port arms, and with fixed bayonets, to take the village of Sosa. They scattered the Korean civilians so that they were out of harm's way. We then charged up and down ridge after ridge on the right of the highway to Seoul.

"Go Go" was hit bad one day at a roadblock, and handed me his field glasses. Until I learned not to use them during daylight, I almost got killed a couple of times. It was impressed upon me deeply in the next few days that when the sun was reflected from them you were, indeed, a target. I took the glasses as a personal gift, and still have them. The 2nd Platoon, including The Private, was now all mine.

We Marines almost always referred to unknown people, enemy or friendly, as "gooks" rather than Japanese soldiers or North Korean Reds (and would later, in Vietnam, as well). The term was not necessarily supposed to be detrimental, but it was often taken so. In fact, in the Korean language, "Me gook" means "I'm friendly."

One morning, some gooks appeared in the brush on the right flank of the platoon. I put my M-2 carbine on full automatic, held up three fingers to Private 1st Class Newman and his Browning automatic rifle on my right, and on the count of three we got up and charged Hell-bent for leather. Suddenly I heard a telltale pop behind me, looked up, and gasped. It was one of our orange hand grenades flying over. (Our ordnance had not been upgraded since World War II, so the grenades were not painted green as yet.) I yelled "Grenade!" as the thrower had failed to do, and hit the deck too late. Both Newman and I were wounded.

You can guess who the culprit was. The Private. The boy was dangerous! I admit, he had delayed three or four seconds before throwing the fragmentation grenade, as he had been taught, and that was fatal for the gooks. It had detonated quicker on target, so that there was no danger of the Koreans retrieving it and tossing it back. But it was bad for Newman and me.

As we approached the city of Yongdungpo on the Han River, across from the capital city of Seoul, we killed more Russian T-34 tanks, took more ridges, and ate raw turnips and anything else we could scrounge while pinned down in the fields that were not paddies, but cultivated. We were continually hungry when in the attack. When later, at Treasure Island in San Francisco Bay, we were all diagnosed with intestinal worms, it was no surprise.

By that time The Private was carrying a heavy BAR (Browning automatic rifle) mainly as a punishment for misdeeds. But to our horror, we discovered this had been a gigantic mistake. His squad leader, Sergeant Jennings, brought The Private to me one day on the side of a hill and handed me his BAR. The operating handle would not retract, and in fact the whole weapon was solid rust and grime. This could not be tolerated, as each Marine Corps squad depended on its three BARs. They were our own mobile machine guns and had to be maintained for the squad to be effective.

We were in the middle of combat with more action coming up ahead, so we held a "ceremony" right on the spot. After The Private dug a grave, we buried the BAR there on the side of a lonely hill in Korea. Somebody even whistled "Taps." The Private's fire-team leader, who was responsible for the actions of the other three members of his team — the rifleman, the BAR man, and the assistant BAR man — was reamed out by both Sergeant Jennings and me. The 2nd Platoon had been getting smaller and smaller with all the casualties, so The Private had remained with us, but with an M-1 rifle and a newly motivated fire-team leader.

We charged through a river, and we were in Yongdungpo. A very unfortunate thing happened just at this time. A replacement Marine was escorted to me by one of my Sergeants. The new Marine had all of his equipment, including his heavy marching order pack, which included the haversack and knapsack. The rest of us had landed with only the combat pack (haversack) and would not see the knapsack part for some time to come. I told the replacement Marine to get at the rear of the platoon and to stay down. But I was told later that he was killed in Yongdungpo.

Meanwhile, we organized and filtered through town, saw gooks on a hill close by on the south, got ready for a *banzai* — a charge — of our own against a railroad embankment (which was called off at the last second), and observed a Jeep machine-gunned as it crossed the bridge into town. We later were told that the Jeep had been carrying our original platoon leader, Lieutenant Waller, whose billet was in the battalion machine-gun section. He was seriously wounded, but not killed.

We received orders to pull back; the Army would take care of the enemy on the hill. They had just come up and had decided that this was in their area of responsibility.

The last time that I dared to use the field glasses during the daytime was at that spot. I managed to locate the enemy from the right side of a hut by using the glasses from ground level.

As I pulled away, the position was blasted as a result of a machine-gun barrage!

The good old 2nd Platoon got in the last licks of this battle, as I had a BAR set up in the second story of a house with a window through which the gooks on the hill could be clearly seen. The BAR man was a crack shot, but his tactics were really bad. I grabbed him away from the window and located him back into the middle of the room behind some rice sacks. He really cleaned house for a while, until our company Commander, Captain Goodwin C. Groff, ordered us down, despite my pleadings. It was indeed rare that one had such a chance to wipe out your foe.

In the lead, the 2nd Platoon slogged toward the outskirts of town, to the Han River. We were on the left side of the street and recognized that this was a pretty important community, as the drainage ditches on both sides were covered with boards rather than open. As Private 1st Class McGarrity (my #1 scout) and I neared the last building before the ground descended into a rice paddy, we saw something written on the wall. It simply stated, "*Run across here!*"

I passed the word to do just that, one at a time. But, sure enough, as we began the maneuver, the spot received machine-gun fire as each man made his move. The Korean had his gun locked down so that all he had to do was touch the trigger. Nevertheless, we were fast, and two squads made it, when across the road, which was about seven feet high, we heard the unmistakable sound of a mortar firing. As I looked up, I could see the shells arcing in the sky. "*Hit the deck!*" I yelled; and we did. Have you ever dived face down into a toilet? Some did, as I could hear all the cussing and sputtering going on around me. In many rice-growing countries of the world, the "night soil" from the homes is collected, carted to the paddies in large "honey buckets," and unceremoniously dumped as fertilizer.

I did a back flop and could see the bombs coming over. The mortar barrage continued with explosions and liquid splashes from duds that had failed to detonate all around us. A slight lull occurred, and one of the Marines yelled from the *"Run across here"* location that The Private had fallen through a rotted board of the drainage ditch and had broken his *"*%#@"_%* leg!" I bet the gooks were baffled to hear the cheering from our rice paddy. I had never seen anything so funny as all those muddy hands clapping and all that yelling. We all knew immediately that we would never see the troublemaker again, as my two excellent corpsmen would tag him and make damned sure that he was carted off to the rear right away.

At this time, we also had noticed some Marine F4U Corsairs orbiting the area, but it was a big surprise to see one come in close on the other side of the elevated road. The mortar fire stopped and soon a flight of Corsairs swept in very low and let loose their payload of large bombs, which we could clearly observe. Some exploded as they hit, but most bounced above the road and failed to detonate. I believe the Corsairs were too low for the fuzes to arm themselves. A small propeller on the fuze has to rotate in the wind so many times for the fuze to become active. Nevertheless, we cheered, and I ordered the remainder of the platoon to follow as we exited the paddy and continued in the attack. We were called the "Stinking 2nd Platoon" for a few days, as we had foul-smelling material embedded on ourselves and our gear. But . . . The Private was history!

Also about this time, in answer to President Truman's speech of September 5, 1950, someone "re-wrote" the Marine hymn:

THE NEW MARINE HYMN

I
From the Halls of Montezuma
To the shores of Tripoli
We'll police our God Damn Navy

As long as they're at sea.
First to Fight the Army's battles
and to win the Navy's fights
And still our old friend Harry
Trys [*sic*] to louse up all our rights.

II

Our flag's been flown from every ship
Since the Navy had its start
A Marine Detachment in their midst
Kept the fleet from falling apart.
Uncle Harry says we're just police
and he should really know
We've arrested wars since we began
and dealt the final blow.

III

We have Honor, we have Glory
We're the finest ever seen
But still our propaganda
Is a second rate machine.
Harry's Army and his Navy
Never look on Heaven's scenes
Cause they know the Angels are in love
WITH UNITED STATES MARINES.

"Devil" Dogs !

Chesty's Tanks Coming Up

On September 20, the 5th Marine Regiment in amphibious tractors had made an assault crossing of the Han River, which protected Seoul, South Korea, on the west and south. They fought hard to clear a safe landing area for us — the 1st Marine Regiment. Early on the morning of September 24, the 1st Marines, under scattered incoming artillery fire, took its

New York Herald Tribune war correspondent
Marguerite Higgins, in Korea.

amtrac ride of about 400 yards. The 2nd Battalion, which was composed of Dog (D), Easy (E), and Fox (F) Companies had been assigned as the reserve battalion for the 1st and 3rd Battalions for the day.

As the platoon leader of the 2nd Platoon of Fox Company, the best in the Corps, I immediately got the men digging what was to be the first of four foxholes we would construct that day, alongside a road just inland from the wide and sandy river shore. With no conceal-ment whatever, it was both interesting and embarrassing to observe all the bare-assed Marines doing their morning nec-essary duty. Suddenly, there she came — Marguerite (Maggie) Higgins — trudging along with her blonde hair shining in the morning sunlight below the edge of her steel helmet. She was right in the middle of the action, doing her sworn duty, cover-ing our operations for the *New York Herald-Tribune*, and was seemingly oblivious to the mundane goings-on around her. I was proud just to see her here in this madness. (Unfortunate-ly, while in Vietnam in 1965, Maggie contracted a tropical dis-ease; she was brought back to the United States, but died in 1966.)

I was in my foxhole when suddenly I heard a gruff voice asking me who I was and what outfit this was. I responded immediately with "Staff Sergeant Farrington, 2nd Platoon, Fox Company, Sir!" The gruff voice had come from Colonel

Lewis B. "Chesty" Puller, the Commanding Officer of the 1st Marine Regiment.

Finally, the day was over. We had spent the previous sixteen hours in accomplishing a shore-to-shore amphibious landing, and running all over the terrain supporting our other two battalions in the attack; we were now dead tired. We were on the right flank of the regiment, digging our holes right up to the Han River. The guys were putting in rice mats and straw for comfort, and we heard that C-rations were on the way. Suddenly, a runner from the company command post (CP) appeared and told me that I was to report to the regimental CP immediately!

After wandering around for about a half mile in the pitch dark, I arrived at the CP to find Colonel Puller, his S-2 (Intelligence) officer, and a Lieutenant. The Colonel told me to take my platoon down-river about two miles, to contact B Company of the 1st Tank Battalion, and, in the morning, to escort them to him personally. In answer to my question as to exactly where that will be, he said, "In Seoul."

The Lieutenant was an engineer, and he would accompany us, with six of his men. I said, "Aye, aye, Sir!" and headed back to Fox Company. Evidently the good Colonel had liked what he saw of my platoon early that morning, specifically — and how should I put this? — that we were busy digging-in and not just lying about. So he had graced us with a choice assignment.

Upon apprising my Company Commander, Captain Goodwin C. Groff, of the Colonel's order, the good Captain immediately yelled something like, "Hell, no! Go back to your Yellow 2nd Platoon and make damned sure my right flank is secure for the night!"

The Captain was a very brave man, but he insulted everyone, including other officers, in order to get action. We knew he was just trying to stir us up! If you realized what he was doing, and that in most cases it was a compliment, it was sort of OK, though his comments often still somewhat stung.

We had earned the name "Yellow 2nd Platoon" on the morning of September 21, after an attack by five T-34 Russian tanks and their accompanying infantry. My platoon was on a steep slope 25 yards above the road on which the attack took place, and as soon as the dawn broke, the Captain yelled: *"Let's go!"* Well, he beat us to the ditch next to the road and hollered for the "Yellow 2nd Platoon" to get down there.

We did, as we were only five or ten feet behind him, and I got some revenge right away. He was still in the lead when I spotted a burp gun up on the road, which I retrieved. It had been run over by a tank and the front sight was really bent over. But it was such a rugged weapon, and it appeared that the cooling jacket was still lined up all right with the barrel, so I fired the remaining rounds in one long burst into the rice field on the other side of the road where the North Korean infantry had attacked. You could hear the cries of the wounded. Captain Groff almost had a heart attack from the distinctive enemy sound of the firing just behind him! Then I shoved the weapon, barrel down, into the mud.

I saw the *same* Russian gun again in 1951 at a weapons exhibition at the Los Angeles County Fair in Pomona, and again at one of the tent camps at Camp Joseph H. Pendleton in Southern California. The gun was too heavy to carry at the time, but later I "liberated" another in Seoul and have it to this day. I registered it with the ATF Agency of the U.S. government.

But back to South Korea and the gruff Captain who was angry about my orders from Colonel Puller. It meant that when we pulled out, he would have to realign the whole company's defensive positions. Nevertheless, feeling that "Chesty" Puller was the greatest Marine that ever lived, I ordered the good old 2nd Platoon to saddle up and stand by to move out. I had never heard such bitching and moaning in my life. While I was gone, the men had really gotten "squared away" and settled in. The C-rations had arrived, had been warmed, and were being eaten. The foxholes were comfortable and "homey," and some men were even fast asleep.

However, we were ready when the runner from the company command post arrived and told us to get going. He also told us that the Captain really got reamed out over the phone from regimental headquarters for our delay.

The 2nd Platoon at that time consisted of 22 members, and we really suffered on the hike along rice-paddy dikes, all the time inhaling the headache-causing smell of the plastic explosives that the engineers were carrying. Following a couple hours or so of slipping, sliding, and splashing through filthy paddies, we arrived at B Company's tank bivouac under a railway bridge on the Han River. After telling my guys to get as much rest as possible, I was whisked away in a Jeep for the tank battalion command post. On the way, suddenly two lines of soldiers appeared on each side of the dirt road going in the opposite direction. The driver said they were just Republic of Korea soldiers, but I pulled a tarpaulin up over my head anyway — knowing, of course, it would not do any good. Upon arriving at the CP, in a tunnel, we poured over a map, trying to figure out the route we should take to Seoul. Because the route taken by the 1st Marines would not allow accompanying tanks due to the unsuitable road and bridges that would not support the M-4 Shermans, M-26 Pershings, flame-throwers, dozers, and retrievers, we came to the conclusion that the only feasible way to approach and enter into Seoul was on the railroad tracks upon which Company B was already astride. Unfortunately, it seemed from the map that the rail line ran behind the enemy lines facing the 1st Marine Regiment on the right — and God only knows where the 5th Marines were on the left. Nevertheless, the decision was made: we would go.

The 2nd Platoon was fortunate with the chow, as the tankers had plenty. However, sleep was very difficult to achieve as we were soaking wet and the weather had turned cold. We were not equipped with long johns, sweaters, or other cold-season gear as yet, and I believed this was the first time that we had tried to sleep with our feet in our empty packs. Marine boon-dockers, the high-topped reverse-leather field shoes, were the best in the world, but useless in cold weather.

When morning arrived, we were off. I had one squad in front as protection for the engineers searching for mines, and two squads behind me. Naturally my best scout, Private 1st Class McGarrity, was out in front aways, but when he was fired on by the tanks' machine guns, I had to bring him back to just about 50 yards. We saw many dead Korean civilians lying all over the landscape, killed by the retreating Reds. Then, suddenly, I heard firing and the detonation of hand grenades just the other side of a small draw. After rushing up, McGarrity told me that the point (scout) had seen rifles stacked in front of some huts to the right of the tracks, and that firing had erupted from the huts. The point had immediately answered the fire; he and some of the engineers had grenaded the huts, and the Lieu-tenant had been hit in the right hand — and he a ball player. Another engineer had been hit also.

As I brought the platoon up, someone said that he saw Marines on the side of the mountain off to our right. Now, al-though I had promised myself never to utilize my field glasses again during the day within firing range of the enemy, I had to. With the glasses I determined that the trees moving down toward us were not Marines but North Koreans covered with bushes and greenery.

The squad leaders were briefed; one yard bird was posted to watch our rear on the other side of the elevated railway, the rest went to find firing positions, and I went in search of the tank Commander. I found the Captain in his radio Jeep parked up against a bank back in the small draw. I asked him to con-tact the artillery or air for support, but to my surprise he yelled at me that North Koreans had us just where they wanted us. *"Let's turn around and get out of here!"*

I could not believe my ears, and from the look on the face of his driver, he could not either. I immediately had no use for this man, and told him to just remain where he was. I used the telephones on the back of two tanks, trying to have them call for support, but to no avail. To this day, I feel guilty about leaving the phones to drag behind the tanks, but I just could not properly replace them with the bullets striking all around. We were definitely on our own.

I worked a squad up a path to the right and a firefight commenced with even some of the lead tanks able to find targets. My scout, McGarrity, was on a ledge, pulled the pin on a grenade, then drew back his right arm and dropped the grenade right next to his head. He remained there with the grenade fuze smoking; there was no time to grab him. But it was a dud! We dragged him down, and I stood over him yelling expletives. He gave me a crazy look and held up his hand. There was a bullet hole right through the palm. We had heard a burp gun fire as he was throwing, but never made the connection. (One of my other wounded, who later rejoined the platoon, would tell me that Mac did not fully realize what had happened until he was told at the aid station.)

We were able to guide a flame-throwing tank up the path, and it really did a job on the gully between us and the far ridge. I asked if anyone knew how to say "surrender" in Korean, and luckily Sergeant Sam Lamb did. He and I commenced yelling "*Sundra! Sundra!*" as loud as we could, and lo and behold a "tree" stood up on the far slope, holding a rifle above his head. I turned around and yelled for no one to shoot, but I fully expected his own men to kill him. We motioned for him to come on in. He started and disappeared down in the draw, but soon reappeared, still holding his rifle high. He marched right up to us. I had him undress completely, in full view of his comrades.

That did it. The others started coming to surrender in numbers, still carrying their rifles and burp guns. As we had done with the Japanese during World War II for our own safety, we stripped each and every one. The only trouble they had was getting their trousers off over wrap leggings!

As the men were escorting the North Koreans down to the tracks, another Korean appeared, stared, and said, "Hey, you.

I want to talk to you!" He was obviously an officer, although he had shed his cloth shoulder boards. All he could see was Private 1st Class Villa (who, sadly, was later killed north of Hoengsong), with the parts of his Browning automatic rifle spread out on his poncho, as he had had a malfunction — and me, one cruddy little mustachioed Staff Sergeant, holding a bayoneted M-2 carbine. I thrust the blade right up to his stomach, told him to immediately shut the "*%#@" up, and to undress as quickly as possible. I called for an engineer, who was armed with a .45-caliber pistol, and told him to march the fellow off and keep him separated from the other POWs — and if he gave any trouble, to shoot him. The enemy officer by then obviously realized that they had surrendered to a very small group. The sound of the tanks, the job done by the flame-throwing tank, and our aggressiveness had no doubt saved our butts that day.

While this action was going on, someone said that he had heard noises behind a door in an embankment. Upon forcing an entrance, a tunnel was revealed, and more prisoners, including two women I am told, were taken, stripped, and lined up. Back on the railroad, I ordered all the wounded, theirs and ours, up on the tanks, and we prepared to move out.

Just as the Marines, tanks, and 129 bare asses moved, North Koreans that had been lying "doggo" the whole time on the back side of the tracks opened fire on us. Ready on the right, ready on the left, we opened up. The North Koreans aborted their charge up the embankment and started to run. What an opportunity to see what my carbine could do. Sam Lamb, on my right, was cursing. He had scrounged a 30-round banana clip for his carbine, which held 15 more than the regular clip, but it was empty, and as he loaded he was missing out on a rare shooting spree. You should see what a 90mm tank shell does to a chicken house; I have never seen so many feathers fly!

Finally, with no more targets, we moved out. I felt sorry for those prisoners without shoes, for I remembered as a kid how coal cinders on railroad tracks can ruin your feet. We finally reached a village with a fairly wide main path that looked like it would accommodate the tanks. We took it, and only a few huts got in our way. As some of their houses were being destroyed, civilian Koreans appeared and cheered us! I could not believe it. It sure made you feel good — but embarrassed at the same time.

We approached a main road and, to our surprise, in the ditches on both sides was our Easy (E) Company pinned down by fire — the same rifle fire that had been following us all the way in. The men appeared sheepish as we walked in with two lines of prisoners and tanks with wounded aboard.

We saw that the wounded were unloaded, so that they could be attended to by corpsmen and evacuated, and we sent the walking wounded and other prisoners back up the main road under guard of two of my men. At the MP (Military Police) station, the two women were provided with long johns. Their picture, along with our man, Private 1st Class Block, appeared later in *Newsweek* magazine. *Newsweek* subsequently received the stupidest letters from Americans complaining about how American Marines were treating women! What would they have done under the circumstances? Who were those women? Nurses? Whores? Soldiers? . . . Who knows? Did they have grenades on their persons? Were we to end up in a free-for-all and lose some Marines? No. A couple of women just might have been embarrassed for a while, but in my book this is justifiable in the face of possible American deaths.

We entered Seoul, and I stopped the tanks and climbed Nam Hill to report to Colonel Puller. As we looked out over a panorama of the capital city of Korea, he pointed, started to tell me where he wanted the tanks assigned, and took a look at me. He simply said, "Thanks." I was to just tell my story to the

Ma Po Boulevard, Seoul, Korea, September 1950. This photo appeared in the *Stars & Stripes* and *Guidebook for Marines, 1962: The Browning Automatic Rifle (BAR)*. On the left is Private 1st Class Newman of Bunkie, Louisiana; on the right is the author, Staff Sergeant Arthur C. Farrington, platoon leader at the time, about to grenade a previously carbined bunker between the street and the sidewalk and retrieve the Burp gun Farrington had hidden. Notice the M-4 Sherman tanks, which had helped Fox Company, 2nd Battalion, 1st Marine Regiment, take the large roadblock obscured by smoke. The photograph above is only part of the complete picture; Private 1st Class Martin, also supporting Farrington with his M-1, is missing here, from the foreground. The complete frame was in the Smithsonian Institution for a few years, and the complete action has been presented on television quite often.

UNITED STATES MARINE CORPS

"I HATE THE WORLD!"

Corporal James Baxter, of the 2nd Platoon, Fox Company, 2nd Battalion, 1st Marine Regiment, drew this discouraged Marine at Inchon, Korea, on September 15, 1950.

Linda Treviño, the author's girlfriend at the time of the Korean War, later his wife.

S-2, the Intelligence officer — location of the action, number of prisoners, casualties (40-50 enemy) — then report back to Fox Company. It is really interesting to me as a trooper to hear what I said go out over the radio to various units. I learned later that the cave had been an enemy regimental headquarters, and quite a few important documents were recovered.

What a 40 hours! We finally located Fox Company long after dark. And the Captain said: "Where in the Hell have you been?"

We then prepared for a night attack down Seoul's Ma Po Boulevard, on empty stomachs.

Shermans, A Burp Gun, and Bad Behavior

The good old 2nd Platoon, a part of Fox Company again, spent the next day's early morning hours in some ramshackle houses about a city block from a large North Korean roadblock that had held us up the evening before. We had not had any chow the previous evening, had moved out in the pitch-black night, and were certainly not going to have chow that morning. An artillery battle had raged throughout the night.

Sure as shootin', at sunrise, the 2nd Battalion was in the lead, with Fox Company up front, and with the 2nd Platoon ahead of the whole kit and caboodle. The street, we discovered later, with a tram line down the middle, was named Ma Po Boulevard. It was cluttered with building material, destroyed trees, and some dead bodies, and at about 150 yards distant was the culprit — an 8- to 10-foot barricade made of — what else — large rice bags.

We advanced down the right side of the boulevard until taken under fire by rifles and an anti-tank gun firing tracers that simply ricocheted everywhere. We dropped to the street, and Corporal Baxter was hit. I told him to stand behind a telephone pole to my immediate front until I gave him the word to *di di* — get going — to the rear. I requested his M-1 rifle, as my M-1 carbine did not seem to be doing the job on the gooks running up and down the stairs of a large hotel next to their barricade. He threw it to me, and it felt great to be firing one again. We were not accomplishing much. The firing had died down, so I bid Baxter *sayonara* and away he quickly went. (He would rejoin us later up north.)

What we needed was support, and we could see it coming. Two big Patton tanks went charging down Ma Po, firing broke out, then two big Pattons came charging back up. One had been hit in the fender, so they called it quits. One of my men went dashing by, although I was screaming at him not to. He unwisely jumped into a gook position just a few yards in front of us; there were many of these positions between the sidewalk and street, all the way to the roadblock. We heard a *bang*, and out he jumped yelling that there was a gook in the hole with him! Well . . . *yeah.*

The upshot of this was the worst thing that could happen to a combat Marine. Private 1st Class Block later received a letter from my wounded man then in a Navy Hospital. He was going out with Block's sister!

Carsanaro, one of our two great corpsmen was wounded there also. Fortunately, to our rescue came an M-4 Sherman and an M-4 Dozer tank. As they headed down the street, we advanced also. I put my carbine on full-automatic, rushed to the dugout that had gotten my man, threw a large rock near the

entrance on the street side, and unloaded the whole clip (fifteen rounds) into the seven-foot-long position. Reaching in, I
latched onto an old Burp gun, then went around to the other
end of the position, and shoved it all the way into the soft sand,
barrel first. I certainly did not want a possible survivor pulling
the trigger.

The two Shermans, and the men inside, did a job on the
gook position. We took it, then went on the defense in some
Korean houses. We still had nothing to eat, except what was in
our pockets. No one had much more than I, and I only dug out
some sugar packets.

At about this moment, the Captain ordered me to grenade
the bypassed sidewalk positions so, I took with me a "Coon
Ass" (a Marine from Louisiana, and not a derogatory term),
Private 1st Class Newman, and Private 1st Class Martin, the
first with his BAR and the second with his M-1. As they covered me, I blasted the positions, including the last one where I
had stashed the Burp gun. Then I retrieved the Russian weapon. The muzzle was covered with human flesh and blood; the
grenade had blown up a body into it. I checked the weapon
later. It was fully loaded but, lucky for my PFC when he had
jumped into the hole, the selector had been set on single fire.

At one point during the long day a couple of us walked over
to investigate the hotel. We went upstairs and I liberated some
German stamps from one of the rooms. Having been a stamp
collector for many years, I knew they were worthless but, hey,
a souvenir is a souvenir.

In the afternoon, a patrol from one of our companies returned with about fifteen to twenty prisoners. They were
marched into the hotel, and a little while later we heard all
kinds of shooting. One of my Sergeants, Sam Lamb, requested to investigate, and I said go to it. A while later he
returned; he was never the same man. He recounted to me
that the patrol had put all of the prisoners in a swimming pool
and shot them to death. I could not believe it. We started up
the street to see our good Captain, but he absolutely refused

to talk to me and ordered me back to my platoon. What he and Lamb discussed was and is unknown to me.

There had been civilians in that hotel, however, who had witnessed this affair, and how long do you think it took for the news to reach the North Korean troops? You can bet that we were not going to be taking many more prisoners the rest of the way through the city, and we were surely going to pay for the incident with some unnecessary casualties.

We had some ferocious battles retaking Seoul from the North Koreans. They had many Russian weapons and were not shy about using them. A large self-propelled gun fired at us, and a piece hit me dead center, right on my Burp gun drum magazine, which I carried in the large breast pocket of my dungarees. Souvenirs just seemed to be coming my way. Outside of Yongdungpo, I had noticed a small hole in the same jacket pocket, reached my hand in, and came out with the steel core of a rifle bullet! The copper covering had been shredded away as it ricocheted.

We made it through the city, hearing on the way that "Dugout," General Douglas MacArthur, was having a ceremony returning the city to the displaced president, Syngman Rhee. U.S. army troops were wearing dress A uniforms with field scarfs, and no combat troops in filthy attire were in attendance. *Whoop de doo!* MacArthur must have thought he was still in Japan! Incidentally, however, I think he did a great job in the land of the Rising Sun after World War II.

Crapped out in a schoolyard eating freshly baked bread with jelly wasn't bad at all on one subsequent pleasant afternoon. We usually had small C-ration jelly containers in our roomy pockets, but the problem was always what to put the jelly on — certainly not the terrible powdery crackers from the rations.

About then, one of my men came up to tell me that the Sergeant in charge of the "killer patrol" had been setting out trip flares for the night when one blew his head off!

We set up defensive positions on some ridges outside the capital city, and the 2nd Platoon was called out to aid Easy (E)

Company in repelling a ferocious attack in the middle of the night. Why were they being honored and no other company? You speculate. Not being night fighters, it was a really scary adventure in strange and unfamiliar circumstances but the 2nd Platoon came out of it unscathed.

With Seoul secured, we held positions on a ridge for a while, and the bottom part of our packs were brought up. As I was looking for mine, I saw a Korean trying on a pair of boondockers. On the back of the Marine dungaree jacket, which he already had on, was a black German cross. That was my marking! I tackled him to get my gear, and some chaplain intervened to ask me what I was doing. *What was I doing?* My first clean clothes and gear since September 15 were at stake. There was a limit to friendly relations. The boondockers I took off his feet also had German crosses.

The 2nd Platoon had a couple small boys doing errands, and one brought me some *kimchi* that his mother had just made down in the valley. Hot! No wonder they have such great teeth, with all those chili peppers, which replace milk in many malnourished areas of the world.

Before we left Seoul, we test-fired our weapons. Our new target was Seoul University, which was still outside our lines. I broke out my liberated Burp gun, attached the 81-round drum, and, standing next to Captain Groff, fired a long burst. He went straight up in the air and got excited. (I was continually trying to get even with him for some of his actions.)

After some patrolling, we were put on trucks and driven back to Inchon. On the way, we passed the 1st Cavalry Division and heard a friendly tale about their patch, which was a very inviting target — it was yellow, with a horse they never rode, and a line they never crossed (the 38th Parallel).

We arrived at Inchon on October 7, 1950, where we were able to get showers and receive some decent chow. Replacements arrived, and in a few days we were nearly back up to strength. One of these new men was Causey, who had been a sheriff in Shreveport, Louisiana. He sported two ivory-handled six-shooters. We really had a ball watching him retrieve the one he lost in a slit-trench while using the facility.

Soon we boarded the USS *Noble*, APA 218, where the 2nd Platoon received a Lieutenant, L. A. Michaux, and we shoved off on October 11 for Wonsan, on the North Korean eastern coast. There we waited for days while the mines were cleared, and then made an administrative landing after the South Korean army had already taken the place and Bob Hope's performances were over. Embarrassing? Nah.

We were informed that our 1st Battalion had run into trouble 39 miles to the south, some men had been killed in their sleeping bags, and others had been thrown bodily over cliffs while still in theirs. Quickly boarding a train, we were in an open coal car with Chesty Puller when we took off. At each of eleven tunnels the train stopped, blew its whistle, and then slowly proceeded. I have never been so fearful of an ambush in my life, and again we were absolutely filthy, so soon after leaving the ship. It seemed that the guerrillas who had hit our 1st Battalion had moved on, so we patrolled.

One day, at Kojo, the city south of Wonsan, on the coast, we were going down a dirt road between two rice paddies, away from the harbor, when a screech and an explosion occurred just yards away from the Captain and my platoon in the right-hand paddy. As we turned around to see where the fire was originating from, a puff of smoke and flame appeared on the deck of an American destroyer. As we splashed down into those filthy paddies, a second shell detonated in the paddie to the left. All I can say is that it was indeed fortunate that neither shell detonated on the hard dirt road. In my mind the worst thing that could happen to a Marine was to be killed by "friendly fire." We were glad to bid Kojo *sayonara*.

Some troops rode the train back to Wonsan, but Fox Company was detailed to march back. Above the track we could see a continuous trench, which could have been the end of us if it had been manned on our train trip down. Anyway, after guarding two parties that were repairing the tracks, which had been blown in the meantime, we made it back to Wonsan, filthy with coal dust, sweat, and mud. We wondered just how our new girl-soldiers would do in situations such as this and after weeks without bathing.

By that time we had sleeping bags, long johns, great Army high-necked sweaters, and gloves, and each squad was issued a parka. We took turns wearing it, especially when two of us would be detailed to ride shotgun on the front fenders of the 6x6 trucks. The Marine Corps field jackets with downy vest suited most of us, and the only time I wore the parka was when riding on a fender, which I frankly preferred, as you could debark quickly when attacked.

Fox Company then moved west a mile or so to a little schoolyard where we received some more replacements, including a veteran of World War II and one of my best friends in the CALVETS at UCLA, Sergeant Mac-Gloughlin. Mac had gone back to Pennsylvania, joined the Reserves, and now there he was. He subsequently made it out of Korea and later became a respected university professor of English. A letter from Linda at this time lifted my spirits, telling me how the gang had gone to The Glen, celebrating a UCLA victory, and a movie star had invited them all to his house to continue the party. He was one of my favorites, Rod Cameron.

We boarded trucks and made our way up into the mountains past Ambush Alley to Majon-ni. It surely was disgusting to see hands reach out from our trucks to tip the belongings off of the heads of women refugees into the yawning chasms. Long before this I had warned my platoon that behavior such as this — not respecting prisoners of war, throwing rocks at kids — would be dealt with by removing them from of the 2nd Platoon. That was the worst punishment that I could think of, and it worked.

We spent the early part of November (including the Marine Corps birthday and my own) defending this road hub, freezing, and being supplied by parachute — a very dangerous task for the troops on the ground in a small area. In fact, we had some casualties as the parachute drops were low-level. All winter I slept in my sleeping bag with my trusty .45 loaded and ready. I have often wondered since then if the bullets would have penetrated through the thick bag material. Anyway, I would have gone down shooting. The sleeping bag zippers would freeze, however, and it was a real balancing act trying to empty your piss-filled C-ration can outside in the snow.

The following was a typical schedule of our patrol:

4:30 — Reveille.
5:00 — Chow, C-rations.
7:30 — On the road. Uniform: field shoes, field jacket, fur cap (mine was Korean, made of dog fur). Ride ten miles, down to Ambush Alley, get off, patrol, and walk back.

While leading this Ambush Alley patrol, a Marine came up to me at the turnaround point with a muffler over his face and addressed me. It was Staff Sergeant Roach's son! They were both in the 13th Infantry, and both were in Korea. This boy had been wounded, evacuated to Japan, and later put aboard a ship for the States. He had gone over-the-rail, made his way back to Korea, was searching for his father, and had joined up again with us. Captain Groff was good enough to allow him to remain with the 2nd Platoon until we were able to find the Staff Sergeant, which we finally did on Thanksgiving Day.

As we began our attack up the east coast toward Hamhung, one incident stands out. (The firefights, patrols, and ambushes are mostly forgotten and would not be very accurate if I were to write about them now, but some incidents I shall never forget.) As we were resting in a ditch, the most comfortable position that an infantryman can find, down the dirt road came a patriarch, just as pictured in *Life* magazine. He was a very old man with the typical black hat, white clothes, and snow-white moustache and beard. He was tending an ox cart loaded with his possessions. Our gunnery Sergeant, who had shot my Corporal Carpenter on our first night ashore at Inchon, got up, went out on the road, and cold-cocked the ox between the eyes. The ox and cart went into the ditch. I took my carbine, fixed its bayonet, got up, and started up the road. Captain Groff yelled at me, and my platoon tackled me. We got the ox and cart on the road, said many *gomenasai*'s ("I'm sorry"), and sent the noble North Korean on his way with heartfelt *sayonara*.

We received Thanksgiving dinner in the most horrendous conditions — cold, rain, and sleet — but ate it anyway. I don't remember when, but mock-fur caps with earflaps and lined shoe pacs made of rubber, which came up half-calf, were finally issued. The latter saved our feet from freezing.

The 2nd Battalion, 1st Marine Regiment, finally reached Koto-ri, the town on top of the plateau at the Chosin Reservoir where most the fighting was to take place. We had learned that the Army artillery, with large guns on our left as we began the climb, were from Puerto Rico. Compared to what the 5th and 7th Marine Regiments, our 3rd Battalion, and other U.S. Army and British Commando units went through, we "had it made," as they were up where most of the Chinese were located. And I was ready.

Above and opposite: A "Safe Conduct Pass" for enemy soldiers who will "cease fighting." It was taken from a Chinese prisoner wearing tennis shoes at the frozen Chosin Reservoir, December 1950. The Korean language is at the upper right, Chinese at the bottom (read from right to left). The "Pass" is signed by General Douglas MacArthur and tells the enemy soldier: *Surrender and you receive Smokes, Medical Care, Chow, and Recreation.*

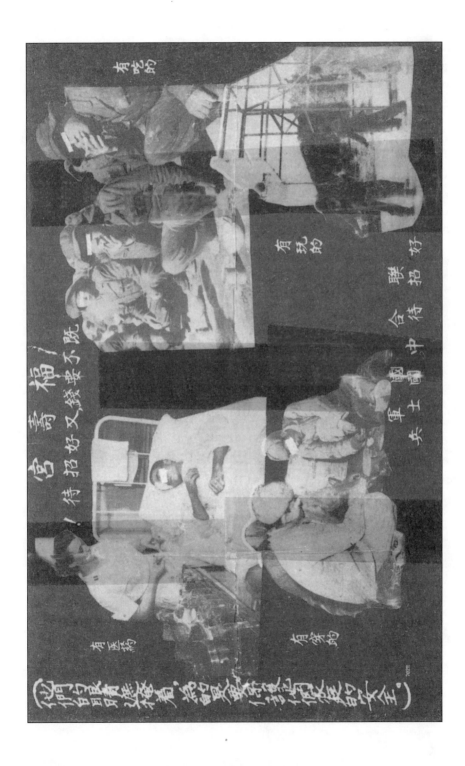

When in a defensive position, I was armed with my full automatic M-2 carbine, my Colt .45-caliber pistol, my Burp gun fully loaded with 80 rounds, and my knife that I had bought in San Francisco's China Town in 1942, along with a "Jap-hunting" license from a smiling Chinaman.

Much has been written about the Chosin Reservoir, so I have little to add. Fox Company had its firefights and patrols there, and we were just about the last to leave. We grenaded and burned blankets and gear that could not be evacuated before leaving Koto-ri. After a long trek to the sea, we once again boarded the USS *Noble*, and arrived safely in Pusan, South Korea. With no food being supplied to us for two days, we finally arrived in Masan and were set down in a bean patch.

I wrote a letter home to Linda from Masan.

Monday, Dec. 18, 1950

Dearest Linda.

I just remembered last night that I haven't even wished you a Merry Xmas yet. Now this probably won't reach you in time. . . . [*After leaving Koto-ri by foot, we had reached Hamhung on Linda's birthday, December 10, and boarded ship at Hungnam.*]

We fooled around aboard ship, slowly starving until 8:00 Saturday night when they announced we would disembark at

10:00 P. M.! So — we saddled up, disembarked, walked a mile through Pusan & boarded a train. We got two dried-up dough- nuts from two men in the dark. Someone said they were Red Cross workers. Half the train windows were out & there were wooden benches. By two in the morning when the train pulled out we were all in our sleeping bags on the floor & benches. (You may have noticed, honey, we always move on Sunday). Well, sometime in the morning we arrived in Masan. We stopped by a freight train full of chow. Well — we ate; cereal, milk, sugar (by the 10 lb. sack), fruit juices, spam, etc.). Honey, they never feed us anymore; we have to steal & scrounge. Well, the train had gone too far, so it took us four miles back up the road & here we are, the whole 1st Division in big tents — except us. We just have a field to call our own. We didn't eat this morning, line a mile long & they gave 1 spoon of eggs & coffee or juice. We had some cereal & milk left so we had our own. We should have plenty of mail soon. They seem to get fouled up worse all the time around here..

Honey, I'm fed up with this & with the U.S. Government. What are we doing here anyway? If only someone would give us some reasonable reasons for being here. The train sounded like a hospital train. If anyone coughed like the guys here do in the States they would be sent to the hospital right away.

The weather is pretty nice here, still freezing but kind of damp. Thank God for these sleeping bags — !

A fellow looked me up yesterday. He just came in with the 3rd. Replacement Draft. Sgt. Wolforth of the Santa Monica Reserves. He said that back at Pendleton they heard that I was wounded twice & not expected to live! How about that?

It looks like we are going to spend Christmas right here. The only future we can see is fight the Chinese here or go to a Pacific base. . . .

I'm thankful I'm alive & fairly well. If they are trying to starve us they sure are succeeding. . . .

Honey, I hope you have a very Merry Christmas. I'll make it up to you one of these days.

All my love & kisses
Your Reggie

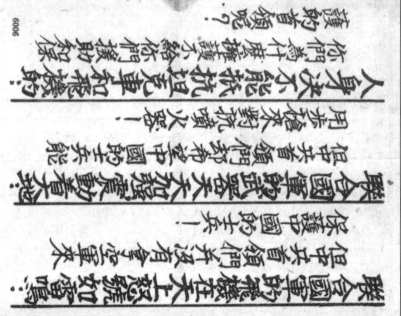

A Chinese propaganda leaflet showing how the United Nations is rolling over its "volunteer" soldiers.

Ever since arriving in Korea I had no trouble eventually getting chow. My mother, from Texas, had raised me on the value of vegetables, and we had always had a garden. Piles of discarded C-ration cans were encountered once in a while, and there was always a plethora of "Chicken and Vegetables," which with some water added to counteract the salt were #1 with me and #10 with most.

Come to find out, the spot we set down at in Masan, South Korea, was the famous "bean patch" that our 5th Marine Regiment had called home when they were in the Pusan Perimeter. We remained there for Christmas and our New Year's Day, hearing and reading that the Chinese were advancing and had even captured Seoul again.

I went on liberty once to Masan with some buddies and had some good beer, dancing, and conversation with the local girls. Upon leaving I gave all my money to a pretty young lady to help with her survival in case of an evacuation. It was a very scary time.

We had a specific deadline for getting back to camp. I think the liberty was for four hours. But we had missed the last "on-time" truck, and I, as a Staff Sergeant, guaranteed Boudreaux (a Private 1st Class "Coon-Ass") and Private 1st Class Newman (also from Louisiana, the town of Bunkie in fact) that everything would be OK. However, I had not factored in Captain Groff. When we arrived late at the bean patch, the good Captain called us in and assigned both PFCs to digging a garbage pit right in front of his palatial tent, which was equipped with toadies — his servile subordinates; but he had no "punishment" for me. I returned to my tent, was issued a case of beer, carried it back to the scene, and sat there popping cans to the Captain's chagrin, as a sign of support for my men. I hope they appreciated it. I know that I enjoyed myself, although I almost froze in place.

In the middle of January, we boarded trucks and moved just outside of Taejon to Uisong (Yusong) where we set up a strong point for a few days. The temperature was way below 32 degrees; your face would freeze if you faced the wind. However, a mortar squad wanted to register its gun. We watched as the men fired the 60mm shell. It went up, out, and began to blow back! Everyone hit the deck, and I swear the shell landed in the crowded firing pit. Amazingly, no one was seriously wounded by the detonation.

We then engaged in "The Great Guerilla Hunt," trying unsuccessfully to wipe out the North Koreans escaping from the south.

Captain Groff and I were leading Fox Company up a small, brushy valley when suddenly a machine gun opened up on us to our front from some distance. The Captain immediately hit the deck and I turned around and laughingly yelled for the whole 2nd Platoon to take a look at our Captain. It was a .50-caliber heavy machine gun, and as I had manned one for three years back in World War II, I was familiar with the sound and had no concern about being hit. Was he embarrassed? Yes! Among others, we lost another 13th Infantry man in this valley. Three of our Sergeants, along with a total of seven kids, had been killed with the 5th Marines outside Seoul.

I now considered the Captain and myself "even," but he managed to best me later on up north. Subsequently, during the hunt, we were in a large meadow and a field telephone began ringing. As no one was near, I answered it with, "Hello. . . . "

"*Hello?*" was the response I heard. "Who in the Hell is this? This is Colonel . . . ."

Needless to say, I hung up and *di di*'d out of the area. I have never liked answering the telephone since, and frequently respond with *Moshi, moshi, anonei?* (*Hello, hello . . . who is this?*)

Kim — A South Korean Boy's Mixed Loyalties

The Chinese Army had chased us from the Chosin Reservoir near the Chinese border back into South Korea. They had, indeed, crossed over the 38th Parallel, had recaptured Seoul, and we were to stop them — "we," being the 1st Marine Division. Having gotten our second wind, we had been ordered to undertake "Operation Killer" to find, engage, and push the Chinese out of the south. Therefore, we had regrouped and were headed north again. After chasing North Korean guerrillas near Taegu, we found ourselves one afternoon in the town of Andong. We could not believe it, but our 2nd Platoon was billeted in a line of small houses facing what appeared to be a soccer field. The houses had small stoves in them, which was

At Andong, Brigadier General Lewis Burwell "Chesty" Puller was officially promoted to General. According to *Marine*, by Burke Davis, the three Marines standing behind the General, who had served with him in World War II, were Master Sergeant Mathew Jacklewicz from New York, Staff Sergeant Vincent J. Lukowski from Massachusetts, and Staff Sergeant Albert J. Salonis from New Jersey. Private 1st Class Robert Y. Gonzales, from Stockton, California, the 1st Marine Regiment's smallest man and a musician, pinned on a jumbo-sized star made from cardboard and aluminum foil by Master Sergeant Joe Guiliano. Guiliano also had Chesty stand on a stone for the pinning. *U.S. Marine Corps*

a Godsend, as we had had enough of living outside in the Korean winter.

A roadblock was set up by Fox Company, and we dug positions between the houses and the large field. A company of U.S. Army tanks moved in between the houses to support us on the line. We sent out patrols, and the off-duty troops stayed warm indoors. Rations were available, and some hot chow was served if you went and got it. The mess Sergeant passed the word that we could have all the cake batter we wanted. Well, we wanted!

I was located with Sergeant Jennings and part of his squad in the platoon command post. We somehow or other had been joined by Kim, a boy of about nine or ten. He was really a big help, and got right into the middle of things. The cake batter was at hand, so as usual a small line formed in front of the stove to take turns making flapjacks, which incidently were excellent with all that sugar and egg in them. It was amazing how your taste buds craved sweets in the field.

Kim was in line, naturally, so I held up my carbine and asked him if it was any good? He quickly came to attention and in a strong voice said, "Burp gun number one, carbine number ten!" I told Sergeant Jennings to get him, and I opened the door as Ivan threw the boy bodily into the snowbank of the house next door. We slammed the door of our house and locked it.

Pretty soon there was a loud knocking, and a plaintive little voice shouting, "M-2 carbine number one, M-1 Garand (we didn't even use the word Garand) number one, Sherman tank number one, and U.S. Marine number one!"

We let the poor little soul back in to cook his hotcakes. You see, we were aware that he had been with the Chinese/North Koreans, and we had taken him by surprise with the question. The Russian Burp gun was one of their main weapons, as it had been for the Russian army during World War II and the Chinese Communist armies during the late 1940s.

A few days later, Fox Company boarded trucks for Wonju, our next "jumping-off" point. We Marines were not allowed to relocate any Korean civilians, so it was really sad to say *sayonara* to Kim.

After the stop at Andong, trucks took us to Wonju. The place was devastated, and we were ready for Operation Killer. Patrols were organized, and we finally dug in on some mountains on the left of the main road. We had no problem keeping warm; all one had to do was walk up and down a mountain during the night rather than freeze trying to sleep or stand guard!

After a few days, we were ordered down to the main road and north toward the city of Hoengsong, with the Som River on our left. One day as we were assuming our positions in the roadside ditches, along came some VIPs. Lo and behold there was General Matthew B. Ridgway, who had taken over from U.S. Army Major General Edward M. Almond, December 18, 1950, when the 1st Marine Division was transferred from X Corps to the Eighth Army, of which Lieutenant General Ridgway was the Commander. I was glad to see him, as I had read much of his actions as Commander of the 2nd Airborne Division in World War II, especially in Sicily. I immediately spotted his famous hand grenade, well-taped to the right side of his paratroop webbing, but I was stumped by the object on his left. Because of the tape, all I could read was "Fir." Until an article in *World War II* magazine just a few years ago, I wondered if it were some type of thermite, white phosphorus, or other type of grenade. Bummer! It was a first-aid pouch!

We were frequently shelled by the Chinese, and firefights were the order of the day. One of my men shot himself in the leg, and I paraded the whole platoon by his hole for the express purpose of humiliating him for letting us down by bugging out.

One cold morning, Captain Groff ordered us to "fix bayonets" and prepare to charge, which we did of course. (We always fixed our bayonets in advancing toward the enemy, but this sounded as if we were in World War I!) Three-fourths of the way across the frozen rice paddy, under fire, he stopped and ordered me to look at the bullet holes in his green wool trousers (there were three). With that, he had one-upped me for the last time. Recently I heard that he had pulled that stunt before — but in a charge, while receiving fire? The good Captain died at Camp Pendleton Naval Hospital on September 15, 1960, ten years to the day after we had landed at Inchon. I was in Haiti at the time, and will always remember a very brave man.

As we fought our way to our objective, a ridge over looking Hoeng-song, we came upon a meadow just covered with the remains of a U.S. Army field artillery battalion, probably the 15th, which had been slaughtered by the Chinese some time before. Horrible.

We occupied a ridge just outside Hoengsong from where I would watch the Korean Marine Corps Regiment attack on a mountaintop the other side of the river. It had been attached to us during the drive on Seoul. I observed the fierce action with the binoculars that Lieutenant Maiden had given me when he was seriously wounded near Sosa. Both the ROKs (Republic of Korea) and Chinese were visible, as were the mortar and hand-grenade detonations. The atmosphere was surreal, as there was no sound due to the distance, and yet those men I was watching were getting killed and wounded.

On my last patrol down into Hoengsong we carried many colored signal panels, as our aircraft were busy overhead. When a plane threatened us, we would wildly flutter the orange and red panel signals. I spotted a dead Chinese out in a beet field, and went out to discover that he was a Staff Sergeant just like me. I still have his padded cap with the Staff Sergeant stripes on the front.

We returned to our lines via the main road and encountered a most horrible tableau. A U.S. Army convoy had been wiped out. At first you don't want to even think that there are Americans involved, but with the first dead blond soldier you encounter, it is all too obvious. A whole convoy of vehicles heading south had been completely blasted and burned, with bodies everywhere, including the horrible compressed corpses in the truck cabs due to the frequently used concussion grenades.

I have always wondered and will never find out why I was selected for rotation back to the States, but I was. I really hated to leave Fox Company as I traversed the line saying goodbye, but orders were orders, and you only had one butt.

Sergeant Ivan Jennings took over as platoon Sergeant, and he at last realized the advantages of making a trade as he eyed the mountains on the other side of the city. He accepted my trustworthy M-2 carbine, and I left the good ol' 2nd Platoon and Fox Company for the rear, carrying his M-1 rifle. To tell the truth, I did not feel safe until the second day, when I was out of Chinese artillery range.

Traveling to Pusan by truck, to Oakland by ship, and to Los Angeles by bus, I finally was home.

Chapter 5

Stateside Duty — Then the Land of the Rising Sun

*I*N OAKLAND, we were warmly greeted on the docks by a great crowd. Incidentally, this was the only time upon returning from three wars that this phenomenon ever occurred and it really felt great. We all were given lifetime movie passes, and then trucked to Treasure Island, a naval station under the Oakland Bay Bridge. I had sold my .45-caliber pistol in Pusan for $100, so I bought a diamond ring in the PX. We all were gathered in a gym where we had to defecate into pint-sized ice-cream containers or fish a turd out of the commode for testing. Everyone had worms, so large pills were taken for a few months.

Arriving home on Sunday, March 26, I proposed to Erlinda, and we took off for Las Vegas the next morning. After getting married on the 28th, we made our way to Mexico, spending our honeymoon in Calexico, Mexicali, and Ensenada. Because it was early spring and the brewery barrels were being cleaned, bock beer was available, and was the order of the day. We purchased a 1951 Buick Special in Culver City, making us a two-car family, and eventually reported in to Camp Pendleton to set up housekeeping in half a Quonset hut near the main

April 1951 in Old Mexico — the author's new wife and his Ford V-8 while on their honeymoon in Cuernavaca.

gate on Vandegrift Boulevard. My job was in Tactics, of the 2nd Infantry Training and Replacement Regiment at Tent Camp #3, 2nd ITR.

We made friends with Gunnery Sergeant Benton R. Montgomery and his wife, and we watched television and drank beer — and later apple cider, with "mother," the apple residue, in it; the beer tended to put us to sleep before the television set. Benton's wife, Shirley, had been a nurse, and because Erlinda was then pregnant, I had no worries when they were off shopping or at the hobby shops making whatever.

While at Camp Pendleton, the movie *Retreat Hell* was made right across the boulevard in the gully leading up to the later-constructed Wire Mountain officers quarters. During the filming, numerous 5th Marines, quartered at Santa Margarita, had to make the hike about nine miles to the movie set, carrying parkas and wearing other cold-weather gear. And it was a hot summer! The "snow" for the movie was pulverized granite; a 1st Sergeant's Quonset was really made over, and the tent area used was also

January 1952 in "Homaja," the housing area at Camp Pendleton. Linda Farrington, a new mother, holds Arthur C., III, in front of their new 1951 Buick outside their first home.

improved for the film. Cinema magic and the Marines produced a very realistic film about our adventure in the Frozen Chosin.

I made Technical Sergeant on August 10, 1951, 0319 (infantryman), and finally caught up with Linda, who then had a rank of 1st Class Storekeeper in the U.S. Navy Reserve. She had served in Washington, D.C., under Navy Captain Hyman Rickover, the father of U.S. nuclear submarines, during World War II.

Reggie Farrington (Arthur C. III) was born on January 2, 1952, and we were transferred to my hometown, Washington, D.C. The V-8 was sold to a Navy corpsman with a bunch of kids, and we were off.

After a visit to Linda's friends and family in San Antonio and Luling, Texas, we reported in to Marine Barracks at 8th and Eye Streets, where I was assigned to the Language Section of the Marine Corps Institute. We taught Spanish, French, and Russian by mail to Marines all over the world. Each lesson as received was personally taken care of by either Master Sergeant Vienneau, Master Sergeant Budkovsky, Master Sergeant Barnyak, Technical Sergeant Flores, or myself. I later was put in charge of the section and wrote new courses for Spanish I and II. One of my students, Sergeant Kim Ki Hong, was an interpreter for the Marines in Korea, and he and a friend later visited my wife and me at our new home at 3 Compass Green, Naval Housing, between Bolling Field and the Naval Research Laboratory, across the Anacostia River from D.C. He and his friend were attending Ordnance School at Quantico, Virginia.

General Lemuel C. Shepherd, Jr., decorating a Lieutenant on June 25, 1954, at the Marine Barracks, Washington, D.C. Arthur Farrington (right) held the medals for the Commandant's presentation. The photograph was taken by the renowned photographer R. H. Mosier.

U.S. Marine Corps

While at the Marine Corps Institute, several significant events occurred in my life:

(1) My divorced father visited — an ex-Marine, who had been born in Greenleaf, Wisconsin, but who now resided in Buffalo, New York, and Daytona Beach, Florida.

(2) I held the medals that the Commandant, General Lemuel C. Shepherd, Jr., pinned on heroes at the Sunset Parade, thoroughly enjoying the comments he made and having a hard time keeping a straight face. One evening I handed out parade programs to the Commandant's guests at his home on the north end of the parade ground. Present was General Krulak, who earlier had been my Battery Commander in Cuba before World War II. He came out arm-in-arm with two tall ladies, greeted me by name, and inquired as to my circumstances after thirteen years! Your spirits are surely lifted by such men. Another was General Freiberg, the original I&I — Instruction and Information — officer of the 13th Infantry Battalion in 1946.

(3) I received my first tennis "Loving Cup" by winning the doubles with a U.S. Navy officer at a Navy tournament in Dahlgren, Virginia. We could not afford champagne, so Linda and I toasted with ale, a higher class of beer.

(4) Promotion tests were given at Quantico right behind C Barracks, where I had been billeted in 1940, and I was on my way to becoming a Master Sergeant.

(5) My father died in Buffalo, in early June 1954, necessitating a trip with only little Reggie and our Siamese cat, Mocha. Linda was due to give birth again in a few days, so it was a hasty round trip.

(6) Rolando Curtis Farrington was born on June 18, 1954, at Bethesda Naval Hospital.

(7) We, at the Marine Corps Institute, were able to visit the architect Felix DeWeldon at his studio in northeast Washington, where he was sculpting the absolutely detail-perfect Iwo Jima statue. One by one the enormous cut sections were chained to the back of an old flatbed truck and driven carefully to Brooklyn, New York, where they were bronzed and then taken back down Highway 1 to D.C.

A Private 1st Class in the 1st Platoon of Fox Company, 2nd Battalion, 1st Marine Regiment, 1st Marine Division, upon returning from Korea in 1951, had been assigned the duty of posing for the statue. He was a handsome Blackfoot Indian from South Dakota named Harvey Owens.

DeWeldon told us that the six men were in the "heroic" style rather than being physically correct. In other words, they all were handsome and very muscular.

I later volunteered and was in charge of the historic flag-raising on the statue in Arlington, Virginia, on November 10, 1954. My entire family was there, and it was quite a thrill to see the three surviving members of the incident, Ira Hayes, René Gagnon, and Jack Bradley, sitting next to the Commandant of the Marine Corps. Satisfying, too, was the realization that my career was not over, as Old Glory went up on schedule and without a hitch on a windy day. Also, no one fell off the extremely slippery Swedish marble that we had to navigate in our double-soled, cleated dress shoes that were the uniform for 8th and Eye ceremonial Marines.

(8) I completed twelve graduate units at American University.

(9) I was selected to tell some war experiences for "Boys' Nation" at the Pentagon; gave a speech on a program with President Harry S. Truman to new citizens; was a guest on a military radio show; spoke at high schools; and accompanied my buddy Jack Lartz, who had been a Marine Raider, on some assignments to properly spell Portuguese and Spanish names when he covered Organization of American States and National Geographic Society meetings. Jack was a reporter and photographer for the *Washington Post* at the time. I was fortunate to meet Professor Preston E. James, the author of the textbook *Latin America*, which I had used while at UCLA. It was also an eye-opener, upon seeing the photo spread in the *Post,* to see how Jack cropped out the not-so-good-looking ladies and manipulated who was with whom. He was talented, and his photos received plenty of exposure.

(10) My "hairiest" assignment was on the sidelines of the Washington, D.C., Redskins team in Griffith Stadium. Jack took photos while I wrote down the numbers with crayons and ran. Eddie LeBaron was the short, brave quarterback. He had to jump up and down in order to see over the large linemen. At the Washington Senators' baseball games, we stuffed cotton in little Reggie's ears.

For a "photo-shoot," Jack had wanted my son Reggie to hang out of the barrel of the first atomic cannon before it was paraded down Pennsylvania Avenue. He wouldn't believe me on the telephone when I told him that the

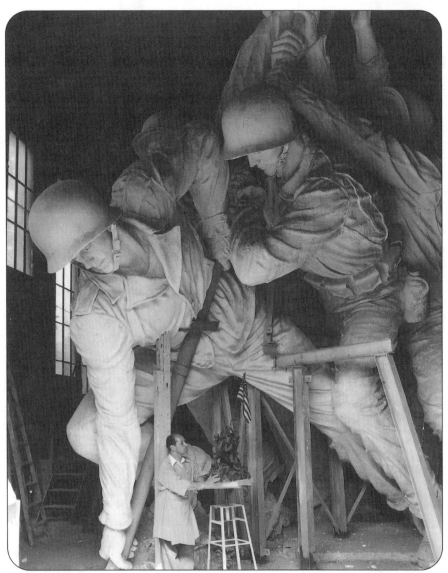

Felix W. DeWeldon, sculptor of the Marine Corps Memorial, puts finishing touches on the plaster model prior to its being cut into sections for bronze casting.   *U.S. Marine Corps*

cannon had a bore of only eleven inches. As we observed the cannon, "Atomic Annie," in the Naval Gun Factory, I asked Jack just how he had intended to get Reggie up to the mouth of the gun. He was ready with block and tackle! He had to settle with posing him under a

Felix W. DeWeldon and his hard-working assistant, who also trucked the sections to and from Brooklyn, New York, for bronzing.   *U.S. Marine Corps*

cow and in front of a Coast Guard poster on 14th Street across from the Trans-Lux Theatre.

I had many good friends at 8th and Eye, but my favorite was gunnery Sergeant Margie Baker, with whom we used to walk about a mile for noon

The Marine Corps Memorial, Iwo Jima statue, in Washington, D.C.

chow at the barracks. Her only quirk — and it really was a quirk — was that she refused to salute officers. At the time, the Marine Corps Institute was located in a Naval Gun Factory building at South Capitol and M Streets SE.

While at the Institute I also met Senator Joseph McCarthy at a luncheon in the U.S. Capitol building. We discussed Wisconsin, and he later came back to tell me that the name Reggie Dwire was familiar and that he had just remembered that he had gone to Law School with him. My father had introduced me to Reggie Dwire, the District Attorney of Green Bay, Wisconsin, in 1933. His first name was given to me as a nickname when I was born. He had been on the Green Bay Packer team and had lost a leg. His wooden leg was propped up in the corner of his office.

Jack Lartz took this photograph of the author's two-year-old son Reggie, in 1954, at 14th and New York Avenue. The original caption reads: "Little Reggie Farrington, 2, of Washington, wants no part of this Coast Guard poster. His dad is a Marine."
Courtesy of Jack Lartz, INP

During this time we visited the Jack Lartz family often, and on one occasion we went to the Great Falls of the Potomac. Jack and I fished from a small boat with an outboard motor. Well, the motor caught fire and we drifted toward the falls. Jack yelled to dump the motor. I knew that he had borrowed it from his brother, so I cut it loose but held on to the tiller as it went down, then retrieved it after a few minutes. We floated 100 feet from the brink of the falls, but made it back. On dry land, amidst all the excitement, little Reggie danced like crazy to Theresa Brewer's great song, "Ricochet Romance."

On Memorial Day in 1953 I was assigned as an usher for President Dwight Eisenhower's speech at the Unknown Soldier's Tomb. This day was exactly seventeen years after I had been on a Boy Scout Camporee in Virginia, so you can probably guess what happened during his address. The seventeen-year locusts (cicadas) came out. Just as in 1936, millions were flying low and fast. Can you imagine Marines in blues grabbing the large colorful missiles off ladies' hair, bonnets, and dresses and launching them higher? It was pandemonium, but Ike took it well, and the affair was more of a success than planned, I'm sure.

Incidentally, in 1937 the Boy Scouts of America held their world Jamboree in D.C., 27 years after being formed there on February 8, 1910. The Jamboree headquarters was located at what used to be the Tiber River, formerly Goose Creek, in front of an estate called Rome, owned by a man called Pope. He had insisted that a Pope living in Rome would have to have a Tiber River! Since 1883, more than 300 acres have been reclaimed from the Tiber and swamp. The Jamboree was "copacetic" for the world Scouts.

In the spring of 1955, I was transferred to Japan. But before reporting in to the 3rd Marine Regiment, 3rd Marine Division, at Gotemba, Japan, I had an assignment to 1st Sergeants' School at Parris Island, South Carolina. I stashed my family in Luling, Texas, drove back to Parris Island, finished the course, drove back to Texas, picked up Linda and the boys, and delivered them to my mother in west Los Angeles.

Japan was my next stop, where I replaced a Master Sergeant who was retiring. The company Commander was Captain "Blackie" Cahill, one of the heroes of the Pusan Perimeter. We got along fine, and I soon made the 3rd Division's tennis team and flew back to Quantico, Virginia, for the All Marine Tennis Tournament. On the way I got to visit Wake Island, Midway Island, Hawaii, and my family.

I don't enjoy flying at all. Over Georgia we kept circling, only to discover that the pilot's house was the target. One of the co-pilots was named Ralph Graniger, a boyhood neighbor. He later fell off a 40-foot ladder (four rungs from the bottom) while decorating the gym at Quantico Air

Station for the Marine Corps Ball and was medically discharged. What a bad break! I looked him up later in Virginia, when I was again playing tennis at Quantico. Incidently, I was beaten 6-0, 6-0 by Lieutenant Spears. We discovered later that we were brother Kappa Alphas, though he had attended the Citadel. He confessed that the reason he had beaten me so badly, besides being much better, was because he had seen a terrible rainstorm coming up the Potomac, and thus the thrashing. He owned a Cadillac, and we made some liberties to D.C.

Spears told me the following story on a trip to D.C. As a jet pilot, he once had to ditch in the Caribbean near Guantanamo Bay. As the plane sank, he boarded his one-man raft. Soon sharks arrived, and he had to lift his butt up each time they passed underneath the bottom nylon straps. He was soon black from the shark repellent, but low and behold there appeared a ship on the horizon. Out went the yellow dye marker for visibility, and he was a black and yellow mess when he was finally picked up.

As it had taken some time for the boat to approach, he had passed the minutes reading a pocket book he had with him. He told me to open the glove compartment. I took out a paperback and read inside the cover: "*When rescued from shark-infested waters Lieutenant Frank Spears, USMC, was reading this book.*"

The Lieutenant said that after the incident he was called the "old lady" because he would walk around his plane like the "old-timers," checking everything. Another time, he had experienced a flame-out coming into the airfield at Guantanamo. I know from having been there that the airfield is up on a sort of plateau above Fish Point Naval Air Station. His jet made it, but the landing gear did not and ended up down the cliff. I sure respect pilots of all kinds. To my satisfaction, he won the All-Marine Tennis Tournament.

And thus, I returned to Japan. What an awful job it was being a 1st Sergeant at that time. A new system of unit diaries had just been designed for use and my clerks were not up to snuff. The diaries would go to Okinawa, Hawaii, and would be returned to I-3-3 — Company I, 3rd Battalion, 3rd Marine Regiment — and its 1st Sergeant for correction of minutiae. I felt certain that I knew why the previous 1st Sergeant had retired. (I met him later serving as a fireman at Camp Del Mar, Camp Pendelton.)

In December of 1955 I learned from my wife that I had been selected for Warrant Officer. She had gotten the word from Duck's wife (Gunnery Sergeant Montgomery). Duck had by then been promoted to Lieutenant Colonel and worked in counterintelligence at Little Creek, Virginia.

The 3rd Battalion then went on maneuvers to Iwo Jima, and the mock aggressors were fitted out with crests on their helmets by Master Sergeant Vick, who also had been selected for Warrant Officer rank. I have two memories of that Iwo Jima maneuver. On an off day I walked completely around the island on the shoreline in a counter-clockwise direction. What terrain! I thanked my lucky stars that I had not been there for the landings in 1945. I have also thanked God that I was on the island of Guadalcanal in the fall of 1942 rather than at Stalingrad.

My other memory of Iwo Jima was the day Captain Cahill had sent me, still the 1st Sergeant, alone to the top of Mt. Suribachi — for what reason I have never been able to fathom. So, off I went. What a view! I investigated the crater, the whole area, and settled in just below the American flag, which at that time flew both day and night. It was cold up there, and rain soon began to fall. What an awful night. Water poured into my sleeping bag, and the large flag just kept flapping and flapping in the cold wind. This was the nearest I have ever come to "losing it." As there was no one within a mile, I spent the night cursing everything and everybody that I could think of. What a long, miserable circumstance.

During those maneuvers, we fought off Master Sergeant Vick and his aggressors by rallying under our "flag," a rocking chair. I have never known what it meant, but the flag was called a *filaloo*, though I am not sure of the spelling, and the meaning involved something about a snake swallowing itself. That never quite made sense to me.

Upon our return to the Land of the Rising Sun, Vick and I were promoted to WO-1 (Warrant Officer-1), moved into officers' quarters, and began taking the bus to Kozu and then the train to Yokosuka to have uniforms made. Our hand-carried bags contained beer, and Vick would say to a can of brew, "Prepare to open . . . *open!*" — to the delight of the Japanese, who had never seen pop-top cans. A drink was necessary on the return trip, as the train ride was uphill all the way and the steam locomotive would really belch black coal smoke, which filled the cars, especially in the many tunnels. Every now and then we would debark, find a bar, and have a really good Kirin, Nippon, or Asahi beer. Unfortunately, my very good friend Warrant Officer Vick later would be killed in Vietnam.

At Yokosuka, the custom tailor's name was Mito. I had all my green uniforms made by him, plus two very beautiful cashmere jackets, one white and one baby blue. I still wear the Eisenhower-style jacket and trousers to the 1st Marine Division birthday balls at Camp Pendleton, and am pleased to stand up as an original member. In 2000, the Division asked the World War II veterans to stand, so that was even better;

The author's All-Marine Corps Championships badge for tennis.

and Erlinda, who had been a WAVE, stood up with me. Incidentally, before each Marine anniversary birthday party we stop off for a couple beers at Carl's in Vista, where Clint Eastwood filmed part of the movie *Heartbreak Ridge*. It is always difficult to leave these "pre-parties."

Warrant Officer Vick was assigned as Commanding Officer of the Middle Camp Brig, and I was assigned to the S-3 (Operations) officer in the Battalion, Lieutenant Colonel Flake, as the officer in charge of the 150-target rifle range at North Camp. Mount Fuji was situated just over the middle of the butts, where the targets are manipulated, and was breathtakingly beautiful in all kinds of weather, which we had. My Sergeant in charge of the pistol range was the Master Sergeant of the infamous Korean ox incident, who I resolutely ignored whenever possible.

In 1956, the best tennis players from the rest of the 3rd Marine Division came up from Okinawa, and we had the playoffs in Gifu on clay with ballboys! Making the team again, I was in for another round trip to Quantico, where I was more successful than the year before. The Marine Corps also hosted the Inter-Service championships in 1956 for the first time and really made themselves proud by constructing Har-Tru courts (green composition) out by the golf club. Crews were provided to rake them down, and there was always a fire truck available to hose them down. Whitney Reed, of the U.S. Air Force, defeated Grant Golden, of the U.S. Army, for the title.

Following the tournament when I returned to Japan, the whole company was sporting Fuji Sticks, the walking sticks with the seal (stamp) burned in it, which the men had received for climbing the holy mountain. To this day I am sorry that I missed that adventure.

More wonderful Japanese duty followed, then my tour was completed and orders were received transferring me back to the States.

Chapter 6

Camp Pendleton Again — and Duty in Haiti

M Y FAMILY HAD been dividing its time between two grandmothers, one in Luling, Texas, and one in Los Angeles, California. Finding them in good shape, we bought a Buick Century and moved into housing on Wire Mountain, just inside the main gate at Camp Joseph H. Pendleton.

I was assigned duty at Headquarters Battalion, Marine Corps Base, Camp Pendleton, working with Warrant Officer Rust on emergency plans in case of an atomic attack, forest fire, flood, or other disaster. Rust was from Detroit, and when we went on active duty back in 1940 I had been his runner. Our picture appears in *The Leatherneck Boys*.

One day at Headquarters down on Vandegrift Boulevard, the crew was listening to the World Series, which had the New York Yankees tied up with the Brooklyn Dodgers 3-3 in the seventh game. A woman Marine screamed as the Yankees defeated the Dodgers, and to our dismay, the Commanding General came down the hallway and really reamed her out — though in a joking manner.

This light duty lasted only a few weeks, and I was shipped out to Tent Camp #2 (San Onofre) as the scheduling officer for the 2nd Infantry Training Regiment. This was a great job for a little over two years, with the best officers ever; and my troops were outstanding. We scheduled everything — chow, weapons, ranges, corpsmen, range-safety officers, transport — for about fifteen companies and were very success-ful at it. Lieutenant Colonel Persinger was in charge. Some other officers included Colonel Masters, the brother of James M. Masters, Jr., who had been the Commanding Officer of the 2nd Battalion, 1st Marine Regiment, for the Sag Sag operation on New Britain Island in 1943. We had been proud to be called "Masters' Bastards." Also included was Major Noble, Captain Cohoon, Captain Heim, Captain Cunha, Master Sergeant Williams, and my trusted Sergeant in charge of the scheduling board, Staff Sergeant Cohee. Cohee was great, as he took over whenever I was called away to be a member of a General Court-Martial, to go out in the field with companies on training, to be range-safety officer for live firing, or to be assigned Temporary Additional Duty to compete in tennis tournaments. Staff Sergeant Cohee was outstanding. On August 1, 1957, I was desig-nated a Marine Gunner (Infantry) by the Commandant of the Marine Corps, General R. McPate.

Our home at Wire Mountain officers quarters was very comfortable. My first daughter, Karen Lisa, was born on July 6, 1958, at the Naval Hospi-tal.

Our 1951 Buick Special had been traded in for a 1952 Special, which was subsequently traded for a '54 yellow and black Riviera, and it for the '57 pink and gray Century. One time, returning from Tent Camp #2 with a carload of 2nd Lieutenants, the large one next to me asked if I had ever used the passing gear. We were climbing the steep hill to Wire Mountain when I said "No," and that I was not aware it had one. The Lieutenant stepped on my accelerator foot, a big cloud of smoke erupted from the rear, and we lunged forward as in an airplane taking off. The Buick had 300 horses under the hood, no doubt about that.

On February 26, 1959, we received orders to the Naval Mission in the Republic of Haiti, with stopovers in Texas, then at Headquarters U.S. Marine Corps, Washington, D.C., and finally a date with an ocean liner in

New York City. A personal memo was sent along from Colonel Robert Debs Heinl, Jr., recommending some books to be read concerning Haiti and its customs. And we were advised not to bring along anything ostentatious.

Unfortunately, the Farrington family had the pink and gray Buick Century! I also had a family of five, including seven-month-old Karen, and our Siamese cat, Mocha, as well as 3,000 miles to travel — and there was a serious time constraint. We discovered much later that it was almost standard operating procedure (SOP) for families displacing overseas to Third World countries to quickly trade for station wagons, which, upon orders to return to the States, could be quickly and profitably sold to the locals to be utilized for public transportation.

We said goodbye to my mother in L.A.; visited for awhile in Linda's hometown of Luling, Texas; got briefed in D.C.; traveled to New York; bought a cat carrier for Mocha; boarded the SS *Cristóbal*; passed the island of San Salvador, where *Cristóbal Colón* (Columbus) had first set foot; and pulled into Port-au-Prince, Haiti, after safely traversing the Bermuda Triangle.

The first words out of Colonel Heinl's mouth as I was coming down the gangplank were, "Well, Gunner, you asked for it!" He was of course referring to my record book, which listed my college major as Latin American Studies, with Spanish and Portuguese.

Indeed, there were a few who spoke French that were assigned to the Mission, but only a few. The rest of us had to take scheduled lessons at Headquarters from a civilian, Mr. Oberstar, who later became a U.S. Representative from Minnesota.

One of the most valuable members of the Mission in my estimation was Sergeant Savoy, from New Orleans. He spoke the exact same Creole as did everyone in Haiti and was stationed frequently on the docks, where he was able to make some order out of chaos with incoming and outgoing Naval Mission cargo assigned to us and the Haitian Armed Forces. Of course, he could do nothing but report the corruption in the *douane* (Customs), which has always seriously damaged the country's economy and continues to do so today.

The U.S. Naval Mission to Haiti, 1959-1963, by Charles T. Williamson, published in 1999, covers this period, but I will add a little on my duties and experiences as a Commissioned Warrant Officer-2 (0302) with designation Marine Gunner (Non-Technical Warrant Officer).

The Farrington family Christmas card, 1961. Left to right: Rolando with Pup-Pups, Reggie, and Karen.

Native artwork the author purchased in Haiti.

My wife Erlinda, sons Reggie and Rolando, daughter Karen, Mocha our cat, and myself were put up for a while in the hotel *Sans Souci* ("Without Worry"), which we enjoyed, in central Port-au-Prince, near American Ambassador Drew's residence. The Naval Mission Headquarters was situated in the old Chrysler building near the Haitian Army Headquarters and just across the street from the National Palace.

I was assigned as the adviser to the *Camp d'Application* about nine miles west on the Carrefour road on Lamentin peninsula. The lighthouse there guides all ships arriving at Port-au-Prince. The *Camp d'Application* offered refresher training for every noncommissioned officer in the Haitian army. During our tour of duty, of course, the army also had the national police duties.

We rented a small house from a nice lady, Madame Malval, out in the jungle near my place of work, in an area called Diquini. Our nearest neighbors were Major Frisbie and his large family; a German, Herr Fisher, who worked for an American tobacco company; and *Ti Barb*, an adviser to Haitian President Duvalier. They were hundreds of yards away beyond fields of *piti mi* (sorghum). We had a maid, Jeanie, and a houseboy named Eléphant Saint Louis.

My counterpart, Major Garcia, was the Commanding Officer, and he was dedicated and pleasant, as were most of the other Haitian officers who came and went. We trained many classes over the next 2½ years in Infantry weapons and tactics. But the most important training was accomplished when I was able to get the men out of the classroom and into the field for combat maneuvers. It seems the classroom was the "French" way.

We always had trouble getting live ammunition, as the Haitians did not want to facilitate any uprising, should such a circumstance occur. In fact, the keys to the ammunition storeroom and the armory in the National Palace were in the President's rooms. Sometimes he handled them personally. If he was sick, some difficulty was encountered in obtaining weapons and/or ammunition. Early on, I had one such typical case. We had scheduled mortar firing at Ganthier to the east, in the country near the Dominican border. We picked up the rounds (60mm French) from the palace and were on our way when I inquired as to the location of the fuzes, which in this case had to be attached to the rounds just before firing them down-range. The answer, of course, was that we did not have fuzes, as they had not been issued to us. No one was going to inform me in advance about this upcoming wasted day.

I had the vehicle turned around, and back to the palace we went. I will never forget the scene in that Colonel's office. He had automatic weapons in the corner and pistols and hand grenades in his desk drawers. After some conversation, he made out a requisition slip; I went down into the cellar, presented it, and was issued the correct number of fuzes. This was the Haitian army's ammunition bunker! Colonel Heinl's son was later locked up down there by President Duvalier's private police, the Tonton Macoutes, until the President's son heard and rescued him.

Major Garcia's official car was a Volkswagen Beetle. I'll never forget the day he made me sit up front with his driver, Private Labbé, who naturally was a fast driver. The rocks hitting the underside and the crowd of people dividing on the roadway just as we raced through were unnerving, to say the least. But I was so impressed by the Beetle that I ordered a black one from Germany and received it on July 6, 1959. We still have the $1,475 VW and have always loved it. In Haiti, the windshield was continually laced with colorful smudges of wet fingernail polish when Erlinda and her girlfriends pointed as they traveled.

We acquired a nice brown hounddog as protection against *voleurs* (robbers), and immediately named him Bugs for his proclivity to have eaten bugs of all kinds in order to stay alive on the streets of Port-au-Prince — and even after he was well-fed. I guess he had acquired a taste for them. We lost Mocha either as a meal for the Haitians or to a mongoose in the area, and were presented with a tiny black and white French poodle by the owner of the property we had been allowed to use for an overnight NCO bivouac. I had admired the pup's mother at the time of the maneuver, and I had even talked the soldiers into throwing limes for the dog to retrieve. It seems that the Haitians have a dislike, and in some cases a fear, of dogs, which goes back to the time of the French landowners who used the animals to chase down runaway slaves and to otherwise keep their property in line.

One day my houseboy came over the fields to excitedly tell us that there was a surprise for us in the jungle. We hiked across, and a small black and white pup was presented to us. At home, we washed him and the black parts came off — they were literally hundreds of fleas and ticks. He was pure white! Later, when I was telling Major Garcia about the pup, I mentioned that we had named him *Ti Roi Christophe* (Little King Christopher). We had just recently returned from a trip with Navy Captain Armington and his large family to the Citadelle, built by the Haitian King *Christophe*. Well, Major Garcia hemmed and hawed as he explained the role of dogs in their history, and requested that I please select another name. I immediately agreed, and so Pup-Pups it was. As a kid, I had a little mongrel named Purpy Durps, but that was a little too much for the rest of the family.

At this juncture it seems that a list of some interesting occurrences in Haiti will suffice for this tale, in no special order. Most of the following information is taken from either my weekly, monthly, or special reports to the G-3 (Operations and Training) officer, Lieutenant Colonel Cain, to Lieutenant Colonel Wilkes, to Lieutenant Colonel Beckett, or to Major Frisbie.

The period of May 8-31, 1959, was spent requesting, arranging, and pleading to obtain some M-1 Garand rifles for the NCOs to fire for familiarization, as the long-term plan was for the M-1s to replace the Belgian FN (*Fusil National*) bolt-action rifles. The Palace issued us 26 M-1s, 26 web slings, and 5,000 rounds of Remington ammunition in five-round clips. The rifles were packed in original Cosmoline and wrapped in waxed

The entrance to Arthur Farrington's duty station in Haiti, *Camp d'Application.*

paper. The only material available to clean the M-1s was a single baby dia-per, furnished by *Ti Fi* (my little daughter, Karen), and gasoline siphoned from my Buick.

We commenced firing at 0630 at the *Champ de Tir* (the firing field). The cartridges, which we had to reload into clips of eight for the M-1s that had been almost impossible to obtain, were very old and appeared to be very bad. Fifty percent failed to fire, and those that did were hang-fires (two explosions instead of one), and five or six ruptured cartridges were encountered. Ten rifles were fired, of which five received broken stocks due to the two separate explosions. Firing was finished (secured) after 100 rounds.

After some investigation by the Naval Mission, it was discovered the cases of Remington ammunition had been retrieved from the ocean, where they had been thrown during an uprising. My diary notes that successful firing was completed only after

> Colonel Cain, Captain West, and myself saw Colonel Neptune, [*the* **Forces Armée d'Haiti** *(FAd'H) G-3 Operations*] and 3,000 rounds of M-2 ball ammunition were drawn to replace the faulty ammunition. Marine Sergeant Beach bought and in-stalled four batteries for the telephones [*connecting the firing line with the butts*]. . . . Around ten o'clock the soldiers become

very weak and tired. At noon they definitely need rejuvenation. Each day the men showed a marked improvement and I am genuinely proud of their shooting. Some had never fired at a target and some had not fired a rifle in twelve years.

Throughout this period, however — and, indeed, always — Major Garcia cooperated to his utmost and was very enthusiastic.

In November I was given an additional duty as Assistant Adviser to the Recruit Depot, which was now at Lamentin, to handle any matters while the Adviser, Chief Warrant Officer Davis, was engaged in his other duties at the *Champ de Tir* most of the time.

Some of the Haitian officers who served at the *Camp d'Application* included Major Garcia, Captain De Chavigny, Captain Scott, Captain Philippe, Lieutenant Edelyn, Lieutenant Lebreton, and *Sous* (Under, or 2nd) Lieutenants Mallet, Benoit, and Denis. The Quartermaster Captain told me that if each soldier was allotted $1.00 a day for chow, he was obliged to pocket 75¢ or he would be replaced and transferred to La Gonâve, an island out in Port-au-Prince bay!

My diary describes the first quarter of 1960 for the NCOs:

Upon the completion of the demonstration by the squad of Marines from Roosevelt Roads [*Puerto Rico*] the NCOs ate "C" Rations with the squad and then, three being assigned to each Marine, closely accompanied them through the live fire problem. . . . The first class of Recruits received their certificates on 26 Mar 60 and were returned to their units.

At about this time, I was advised by the Naval Mission not to participate in any training of Tonton Macoutes, the Haitian President's hated secret police; it was discovered that they had been infiltrated into the ranks of the recruits.

During our time in Haiti, Haitian officers were sent to various officer schools at Quantico, Virginia. Competent NCOs were dispatched to the Recruit Depot in San Diego and, upon completion, the best went to my old bailiwick, the 2nd Infantry Training Regiment up at Camp Joseph H. Pendleton.

Unfortunately for the success of our Naval Mission, upon returning to Haiti, they were either assigned inferior positions, they and their families were threatened by the Tonton Macoutes to resign, or they were just kicked out (reformed) of the army. After all, how can you have a successful dictatorship if your officers and NCOs have been "brainwashed" by outside influences and better trained in their military duties?

Army Day in Haiti is November 14. It is the occasion for the celebration of the 1803 overthrow of the French Expeditionary Army. The members of the Naval Mission were invited each year, and we had great seats in the grandstand on the *Champs de Mars* near the palace. The Haitian Armed Forces paraded well, and for a couple of years a reception in the palace was held after the parade. My most recollectable memory of this affair was that the Haitian bands just loved to play "Red River Valley" — even at religious events.

After some months in the country, Colonel Heinl announced that the Haitians would appreciate our retirement of the pith helmets (elephant hats as we had called them, ever since that awful day in the spring of 1941 when they had replaced the prized campaign hats). They requested that we wear the campaign hat, the same headgear that the *Gendarmerie d'Haiti* had worn while in Haiti fighting the bandits. All hands had to order theirs from the States (Quantico), but all I needed was an officer's accoutrement to replace the enlisted strap on mine, which I had with me. We looked snappy and wore them with pride.

One day I asked our landlady why she drove a Morris Minor, an English car, instead of a Volkswagen, which I had fallen in love with. She turned, showed me her profile, and I immediately understood; her nose looked just like the front of our Beetle!

We spent many an enjoyable day at Kayona, a good twenty-mile ride north of town on the St. Marc road. It provided a small bar, clear water, barracudas, octopi, moray eels, jellyfish, and a rare sandy beach; and the area never had many sun-worshipers. It was great, and the only trouble we got into was being ink-sprayed by the octopi, threatened by a smiling barracuda who was always present, scared by the sight of shark fins, and face-to-face encounters with moray eels. One fine day, however, Lieutenant Colonel Tighe, our G-4 (Supply, or Logistics) officer, came in out of the surf and over to me with a bent spear from his spear gun. He convinced me to go with him to the site of his confrontation, and I did. It was horrible, as we had to snorkel through a mass of jellyfish, and I was petrified. We arrived at the scene, and I retrieved some of the scales that the spear had dislodged; they were really large, silver, tough, and round. I told

The author (center, with pointer) and Haitian officers at a map exercise at *Camp d'Application*, Haiti. Left to right: Lieutenant Mallet, Lieutenant Lebreton, Captain Scott, Chief Warrant Officer Arthur C. Farrington, Captain De Chavigny, and Lieutenant Delbeau.   *U.S. Naval Mission*

him that he had probably hit a Tarpon, a large, tough fish, the likes of which I had seen while fishing with my father in Florida, or the spear might have glanced off the fish and hit some coral.

We flew a 48-star flag in Haiti on special days, but then Alaska and Hawaii became states, and immediately the Haitian fashion was to wear new 50-star flag bras and skirts, among other things. We could do nothing about that, and even when we started reporting that the flag was being used for tablecloths on roadside fruit stands, besmudged with juices of all kinds, nothing could be done. One such stand was situated on the way home from my duty station, and it really bugs me to this day.

Nevertheless, we went out of our way to be respectful to everything Haitian. Erlinda got in trouble once, however. While driving the VW one day, she happened to be right in front of the National Palace, when the

Parade and Review, October 14, 1959, in honor of the visit of Brigadier General William J. Ryzin (USMC). Haitian and American Naval Mission representatives salute the passing colors on the grandstand at the *Champs de Mars* near the palace. Chief Warrant Officer Arthur C. Farrington is at the upper left, immediately to right of the grandstand post, with elephant hat and field scarf. Note our 48-star flag.

Haitian flag went up. As we had been taught, the automobile was stopped and she remained seated. A Haitian soldier ordered her out of the car, but she remained seated in control of the car. (We had seen Haitian drivers debark, and their vehicle hijacked.) To this day, my son Reggie and I kid her that perhaps she was not sitting at attention!

On February 19-20, 1960, we conducted an overnight "tactical problem" with the Haitians. We had been asked to submit reports to the Naval Mission G-3, the Operations and Training officer, regarding our observances of how the Haitians behaved in certain instances. After all, one of our purposes in Haiti was to prepare the Haitian army for an invasion by Fidel Castro's Communist government.

According to my report, prepared on February 26, 1960, on Friday, the NCO School had essayed on a four-mile march and overnight bivouac/night patrol problem. The departing time of 1400 hours was not adhered to due mainly to logistics problems; the troops cleared the gate 55 minutes late. Allowing time for the column to clear Carrefour, I departed by Jeep with three "invaders" (artillery members of the interior guard). I took a different route and set up in previously reconnoitered positions on the first rest stop, 300 yards northeast of the intersection of the Carrefour-Mahotiere roads near Riviere Froide.

The NCOs up to the intersection had maintained two columns right and left of the road at a three-pace interval, putting out road guards, etc. They carried normal equipment with the addition of the old-type marching pack with tent, blanket, and entrenching tool. The squad leaders and officers had Marine Corps camouflage covers on their helmets.

From the intersection on, security was used. We showed surprise upon the point reaching us at a distance of ten yards, but even so got off the first shots (operated bolts and hit helmets with stones). The first three members of the column hit the deck, and we pulled back 35 yards and continued firing for a few minutes. The column was stopped. As our escape route was precarious, we pulled out for our next position down the road some 400 yards. This was the first time that the NCOs had met an "enemy" in the field, and they had not been briefed on what to expect. In addition, this close but quick contact was not reported along the column. A ten-minute break was taken, which extended itself into an hour before proper security measures were achieved.

We established an all-around position 100 yards from the road with a machine gun covering 35-50 yards of the road. Letting a squad pass, we opened fire on the staff, dispatching them soon enough. Excellent principles of movement, especially through cane, were employed in a double envelopment, which took care of us.

The Captain then requested another problem, even though time was getting on. He designated a crossroad, and we Jeeped there. Two men were placed in concealed positions five yards from the crossroad, and the Jeep was backed into a semi-concealed position with a man in the back seat. The point approached from the wood, instead of along the road, and both men stared at each other, although they were prepared to fire. Three times, I urged the man to shoot before he did so, and we got out of there, moving 75 yards, concealed the Jeep, and observed the action as the two hidden men raised havoc with the middle of the column. These actions were subsequently to be critiqued later that morning.

The Farrington family in their front yard in Diquini, Haiti: *Ti Fi* (Karen), Rolando, the author, Pup-Pups, Erlinda, and Bugs.

The column then proceded to the bivouac area, on M. Assad's property; the squads were assigned areas, and tents were pitched and ditched.

Evening chow consisted of very spicy Cabrite (goat) stew brought from Lamentin by the quartermaster with the help of soldiers and prisoners. It was served in mess gear, which was then taken back to camp. While the officers ate non-tactically at a table with an overhead fluorescent lamp, the NCOs were briefed on the forthcoming night reconnaissance patrols. The officers received an added ration of very good pork and cooked banana purchased locally, and cold drink.

The squad patrols were completed in two hours. The NCOs had a good sense of direction, moved quietly and quickly, and played the game realistically. They worked well at night. In the meantime, the sleeping bags had arrived, and the officers' tents had been pitched. All hands slept heavily with security being maintained all night.

Reveille was at 0600 hours the following morning. Breakfast was held immediately and consisted of milk, bread, orange, banana, and "AK 100" (a prepared breakfast cereal). Major Garcia arrived and inspected all tents and weapons; critiques were held on each patrol, tents were struck, and the troops boarded buses for Lamentin at 0930 hours.

A Haitian ammunition box.

.30 SPRINGFIELD (1906)
POINTED   IN CLIPS
20 CARTRIDGES

Trademarks Reg.
U.S. Pat. Off. and
other Countries   KLEANBORE   Marca Reg.
Marque Deposée

150 Grs. METAL CASED BULLET
REMINGTON ARMS COMPANY, INC.
AMMUNITION · BRIDGEPORT, CONN.
Remington, FIREARMS-ILION, N.Y.   DUPONT
MADE IN U.S.A.

The author and 1st Sergeant Walter Stipanovich instruct Haitian NCOs in the art of bayonet fighting. Note the Belgian bolt-action FN rifle.

As the double envelopment took place, the soldiers in my "ambush party" had wanted desperately to bug out, but I continued having them hurl rocks as grenades and to bang on helmets, as rifle and machine-gun fire. The NCOs came out of the cane red-eyed, sweating, filthy, highly excited, and yelling. One grabbed me, bent my arm behind my back, and I could only guess what was coming next. My three troops came to my rescue yelling, in Creole, and were able to settle down the NCOs. To me this scene was perfect, as we had always had a difficult time getting them into the attack mode. I shook their hands and congratulated all of them — and later the officers on the maneuver as well — and the others back at the *Camp d'Application*.

While we were in-country, we took some pretty adventurous trips. We drove to Cap Haïtien where, just off the coast, one of Columbus's ships, the *Pinta*, had foundered. With the Armingtons, the Farrington family arrived at the base of the mountain upon which King *Christophe* had built his Citadelle. As was the case in every instance, at least one non-commissioned officer manning the post had or was about to attend the *Camp d'Application*. We were rented nice horses, and Captain Armington took a mule. The climb was dangerous, more so on the descent, but we succeeded and were just flabbergasted. The large lime pit was there, where the dead were disposed of, and we could see Maman, the super-large cannon that *Christophe* had made, deposited in a ravine far below, where it had landed upon being test-fired. I had volunteered at this point to escort one of the Captain's sons, Pedro, to "do his business," and I can never forget the large pile of worms he left. Obviously everybody had them, if the doctor's son did.

My family also visited missionary/physician Dr. Albert Schweitzer's compound on the road to Hinche. He was not there, but some of the people who had worked with him were. The very old crank-telephone operator remembered when President Teddy Roosevelt had visited. The buildings were on the shore of a smooth and wide river, and the whole area appeared to have been lifted right out of Africa.

Each family drove a vehicle — a Jeep and a recon truck — out past Lake Saumatre and up to the Pine Forest in the high mountains overlooking the Dominican Republic. We traversed unpaved roads, trails, and even rocky stream beds. While there, a foreign professor arrived with some Haitians and assorted recording equipment. As we camped around a fire, eating together, he informed us that he was there to capture the song of the musician bird, La Selle Thrush. The Haiti *Blue Souvenir Guide* (1957) states that no one has ever seen the bird, and that it was "the most perfect singer ever heard." When the professor took off with his recording gear for an even higher mountain shrouded in mist, we wished him and his party good luck.

Almost every rock we turned over revealed one of the most unusual sights: deathly white scorpions. There may not be any poisonous snakes in Haiti, but these guys looked deadly.

Just before Christmas in 1960 we packed up edibles, presents, and cold drinks and trekked some miles back into the hills behind our house to a desolate village. From the way the villagers acted it appeared that they had never seen a white person before. By this time, Erlinda was good at speaking Creole, which was fortunate, as French was unintelligible to these people. We got along fine and enjoyed their hospitality.

Upon relating this safari to Major Garcia later, he had this story to tell me. As a young Lieutenant he had been assigned to aid in taking the census. After the census party had completed the count at a remote village, he had asked about a long building upon a nearby hill. The government official offered to take a look. The building's door had a hasp secured with a wooden stick, through the staple. The village headman removed the stick and Lieutenant Garcia was allowed to look into the dark enclosure. On each side was a long row of sitting men who appeared to be in a trance. As the Lieutenant and the official left, the government man said, "They don't count."Apparently they comprised the village "workforce." The Major then asked, "Zombies?"

You make up your own mind.

As to voodoo, just 200 yards down the road from our small cottage was a *houngan*, a voodoo priest. Every Friday night and on the many holidays, voodoo ceremonies would take place at the cottage with much drumming. They would spill out, parade to our house, a pretty girl would come up on the porch, I would present her with a bottle of Barbancourt Rhum, then she would place it on top of her head and dance off with the crowd. When in Rome. . . .

All hands took tours of the Barbancourt bottling facility just to the east of Port-au-Prince, perfectly situated near HASCO (Haitian-American

212   PACIFIC ODYSSEY

Sugar Co.). The employees told us that little was exported, mainly to New York City and Miami, as production was not that large. I'm proud to say that while the Marines were there, its export suffered. The best rhum was classified as *cinq étoile* (five star). *Trois étoile* (three star) was next, and the cheapest was *une étoile* (one star). *Trois étoile,* at a dollar bottle, was the most popular, with *cinq étoile*, reserved for Bridge and Poker parties, a whopping two dollars.

While we are on the topic of alcohol, Mill beer from Holland was eleven cents per bottle in Haiti, and Heineken was very reasonable. For me, the best after-work club was the *Cafe de Port*, on the waterfront. The beer mugs came right out of the freezer, which was perfect on a typical scorching day in the tropics.

But getting back to trips, one time a few Marines and I went by Jeep over a very circuitous route. It was an official trip to make a "reconnaissance" between the "main road" to the west and the town of Jacmel on the south coast. There was practically no "road," just rocky stream beds, and I came out of that trip feeling sorry for the very friendly and nice people, considering the state of affairs in Haiti.

During this trip, I also discovered hundreds of pounds of deteriorated dynamite under the Haitian army post. The explosives had obviously been there for many years, as the nitroglycerine had long ago seeped out of the sticks but was still present. All I could do was advise the senior Naval Mission officer and the Haitian Commanding Officer of the ever-present danger.

Part of our mission to Haiti included our attendance at parties, dances, and Marine Corps balls. The first Army Day on November 14, 1959, was celebrated at the *Camp d'Application*, and Erlinda and I were glad to accept an invitation to participate. The hall was decorated, and the five or six officers comprising the staff of the base were present, as well as the enlisted staff and the class of Haitian NCOs. A couple of Haitian officers' wives attended also. I think it was Major Garcia who had asked me if perhaps my wife would like to dance, and when I said, of course, Captain Monod Phillipe asked her. They had quite a time, and the soldiers' mouths were agape. Erlinda and I thought nothing of the incident, but it sure had repercussions.

Capitaine Phillipe, as a young Lieutenant some years before, had been stationed at Fort Dimanche when an American citizen of Syrian descent (there was quite a community of Syrians, mostly dealing in clothing and

The Marine Corps Ball in Petionville, Haiti, November 10, 1961, the annual celebration of the Marine Corps anniversary. The American Ambassador to Haiti attended (front, left), as well as Colonel Henry H. Reichner, Jr., USMC, Deputy Chief/Chief of Staff of the Naval Mission (center), and Haitian General Jen René Bouiciaut (*FAd'H, Forces Armée d'Haiti*).

material) was accused of a crime, and he had sought sanctuary in the American Embassy. The two governments conferred, and the Embassy released the man to the Haitian army on good faith. Well, he was beaten to death at the fort, and the officers deemed responsible were assigned *persona non grata* status, including then-Lieutenant Phillipe. He had told me the story, and although he was bad-mouthed by most, I found him cocky, intelligent, sarcastic (like me), and interesting. He asked Erlinda and me to be his guest at a following gala down the Carrefour road at the *Garde-Côtes*. As we knew the two mission officers, Captain Treadwell of the U.S. Navy and Lieutenant Mihlbauer of the U.S. Coast Guard, and because it was not far from our house, we accepted and had a great time. For the next two years, I would kid him about his experience with the Haitian Rifle Team's trips to Panama in the summers of 1960 and 1961. Being out of favor, he was not allowed out of Customs on their stops in Miami,

The "best" table at the Marine Corps Ball, November 10, 1961, in the *Cabane Choucoune*, on the hill in Petionville, Haiti. Clockwise from the bottom: Monsieur James Oberstar (the French instructor), Madame Simpkins, Madame Farrington, Madame Mihlbauer, Lieutenant Martinez (USCG), unknown couple, Madame McCall, Storekeeper Chief Otis McCall (USN), Lieutenant Mihlbauer (USCG), Warrant Officer Simpkins (USMC), and Chief Warrant Officer Arthur C. Farrington (USMC).

as the other team shooters were, to purchase U.S. merchandise. However, he captained the Haitian team to a second place, just 13 points behind the USARCARIB team from Panama, and 30 points ahead of Peru, in third place.

Members of the Naval Mission also would hold card parties, and Linda and I enjoyed learning to play Bridge and preferred it to Poker. I will never forget Madame West, a beautiful woman married to Captain West, making a grand slam. The Captain and Lieutenant Colonel Redalen were our helicopter pilots. They would go out on hunting expeditions, and one time Captain West related to me the following story. A duck had been shot, the dog had retrieved it still alive, and the Haitian guide had immediately broken its wings, but one of the officers said, "It can still walk." The next sound they heard was *"crack . . . crack."* The Haitian had broken the poor thing's legs.

"Mess Night" at the Hotel *San Souci*. Left to right: James Oberstar, Captain Ivan F. Horne (USMC), Chief Warrant Officer Arthur C. Farrington (toasting MATS), a Haitian officer, and Lieutenant Louis Pelletier (USN/MSC).

The Marine Ball, held annually on November 10th, included invitations for all Haitian military officers, as well as select NCOs, dignitaries from U.S. and foreign governments and companies, and friends. The *Cabane Choucoune,* with a large ballroom, upon the hill in Petionville was the location one year. In addition, Colonel Heinl loved to have Mess Nights, and so we had a few of them. One time during the official toast and no doubt after much previous imbibing, I acknowledged MATS — the Military Air Transport Squadron — rather than the Haitian President and other officials, to the chagrin of some present. It seems that a Marine 2nd Lieutenant had hitchhiked his way via MATS to Haiti to visit his friend, one of our Lieutenants, and the Marine was present and obviously in the forefront of my mind. These "Mess Nights" often were the nearest thing to a bachelor party — minus the girls and the movies — that I ever want to experience, with heavy drinking all around. Back at UCLA, my fraternity brothers had talked me into a stag party out in Santa Monica, and I was so disgusted that I walked out within minutes.

While in Haiti, I joined the Port-au-Prince Tennis Club for three dollars a month and played about twice a week to keep in shape and for the enjoyment. I was the only American member. Being # 1, I was hoping to be able to play Althea Gibson when she visited a year or two after winning Wimbledon, but a Haitian was chosen and she trimmed him easily. Karol Fageros was with her, and a Haitian newspaper ran her picture with her measurements and vital statistics along with the following:

> *Cette beauté, plastique du tennis international exhibera same-di prochain sa "culotte en lamé d'or" qu'elle porte toujours.*
> Translation: This impressionable beauty of international tennis shall exhibit next Saturday her "gold lamé" panties, which she always wears under her short tennis dress.

Our parties and celebrations in Haiti were always affected by the terrific rainstorms, which would bring rocks down, blocking the Carrefour road. Guests either had to stay the night or simply climb over the road-blocks with their cars, which we all did frequently. On one occasion, at night, on the way to a party in Petionville, we were really dressed up and had the Frisbie couple in the back seat of the Volkswagen. It was quite a load, and while driving through Port-au-Prince in a heavy rain, the headlights went dim. I slowed, to not make waves and disturb the floating garbage, and we continued on with no problem. Later we observed that the mud line was over the engine compartment and nearly up to the door handles. *Sous* Lieutenant Mallet told me that when he was taking his wife to have a baby, in a downpour, they were swept away in his VW. But, *no problema*, the car floated until they hit dry land! Mallet was stationed at Hinche at the time as a Commanding Officer.

Lieutenant (Junior Grade) Louis Pelletier, U.S. Navy/Medical Service Corps (USN/MSC), was the hospital administration instructor, and he owned an Edsel. At a shindig up in Petionville, he had parked nose-first into a large tree. Subsequently, his reverse gear would not operate, and it took a number of us to position the car so that he could proceed home.

I also recall that gasoline was cheap in Haiti, and that a recall by General Motors on my Buick was handled well by Haiti's mechanics. In addition, on my way to work one morning I had to drive out on the shoulder to avoid a mule train and my tire blew. The Haitians always enjoyed seeing us fall down, trip, or otherwise be in difficulty, and this was no exception. I had run over a water faucet lacking its handle and had a very large hole in the tire. I changed it, and the puncture was later vulcanized. The Haitians were amazing at repairing auto and bus tires, using nuts and bolts and many other methods.

One of the interesting events at *Camp d'Application* had occurred on April 22, 1960, when German film makers were to visit and record the recruit class doing close-order drill with and without arms, as well as their dormitory.

I was so proud of this class of NCOs. They put on an exhibition right in front of the cameras that was second to none. In an operation of musketry, they advanced wild-eyed with fury; they hit the deck in order with knees, rifle butt, and body, rolling, aiming, and firing blanks; and then they continued with fixed bayonets right across our front and literally destroyed the target dummies using both the bayonet and rifle butt. 1st Sergeant Stipanovich and I had taught them the principles, but some of their fellow NCOs had really motivated them, and frankly I was a little taken aback and impressed with them that day. When properly trained and led, these men were indeed battle worthy in my humble estimation.

After all was completed, we retired to Major Garcia's office for refreshments — Barbancourt Rhum with coconut water (obtained by our own private prisoners from the palms in our camp), Heineken, and Haitian coffee with *beaucoup* sugar. The German film maker in charge told me he had been a Stuka pilot on the Russian front in World War II and had flown 187 missions. He said it was true that the ground crew would cut parts of the spinner (propeller), to make horrendous sounds when the plane dived. I told him of my experience on Guadalcanal, when we were attacked by three Messerschmitt 109s. He immediately put his arm around my shoulders and said that he was very sorry. But when I told him that although I had my .45-caliber pistol out and cocked, I did not fire at the one just over my head as it was so pretty, dark green or black, with pointy nose, liquid-cooled engine, and flying like a sled. He immediately shook my hand and thanked me! Those Germans sure love their machinery.

Interestingly, we knew many Germans in Haiti, but not one would acknowledge that he had fought Americans. And although it had been reported that the Me-109s were shot down, I did not have the heart to tell the German film maker.

Speaking of machinery, the following vehicles were assigned to the NCO school and recruit depot by the Haitians:

Type	Year	Condition
Dodge 6 "500," Bluebird Bus	1958	Good
Volkswagen Camionette Van (being repaired)	1959	Good
Truck	1955	Poor
Volkswagen Beetle	1958	Good

On May 16, 1960, Major Garcia asked if we could have a course on amphibious training for the NCO class. I said I would be glad to, and would check on availability with Commander Treadwell, the U.S. Navy adviser. He had promised the previous summer to support us in any such venture. But due to motor trouble, it was determined that a boat would not be ready until the week of May 30. Accordingly the first, second, and third of June were selected for the presentation of the course. The course schedule was published, with four hours each morning allotted to the training.

I made three visits myself and one with Adjutant Enoch, the course instructor, to the *Garde-Côtes*. We effected liaison with Commander Martin, the Haitian Commanding Officer, regarding classroom spaces and permission to enter, and with the Naval Mission on boat specifications and training aids.

Lesson plans were made and translated into French. The situation, plan of attack, and related papers were also translated. The schedule of events for the June 3, 1960, exercise was included in the Naval Mission's schedule. Members of the *Forces Armée d'Haiti* were invited by my counterpart, Major Garcia, who by the way was Haitian, and thus there was no accent on the letter "i" and both syllables were pronounced evenly. The boat, crew, and life preservers were promised the week of May 23rd, and I was told that Lieutenant Martinez of the U.S. Coast Guard would be in charge.

The boat was to be at the pier at the *Camp d'Application* the morning of June 2 for practice embarking and debarking, and would be available at 0800 on June 3 to transport two boat teams to the *Plage Rouge* (Red Beach) at our *Camp d'Application*.

On June 1, the course was begun. The first four hours were devoted to boats, boat teams, and practical work on loading and debarking from a simulated LCVP (Landing Craft Vehicle, Personnel). I then went to the *Garde-Côtes* to check on final arrangements for the next day, where I was informed by Chief Owens that Commander Treadwell was in Key West and that Lieutenant Martinez had the duty at the Naval Mission headquarters. At 1430 I contacted Lieutenant Martinez and the whole show was a complete surprise to him. He gave me a note for Chief McCall, to arrange for gas if necessary, and to alert the boat crew. He figured that the boat would arrive about 0830. It was deemed unnecessary for me to go to the *Garde-Côtes* in the morning; if any trouble developed, the *Camp d'Application* could be messaged. Chief McCall said he would check on the gas and crew in the morning first thing.

The second part of the course was begun at 0800 in the beach area. By 0945, neither the boat nor a message had arrived. At 0947, Commander Martin and Lieutenant Martinez drove up. The boat was full of water! It was stated that the amount of damage would be known by the afternoon, and I would be able to tell Major Garcia the following morning whether it would be feasible to postpone the final rehearsal and exercise until the following week. Needless to say, the whole thing was canceled. Major Garcia cooperated as always and the NCO class completed the problem beginning at Red Beach, maneuvering, using simulated demolition charges, and routing the enemy. (I have the SECRET document prepared by the FAd'H for this amphibious operation.)

Official reports of inspections of the various forts (*casernes*) and posts throughout Haiti were indicative of the overall situation there. Following is a portion of one of the Naval Mission's reports:

> Sub-District of Thomassique. Lieutenant Francois Sylvestre. Four Colt Automatic Machine Rifles Model R 75. The magazines for the Colt ARs are for the FN [*Fusil National*] AR and

A nine-man Haitian squad at the *Camp d'Application* — all NCOs — in the "approach march." At the right are Chief Warrant Officer Arthur C. Farrington and 1st Sergeant Walter Stipanovich (far right).

will not fit. Is the sewer system adequate? No. In one place the pipe from the second deck urinal empties into the first deck shower stall.

The comment by Colonel Heinl, who headed the inspections, "Some shower. . . !"

Other reports of inspections of the various posts throughout Haiti were often amazing, but I shall only include two more, one satisfactory and one pretty poor.

District of Prison of Cap Haïtien. Lt LEMOINE, Joseph, 26 Jul 61.

The command is to be congratulated on the condition of this mess. It is proper and well squared away. It could well serve as an example for many enlisted messes, much less prisoner

Lieutenant Delbeau, *Forces Armée d'Haiti*, and Chief Warrant Officer Arthur C. Farrington and 1st Sergeant Walter Stipanovich (far left), at their camp at the Lamentin Lighthouse.

messes. It is reported that block one dates from the French days and the cells are original. A solution must be found to the problem of the incarceration of tiny babies with their mothers and very young boys. FAd'H regulations have nothing to cover this problem except that minors must be separated from adults. Cap Haïtien's solution to the latter is to put [*the boys*] in solitary.

District of Hinche. 26 Sep 60, Capt. Marcel CHERUBIN.

Notes of interest: The emergency plan is only on paper and cannot be considered at this time as capable of being executed. . . . It seems that the storerooms are only visited when the officers need something. ARs [*automatic rifles*] evidence no maintenance. The bores of the officers' weapons (M1s and carbines) are closed with rust. There is no care taken at all of any weapon in the storeroom. There are 20 offensive (concussion) grenades and 23 tear gas. The tear gas grenades are so completely corroded that the fuzes are welded to the body. Ammunition is all piled together in a corroding mass.

Most of the army posts and many other public buildings had been built when the U.S. Marines had been in Haiti from the early 1900s to 1934.

Of interest is that although on April 14, 1961, U.S. Marines were aboard ship in the area at the time of the disastrous Bay of Pigs invasion of Cuba, they were never called upon to land, and Castro's troops quickly repelled the U.S. incursion. We all took a lot of kidding from the Haitians regarding this fiasco.

When the Dominicans threatened Haiti, as they did twice while we were there, General Merceron placed oil drums all over the international airport to prevent any planes from landing and made the statement: "There is room in Haiti for only one General, and I am he." We loved that. He was not going to allow any Dominican Generals to invade.

The Haitian soldiers' position was built right on the border with the Dominican Republic; and the Haitians had poor arms and equipment. The Dominican's position, however, was well back, hidden in the trees. They could have walked over behind their tanks at any time they chose.

But back to the training of the Haitians — I remember the following events very well, having recorded them for the Weekly Report:

013/acf

NCO School/Recruit Depot, Weekly report

The 18th week of training for the 7th NCO Class included the light machine gun, leadership, and field fortifications. The latter course was very well presented. One- and two-man fighting holes and positions for machine guns were located on a platoon defensive perimeter. All holes were correctly constructed and camouflaged. Two were covered, one for protection from the weather and one from air bursts. One squad was completely outfitted with helmet covers and all automatic riflemen wore red covers. A defensive fire plan was arranged and the location of obstacles was covered. On Friday the Commandant of the Camp, the OinC [*Officer in Charge*] of the NCO School, and

A field class in defensive positions. Lieutenant Delbeau (far left), *Forces Armée d'Haiti*, observing and remarking on the results of Sergeant Decastro's and author Arthur Farrington's labors. The Lieutenant was quite a character and well-liked by all. Chief Warrant Officer Arthur C. Farrington stands to the right of the tree. Left to right, front row, in trench: M. Pierre, A. Germeil, J. L. Pierre. Second row, kneeling: K. Cayemitte, G. Chounoune, R. Jean-Charles, C. Pierre. Back row, standing: M. Eugene, J. Marc, J. Jean. These troops were equipped with automatic and Mauser rifles of Belgian manufacture.

the Adjutant were brought to the area to see the results of a well-organized course. The instructor for this course, Sgt. DECASTRO, told me that even if there is no member of the Naval Mission present the next time this course is scheduled, he will attempt to present it in the same manner. Let's hope he will be permitted to do so. Many of these NCOs had never heard of a foxhole, much less dug and occupied one. The seven corpsmen assigned to the *Camp d'Application* for five weeks were given four hours of instruction on their duties if assigned to an infantry platoon.

The 4th Class of 93 Recruits wound up its 9th week with two days on the rifle range. The other three days were spent snappin-in and carrying out extended order drill.

10 April 1961   A. C. FARRINGTON

An interesting episode happened over a couple days when a detail came down from the States (Quantico?) and requested that some expert shooters be made available to test-fire the .45-caliber pistol using a new method: two-handed. They had us fire using both hands from the off-hand, kneeling, and prone positions. We fired not just one round but three or four in rapid succession. We had excellent results and approved wholeheartedly. A new method of pistol-shooting was being born.

Events moved along on the personal side of life in Haiti as well. In the fall of 1960 Linda and I had traded in our 1957 Buick for a 22Sb Mercedes sedan. It was *ivoire* (ivory) and came with matching luggage. Our short-wave radio could pick up Armed Forces Radio, and we heard Roger Maris hit his 61st home run. Our bathtub was big enough to float my rubber boat in, which we did until it went down with my kids in it. We burned it as an offering to the Gods.

Outdoors, we planted banana trees all around the house, bought some cement, and had a ball building canals, dams, and lakes around the trees when it rained. One night I smelled the "ripe" body of a *vouleur* (burglar). I got up and chased him out the way he came in, where he almost killed himself when his neck collided with the wire clothesline hard enough to bring the whole thing down. All I could do was cuss him out as he made his getaway. It was time for some shells for my .410 shotgun.

When Navy Captain Fred W. Armington, our senior medical adviser, was transferred back to the States, his replacement had a large "reefer" — refrigerator — shipped down on one of two World War II LCIs (Landing Craft, Infantry), owned by a Haitian. However, it sank off Cuba, in the Bermuda Triangle.

The new doctor, Lieutenant Commander Richard H. Barrick, moved into the house that had been the abode of *Ti Barb*, an American adviser of President Duvalier. My kids and I were playing in our front yard one evening when we heard the Lieutenant Commander test-firing a shotgun. The pellets began to land around us, and after we sought shelter and he quit firing, we collected eleven pellets in case he didn't believe us when we told him later.

Jeanie, our maid in Haiti, was a good cook and we ate well. Some favorites were lobster, plantains, bananas, pineapples, papayas, and — Linda's favorite — mangoes.

Linda drove all over in our Volkswagen, and her favorite shopping partner was Judy Reichner, the wife of our Executive Officer. They would shop at the American Embassy store, but I do believe that their favorite place was the Iron Market in downtown Port-au-Prince near the horrible outside *abatoir* — the cattle slaughterhouse.

We frequently went to the movies down at the *Garde-Côtes* where the nightly blackout would have us sitting for quite a while waiting for the Coast Guardsmen to fire up the old generator. One evening as we were coming home, after we had passed the voodoo meeting house, someone shot at the car. I recognized it as a .45-caliber and the bullet made quite a commotion as it passed through the fields of growing *piti mi* (sorghum) to the starboard side of the car.

Erlinda and I also enjoyed taking dance lessons from a famous American instructor. She taught us the Merengue, and when Chubby Checker's Twist arrived on the scene, we had quite a repertoire of moves. While in Haiti, we attended many formal military events where we could use our newly learned dancing skills.

In July 1961, the Naval Mission in coordination with the *Forces Armée d'Haiti* planned and scheduled a Grand Maneuver involving the military academy, the *caserne* (the barracks at the palace), various other detachments, and the NCOs and recruits under training at the *Camp d'Application*. The rolling hills area near the town of Mirebalais, about halfway between Port-au-Prince and Hinche, was selected. For our part, we stressed physical training, small units in the attack, and living in the field. The following is the general schedule for the seven-day operation:

Sunday	23 Jul 61	Convoy Establish Camp
Monday	24 Jul	Approach March and Occupation of Assembly Area
Tuesday	25 Jul	Daylight Reconnaissance Patrols and Night Attack by Company
Wednesday	26 Jul	Daylight Reconnaissance Patrols and Night Attack by Company

Thursday	27 Jul	Organization of Defensive Position by Day. Night Relief, Night Patrols (Company will pass the night on position)
Friday	28 Jul	Company Daylight Attack
Saturday	29 Jul	Inspection and Convoy

In my two-page final report of the Mirebalais operations, my last line was: "The soldiers were proud to see their army actually in the field at work." It seems, however, that others were not. All of a sudden our stay in Haiti began a downward slide, as evidenced by the following examples from my reports to the G-3 (Operations and Training) officers, Lieutenant Colonel Wilkes and later Lieutenant Colonel Beckett.

14 Aug 61 The morale of the officers is at the lowest point yet observed. The preparation for civilian life is the primary occupation of the senior officers and the junior officers have adopted a sort of forced happy-go-lucky attitude.

⋅⊷⟹⟸⊶⋅

5 Sep 61 LtCol GARCIA was reformed [*dismissed from the army*]. Capt. Frank ROMAINE, who has been the quartermaster since March, is now the commanding officer. I have been told that Captain DE CHAVIGNY was his instructor at the Military Academy. If this is true, watch out! [*De Chavigny became the Commanding Officer of the Recruit Depot, and a finer officer there never was.*]

⋅⊷⟹⟸⊶⋅

11 Sep 61 The commanding officer of the *Camp d'Application*, Captain ROMAINE, was promoted to the rank of major. Captain DE CHAVIGNY was transferred to the Military Academy, 2nd Lt DELBEAU taking over as Officer in Charge of the Recruit Depot. Adjutant ENOCH is now the camp adjutant, 2nd Lt APPOLON was transferred and 2nd Lt CLERMONT was joined.

⊹⇒◯⇐⊹

30 Oct 61   From: Advisor NCO School/Recruit Depot
                 To: G-3
                 Subj: ST PREUX, Wilfred, Sgt FAd'H, case of

1. This information was given to me by ex-Lieutenant LEBRE-
TON whose last post was Hinche.
2. He said that he was informed that Sgt ST PREUX was to be
discharged from [*thrown out of*] the army. This was news to
Department commander, LtCol DEETJEN, who said that he
intended to consult the General concerning the matter. Evidently nothing was or could be done and he was discharged.
3. Corporal BEAUSEJOUR told me that ST PREUX was first
transferred to the Caserne Dessalines and discharged from
there.

A. C. FARRINGTON

Sergeant St. Preux had been one of my candidates and had attended the
Marine Corps Recruit Depot and 2nd Infantry Training Regiment in California in 1960. Just two months before this, in August, the following
occurred at the home of another Marine-trained NCO serving as a drill
instructor at the Recruit Depot at Lamentin.

28 Aug 61 Last Saturday at one o'clock in the morning one of
the drill instructors was wakened at his home and warned by a
person armed with a rifle [*Tonton Macoute no doubt*] not to
bother a relative of his who is in the present recruit class. It was
said that if the recruit were bothered the DI and his family
would be shot. The soldier's wife had to be revived by friends.

A. C. FARRINGTON

⊹⇒ ———— ⇐⊹

My Weekly Report dated October 16, 1961, indicated the status of the
training at the final week of the program.

013/acf

Weekly report, NCO School/Recruit Depot

The 30 members of the 8th NCO Class finished their 22nd
and final training week. The courses on small unit tactics and
technique of military instruction were finished. The M1 familiarization course was held with the Naval Mission advisor as
the instructor. A total of four hours school was held at which no
Haitian officer was present. The NCO instructor assisted however and is qualified to hold the next class of this sort. Two
Haitian officers (Capt VAVAL and SLt CLERMONT) were present for the firing and the Haitian Range Officer was even
around for a while. The firing was very successful. Twenty-
seven men in four relays of eight men each fired 30 rounds
apiece. The course was as follows:

3 rds	Sitting	Zero	200 yds	"A" Target
10 rds	Sitting	Rapid	200 yds	"
2 rds	Prone	Zero	300 yds	"
10 rds	Prone	Rapid	300 yds	"
5 rds	Prone	Slow	500 yds	"B" or "D"

Two hours and forty-five minutes were needed for the firing
which was carried out in the afternoon. American cartridges of
a recent lot were used. Old Remington or FN ammunition must
not be used as the former will break the stocks and the latter
will not fit clipped into the magazine. A requisition for 900 cartridges was made to the G-3 over a week in advance of the
scheduled firing. No cartridges were made available. The ones
used were from our machine gun allotment.

No mortar ammunition was made available from the palace
for the scheduled mortar firing at Ganthier. Luckily some shells
were on hand in the depot and we had some cartridges and
fuzes left over from the last firing. Of the eight French 81mm
shells fired only one missfired [*sic*]. With the complete NCO
Class gathered around, the tube elevated, and the shell sliding
toward the mouth of the tube, the soldier, whose duty it was to
catch the shell, took off! The Haitian officer, SLt MALLET,
managed to catch the shell to everyone's relief. It missfired

again but went safely on its way the third time. One 60mm shell was French and fired well. Of the 17 corroded American 60s of 1942 vintage all fired but only two detonated. All hands fired a light Browing machine gun at two targets at a range of 8-900 yards. Over 3,000 rounds were fired through this weapon as the French gun had had an unclearable stoppage on its fifth round. The American gun was so hot that the FN ball ammunition smoked in flight and many exploded, one only 50 feet from the muzzle. Good, accurate firing was held and the targets were well riddled.

The 9th training week for the 5th Recruit Class of 87 men saw the second group, with 8 unqualified men of the first group, at the rifle range. Trouble was had all week with communications despite two trips to Transmissions. On record day there was none at all although the range officer had been kept informed. It is my humble opinion that clothesline is not a very efficient communication media. Anyway, rifle shots, runners, and the Jeep were used satisfactorily (we certainly could have used some wig-waggers [*flagmen*]). No ammunition problems were encountered for this course. Sixteen FNs were repaired at Ordnance before the course of firing.

16 October 1961   A. C. FARRINGTON

In November, it seemed as though the wheels were in motion for the Farringtons' tour of duty to end. But it just didn't seem right somehow or other. This was the most fulfilling duty that I had had since serving as a platoon Sergeant/leader in Korea during 1950-1951. In both experiences, I knew that I was making a difference, and with many more people in Haiti. As Dinah Shore would later sing, "*Que Será Será.*"

Sous Lieutenant Clermont, a graduate of the *Camp d'Application* in April 1959, had joined us in August. He was a recent student at the Quantico schools and had told me that he had spoken to my replacement at the Camp Pendleton 2nd Infantry Training Regiment. I thought it might have been Chief Warrant Officer Rust. My immediate inclination had been, what a waste of an excellent Marine, as the Haitians were going nowhere.

Well, at the end of November I was informed that Captain Klinedinst would takeover, but that was changed and Chief Warrant Officer Sheridan took the position in December.

Before this came about, however, a few things had happened in the fall. My houseboy, Eléphant, had been accused by a large girl of being raped in his room next to the kitchen in the back of our house. She was from the village near us where a farmer had previously tried to extort money from me for claiming that I had accused him of eating our cat Mocha. My friend, Lieutenant Mallé, had taken me to the police depot in the village of Carrefour, near our camp, to report the disappearance of the cat, and a couple NCOs from there had investigated that very same village. But I had never accused anyone.

The Mission had warned us when we had first checked in that we might be subject to shakedowns, and to be careful. Thus, when Eléphant had been arrested and taken to the main police depot downtown, I immediately stopped at the Mission and told them that I was going down there posthaste.

I arrived, was told to have a seat, and saw Eléphant in the next room with a cocked .38-caliber pistol to his head. The policemen were yelling at him, and the poor kid was scared to death. I made them stop the interrogation and told them that he was my houseboy and that he was innocent. But that was it; there was nothing more that I could do. He was thrown into the horrible National Prison in downtown Port-au-Prince. The mission had told me not to pay any ransom or shakedown monies.

We were devastated. Then, in December, a Haitian delivered a letter to me written in French. Eléphant had found someone to write it for him. Briefly it said that due to the Christmas season coming up, favors were sometimes given at the prison.

I drove down there immediately, and I cannot describe the terrible smell and the sight of the filthy prisoners. Upon being ushered into the main office, who should I see sitting there but the Commandant of the prison, Major Monod Philippe, formerly of *Camp d'Application*, surrounded by subordinates. I knew that he had to maintain "face," so the whole conversation was conducted in his beautiful and my passable French. I explained the circumstances of the alleged rape, her size, the room next to Jeanie's, and such other information as I thought pertinent. I explained Eléphant's service to us for the past 2½ years, and that if he were released I would rehire him immediately and trust him implicitly with my boys and 2½-year-old daughter *Ti Fi.*

I thanked Major Philippe for whatever he could do, immediately reported the affair to the Naval Mission, returned home to Diquini, . . . and there was Eléphant, smiling from ear to ear, standing on the front veranda. *Vive Philippe!*

Later, in April of 1963, one former Haitian army officer suggested that on President Duvalier's orders the Major had shot and killed the bodyguards of the President's son, Jean Claude, and daughter, Simone, for what reason no one knew. I doubt that and sincerely hope that he and all the other Haitian soldiers that I knew, enlisted and officer, are living long and successful lives.

On December 7, 1961, I received orders detaching me from the Naval Mission and assigning us to the Marine Corps Air Station at Cherry Point, North Carolina. During our last months in Haiti it was satisfying to see our pink and gray Buick Century sitting in front of the President's Palace, being washed and buffed continually. The Buick surely deserved it — rather than hauling peasants all over the countryside.

Colonel Garcia and his wife had visited us almost every evening out in Diquini. We played Pinocle, and Erlinda served a cake that they loved made out of good old American mixes — rare in Haiti. Colonel Garcia gave me the Haitian flag that he had flown over his first post as an officer many years ago. Incidentally, he had told me about his tour of duty in the United States as a young officer and how he had experienced the — unknown to him — existence of segregation. He had also been involved with a battery of artillery firing at the palace from near the American Embassy back in the 1930s or early 1940s during a rebellion, when the ammunition was thrown into the sea.

I have always regretted not being able to write or contact the Colonel or other Haitians, as any such action could have placed them and their families in personal danger and/or crimination from Papa Doc, Baby Doc, or the various other regimes since. But before I left, we congratulated each other on having such a good relationship and having been involved in the schooling of almost every NCO in Haiti.

After I had received my orders, the following actions soon occurred:

(1) The Seventh-Day Adventists packed our belongings for shipment, and we bade sad farewells to Jeanie and Eléphant.

(2) I drove the Mercedes to the docks in preparation for it to be loaded aboard a ship for transport to Fort Lauderdale, Florida.

(3) We moved to the Carib Hotel on Truman Boulevard in town, where the Garcias still visited, as did Major Varge Frisbie and his wife. We played Bridge; but I haven't played cards since, as once you've played Bridge, all the other games seem vapid.

(4) A gentleman from South Africa was staying at the Carib Hotel who owned a Rhodesian Ridgeback lion dog. We were careful not to introduce Pup-Pups to him as the Ridgeback was ferocious.

(5) We drove the Volkswagen around, saying our goodbyes to the *Camp d'Application*, good friends in the Naval Mission, and others.

(6) Our last visit was to Colonel Heinl and his family in Petionville. I will never forget him having his houseboy go to the freezer and bring us two frozen rum cocktails, and sodas for the kids.

(7) The boys and I drove the Volkswagen to the docks where we turned it over to the owner of the remaining LCI for transportation to Miami. The government only paid for one motor vehicle, so this one was on us. The owner of the LCI promised not to let his craft go to Davey Jones' Locker in the Bermuda Triangle, as his other one had.

On December 19, 1961, we were driven to the international airport. Madame Malval, from whom we had rented the bungalow in Diquini, was there running her large souvenir concession, so we had a fond farewell. She later wrote to us in the States that Eléphant was working for her in the shop. The Farrington family, including Pup-Pups, but unfortunately not Bugs nor Mocha, boarded Pan Am flight #432 and left Haiti at 10:15 that morning. My attempt at a "poetic" evaluation of Haiti, as we departed, comes to mind:

Untitled, December 1961

Mine eyes have seen the glory of
And I've also heard the story of — Haiti.

Oh take me back, please send me back
I've had enough, yes had enough of — Haiti.

They have their voodoo, let them keep it
I'm not obsessed to be possessed in — Haiti.

You must believe me when I say it
J'en ai assez [*I've had enough*] and really mean it, of — Haiti.

Oh tourist, tourist never mind
Pay no attention to this rhyme of — Haiti.

Go see the Cap, the Citadelle
Kenscoff, Furcy, all the rest of — Haiti.

Remember well what you have seen
For pretty soon, next year perhaps
The whole damn place will turn into
      A Garbage Dump!

                     — ACF

Arriving in Kingston, Jamaica, we did a little shopping and were happy to see a crewman walking Pup-Pups around on the tarmac. We arrived in Miami at three o'clock that afternoon, where my mother and stepfather picked us up. They drove us to Port Everglades, just south of Fort Lauderdale, where we collected the Mercedes. We "convoyed" via Alligator Alley to their home in Bradenton, on Florida's west coast near Tampa.

On December 23rd, I phoned the docks in Miami and asked if our Volkswagen had arrived yet. The polite Haitian said, "Wait a minute." A moment later he was back on the phone saying something like, "Our LCI is coming up the channel, and there is a black VW on the deck." Well, the next day, Christmas Eve, the boys and I took the bus to Miami, stood by while Customs searched the Volkswagen, and then drove via the Tamiami Trail back to Bradenton.

Leaving the Volkswagen with my Mom, we drove north and stopped briefly in Kinston, North Carolina, where we ate at the Kinston Cafe. I asked the owner why he had not had a certain stool bronzed. As he was nonplused, I told him that I had been sitting on it December 7, 1941, when the news had come over his radio that the Japanese had bombed Pearl

Le Chef d'Etat-Major Général des F.A.d'H.

a l'honneur de vous inviter à la grande Revue Militaire qui
aura lieu sur la Place des Héros de l'Indépendance

et sous la haute direction du Chef de l'Etat

le samedi 18 Novembre 1961 à 9:30 a. m. à l'occasion

de la Commémoration de la bataille de Vertières

et du "Jour des Forces Armées d'Haiti."

EMBASSY OF THE
UNITED STATES OF AMERICA

The American Ambassador

and Mrs. Drew

request the pleasure of the company of

CWO and Mrs Arthur C. Farrington

on the occasion of the

One Hundred and Eighty-fourth Anniversary of the

Independence of the United States of America

on Monday the Fourth of July

from 11 :30 a. m to 1 :00 p. m.

at the Embassy Residence in Bourdon

Some typical invitations that the Farringtons received while in Haiti.

Harbor. A bunch of us had stayed the previous night across the street in one room of the Kinston Hotel, and my buddy R. D. Phillips and I were having a very late brunch, trying to recover from our White Lightning tasting the day before. It was an occasion for my first cup of coffee! After hearing the news of the Pearl Harbor attack, we immediately hitchhiked back to Tent Camp and were back in Kinston the same night.

The Farrington family reported in to the Marine Corps Air Station, Cherry Point, North Carolina, at 6:15 p.m., January 25, 1962, to start a new period in our lives.

I would like to add a bit of commentary here. For the past 40 years, the United States has been pouring time, money, and effort into Haiti. When I left that poor, misguided country in 1961, I wrote the following, to no avail. I believe its message is still apropos today.

Let's Use Our U-2s

Let's set up a system ensuring every individual Marine and adult dependent returning from a non-FMF (Fleet Marine Force) post overseas be interviewed. The results would be useful not only to the Marine Corps but also to the State Department and other governmental agencies. A well-organized interview by well-trained personnel would glean much information from persons who have been on the scene for two or more years. Combat patrols are interviewed after each mission. Every member is not a trained Intelligence scout, but each member has his chance to contribute his observations. The S-2 (Intelligence officer) on Guadalcanal or Korea would hardly miss a patrol debriefing. A patrol that is not debriefed is dangerous. Rumors, the breakdown of morale, and fear appear. The troops must be confident that their superiors have every scrap of information available and are working on it.

Inspection teams and visits to overseas posts are like

reconnaissance patrols, except that they are expected. So camouflage and window dressing are encountered by the inspectors rather than the real stories. The results are invariably nice. Overseas personnel, on the other hand, are like combat patrols that stay on the objective, struggle, and obtain the true facts.

The Ugly American, by William J. Lederer and Eugene Burdick, put in print some of the things that observing Americans have known for years. We love our country and want to be proud of it overseas. We want to see good, sound policy carried out well. A good campaign is waged only with good, continuing Intelligence.

As to the interviews, they should be held as soon as possible upon return to the United States, and must be confidential. The interviewer will be after frank, truthful answers or opinions, and he will get them only if the interviewee has no fear of repercussions.

Freedom of speech has become so entangled with loyalty these days that it is disappearing and usually must be paid for. Americans, of all people, should be able to speak their mind. We must enjoy our freedom and not suffer under it for fear of criticism.

As the results of interviews from the same areas are tabulated, patterns will form. In some cases these patterns will be startling, in others they will serve only to reenforce or dictate slight changes in our aims or methods. Personnel returning from overseas have recorded in their minds, souls, and consciences information, criticism, praise, and suggestions. The mission's complete; let's read the tapes and profit from our U-2s.

Semper Fidelis

Chapter 7

Cherry Point — and
Explosive Ordnance School

W E SETTLED IN AT Marine Corps Air Station Cherry Point, just outside the fence in public quarters. The address was 42 Kimes in Havelock, North Carolina. The duty assigned me was the Guard Officer/Assistant Provost Marshal. In other words, I was now an MP with badge. My immediate superior was a Captain, later Major, Bushwitz. Reggie and Rolando, my two sons, were enrolled in grade school, and the year 1962 proved exciting to say the least. I had never realized that there was crime involving Marines and their families aboard and off base. It just is not publicized in the base or local newspapers. The following is just a sampling of the events that were written up in the Desk Sergeant's log; these reports were meticulously checked by my Chief Clerk, Sergeant Winters, and myself before being sent on to the Provost Marshal and Headquarters, Marine Corps Air Station, every morning.

(1) In the enlisted housing area a cat had attacked a small baby. The father came out and kicked at the cat, but instead killed his baby.

(2) We had a small detachment, under a Sergeant,

stationed at both New Bern and Morehead City, and two-man motorized patrols in Havelock and on Highway 17. One night a patrol noticed an automobile stopped off the highway with its parking lights on. They continued on, but when they returned, decided to check, as the fogged-up vehicle was still there. They discovered a male and a female Marine. The female had on only her shoes. We reported the woman to the female Captain of the Women Marine Detachment as "being out of uniform." The Captain later called me to thank me for my men's care in checking and our conscientious report.

(3) A "quick-draw" contest in the Main Gate booth resulted in one man being shot in the leg with a .45-caliber Colt pistol.

(4) Two of my men in a patrol car robbed the officers swimming pool of beer and ice cream.

(5) Two of my animal-control men were gassing a vicious dog with carbon monoxide from their patrol car when the dog broke loose. Someone witnessed them hitting the poor thing over the head with lead pipes. Their explanation was accepted.

(6) The woman Marine Captain called me one day to inform me that a Marine had offered one of her Marines a typewriter for sex. I assigned a Staff Sergeant to accompany the woman Marine to the assigned rendezvous in the garbage dump. When the "bad guy" approached with the typewriter, my man jumped out and yelled "Halt!" three times, as the man fled. The Sergeant fired into the ground, the round ricocheted, and hit the suspect in the leg. Both the woman Marine and I stood up for the Sergeant when someone was trying to court-martial him for shooting the man. And because he was getting transferred soon, and because these things take time, I wrote a long and detailed letter of recommendation to the Sheriff in either Kentucky or Tennessee where the Sergeant was going to apply for a job after getting discharged. As this was the second time that a ricochet had hit someone (my Lieutenant had the same experience in Otsu, Japan, in 1950), I advised changing the warning shot target to the air.

(7) Domestic disturbances were frequent and touchy. And we also had our quota of drunk drivers. We had just installed a

new traffic sign down near the Officers Club when a Colonel completely wiped it out.

(8) A horrible accident occurred early one morning about 0200, but upon first approaching the scene out in Havelock, it did not seem very bad. A car was upside down in a ditch alongside the road. However, the two Marines inside had drowned, as the ditch was full of water.

From that year on, I have appreciated the problems dealt with by law enforcement officers of all kinds.

In August of 1962, my second daughter, Lynn Kay Farrington, was born, and my son Reggie's eyes were getting bad. His ophthalmologist at the Naval Hospital was Dr. Raskin, a male, later to be a successful professional tennis player on the ladies tour under the name of Renée Richards.

A few weeks after our arrival in Cherry Point, one of my Sergeants was driving to Florida and I went along to pick up my Volkswagen left with my mother. I returned with the Volkswagen in good order. The Marines meanwhile had scheduled a demonstration of one of our newer airplane types operating out of a short airstrip a few miles away down at Bogue Field, near Camp Lejeune, North Carolina. President John F. Kennedy, was invited, and he showed up in a helicopter. As I was in charge of his security, along with the Secret Service and the FBI, I was present when he debarked, and we exchanged salutes. I swear, he was bigger than life with that hair and large head. Right behind him was my boyhood buddy and ex-Marine Raider, Jack Lartz, who then was a United Press International (UPI) reporter. I saluted him, too, and got a scowl. He disliked officers, so I kind of "got him." We all remembered JFK and his experience on PT-*109*.

What an air demonstration that day! Some Marine Corps GV Lockheed C-130 Hercules aircraft came in, reversed their four engines, and stopped on a dime, compared to other large aircraft. Henceforth, I trusted the C-130 for the remainder of my time in the Marine Corps, especially the one that took my butt out of Khe Sanh, Vietnam, in 1968. Not only were the landings spectacular, but the takeoffs also. Using JATO (jet assisted takeoff) bottles, they simply leaped into the sky.

While at Cherry Point, I played on All-Marine and All-Navy tennis teams at Norfolk, Virginia, and Camp Lejeune, and even traveled all the way to Newport, Rhode Island, in a convertible (an MG if my memory is correct) driven by Colonel Tuma, who had been in JASCO — Joint Assault Signal Company — responsible for relaying air support missions from ground units to aircraft carriers during World War II. I will never forget the foggy and miserable atmosphere when we arrived. The place was like a morgue. It seems that the Admiral's daughter had been killed the day before by her surfboard, there in Newport.

I began brewing my own beer at Cherry Point. I had obtained the recipe from Lieutenant Colonel Benton R. Montgomery, my buddy from Camp Pendleton, who was at the Pentagon at this time in counterintelligence, planning for worldwide war contingencies.

In the fall of 1962, the Cuban missile crisis arose. The 2nd Marine Air Wing was involved, consisting mainly of MAG-14 (Marine Air Group) and MAG-24 with A-4 Skyhawks, F-9 Cougars, and F-4 Phantoms — fighter aircraft, and attack aircraft with bombs, rockets, and napalm.

One day we were tasked to protect some incoming trucks, which soon came onto the base in a well-protected and secret convoy. We took over from the North Carolina Highway Patrol and escorted the trucks to the flight lines. Interestingly, their cargo consisted of the only Shrike missiles immediately available. The weapons were soon hung under the proper planes and flown to Florida, where they were available to wipe out Cuba's radars used to direct SAMs (surface-to-air missiles) and ABMs (antiballistic missiles).

In 1962, the Marine Corps Ball at Cherry Point was the first time I ever thought about retiring from the Corps, because I had such a terrific hangover the next day. At midnight I had stood up and announced, as I had many times before, that now it was my birthday we were drinking to. November 11, 1971, after my retirement, was the first birthday I spent out of combat without a hangover since joining the Marine Corps.

About this time, somehow or other I discovered that my buddy who had made Warrant Officer with me in Japan, William Vick, was now in explosive ordnance disposal (EOD) and that it paid $120 extra each month. I put in a request for transfer to the EOD School at Indian Head, Maryland. I was accepted and approved for "bomb-squad" school.

The U.S. Navy Propellant Plant at Indian Head, Maryland, is about 25 miles south of Washington, D.C., on Route 210. It contains the Explosive Ordnance Disposal School, and the propellant plant, including a nitroglycerine plant, and other commands. In the late 1990s, the EOD school was moved to Eglin Air Force Base, near Pensacola, Florida, as I much later discovered, on May 15, 2001.

The U.S. Marine Corps Explosive Ordnance logo.

I reported for an approximate six-month training in basic and nuclear ordnance. My family remained in our Cherry Point bungalow, and I would drive the 300-odd miles every now and then in my Mercedes. I discovered that a Sergeant from Cherry Point was enrolled also, so we drove in his Chevette once in a while, a rougher ride.

At the basic ordnance school I discovered that Chief Warrant Officer Vick was actually on the staff. And to my horror, I learned that chloropicrin had been the filler for Japanese hand grenades and mortar shells. It was very dangerous, especially when old and crystals had formed. I had believed that the yellow filler was TNT and relatively safe when I had taken so many explosive items apart on New Britain Island in 1944.

The basic ordnance course was difficult, requiring a great deal of memorization, as much of the information was Top Secret and not available to you once you got into the field. The course was very interesting, however, with all the discussions on the British experiences in bomb disposal and the various devices used by the enemy. The German mines — "horse-shit" mines — made in the form of a pile of manure, that were laid on the roads and paths in Belgium, Holland, and France, are never to be forgotten. The defeating of booby traps was especially important with the Vietnam War going on.

The most interesting thing about the course, however, was when my class, consisting of about 22 members — U.S. Marines, U.S Army, U.S

Navy, U.S. Air Force, Canadians, and others — took a trip to the Army's Edgewood Arsenal above Baltimore on the Chesapeake Bay for Chemical Warfare Training. Everything proceeded smoothly until we went along reluctantly with the Army Lieutenant's instructions on the procedure for disposing of Sarin, a nerve gas. It was the middle of winter, and we were operating out of a heated Quonset hut. We donned all of our protective gear: gas-proof rubber suits, oxygen breathing apparatus (OBA), and rubber boots. After taping up all seams on each other, we were ready.

Outside was a large nerve-gas projectile in a shallow hole. We knew full well that the proper procedure was vent and burn. We installed the shaped charge on the shell and a charge for the fire. The Lieutenant ordered us to use non-electric detonation! Under protest, from inside our suits, we tried to cut the fuzes exactly the same length, but you know that is impossible. The detonation proceeded, and the Lieutenant ordered us up to see the results. We saw a beautiful hole in the nerve-gas shell, and the fire burning brightly. We washed our boots in the prepared wash bin and re-entered the Quonset hut to take a written test. Soon people were complaining of splitting headaches and a loss of vision. We stared at each other and almost in unison stated that we had been nerve gassed: the pupils of our eyes had constricted so much that we had large colored orbs, like owls.

After changing to our Class A dress uniforms, we were loaded aboard our bus and given the "heave-ho" from the base. They wanted to get rid of us — we had been gassed and were a problem. No one felt like stopping for chow on the way back, and the bus driver, who was not a student but a Navy enlisted man, complained about his eyes, but got us home safely. He had been in the Quonset hut with us.

Sure enough, specialists were called in from the Pentagon, and some of us got Atropine shots and spent the night on mattresses in the small sick bay on base. Our drivers' licenses were taken away so that we couldn't leave, and because we did not trust the clothing that we had worn, much of it was burned. As far as I know, everyone recovered, not with flying colors, however, as our peripheral vision only returned slowly.

At the investigation at Indian Head, we all gave our eyewitness accounts as to what had caused the contamination:

(a) Non-electric rather than electric priming was used.
(b) The nerve gas was vented before the fire ignited.

(c) All of the scattered Sarin was not burned.

(d) While we gathered around the site as ordered, mud had gotten on our boots (the frozen earth had been melted by the fire). Proper washing of the boots had not been done.

(e) Upon entering the heated Quonset hut, the Sarin had been released from the mud and immediately infected us.

I don't know the repercussions of this affair, but I would bet the farm that a new SOP — standard operating procedure — for disposing of nerve gas was written up that the military is following these days at the various nerve-gas depositories.

While at the Explosive Ordnance Disposal School, I met "Blackbird" Byrd, a Navy Chief, who I was told was the first black EOD diver, or something like that. He was a great guy, like most of the other instructors at Indian Head. The Navy divers had a deep tank at the school, and also dove in the filthy, littered Potomac River.

Our EOD class flew to Eglin Air Force Base in Florida, where we destroyed all kinds of large duds, including 500- and 1,000-pound bombs, napalm, rockets, missiles, JATO bottles, bomblets, and other large ordnance. We had liberty a few times while in Florida, and so one day a buddy and I happened to be in Niceville. We wandered into a bar and asked the owner how the town got its name.

"Hell, I don't know," he said, "I'll ask my wife. . . . Hey, George!"

Upon completing the basic ordnance course I was enrolled across the parking lot in the nuclear facility. This was interesting, as I had no idea that so many accidents had occurred that EOD teams had taken care of, especially in the good old USA. Also enlightening was how our government was getting shafted over the price of nuts and bolts (literally) that go into the building and maintenance of nuclear weapons.

I cannot go into any of the training at this facility, as it was and is Top Secret. One thing, however, is not. The facility had a Russian manual that showed the secrets the Rosenbergs had sold to that country, and I never doubted their guilt and execution. The illustrations have been printed many times since in newspapers and magazines.

You might find interesting the following EOD abbreviations for dealing with unexploded ordnance (duds):

BIP	Blow in place, which is the most desirable.
BTBU	Blow the bastard up (likewise).
PUCA	Pick up and carry away (if safe to do so).
DDOT	Don't drop on toe (referring to a very heavy Japanese fuze used in a battleship shell).

While at Indian Head, a young Navy Lieutenant and I were talking one day when the topic of "home brew" came up, and he bragged how he knew all about it from his younger years in Oklahoma. Well, I informed him of my hobby, and promised to bring him a bottle, which I did on my next trip. I presented it to him the evening I returned, and he put it in his refrigerator in the Bachelor Officer Quarters (BOQ). You should have seen him the next day in the schoolroom; his bloodshot eyes explained all. He had drunk the quart the night before, without giving the dregs time to settle after the auto trip. I don't think he was a real backwoodsman.

Upon graduation from EOD School, I was assigned as the EOD officer of Marine Air Base Squadron 14 (MABS-14) at Cherry Point, and thus returned home in June 1963 to 42 Kimes, in Havelock, North Carolina.

Chapter 8

The 2nd Marine Air Wing — and Two Top Secret Years

A S A RECENTLY promoted Commissioned Warrant Officer 3 and graduate of the Explosive Ordnance Disposal School, I took over as Marine Air Base Squadron 14's EOD officer at Cherry Point, North Carolina. In addition, I had assorted other duties, as emergencies did not happen all of the time, though I was on call 24 hours a day. The EOD personnel aboard the base had a common shack out near the rifle range where we got together for schooling on new weapons, and for inspections by the Inspector General (IG) teams on our handling of staged emergencies, both nuclear and standard.

Thankfully, while I was there, the 2nd Marine Air Wing, of which I was a part, did not suffer many horrible accidents. The one that stands out was the death of a Reserve Captain on two weeks of summer training, who had been in a terrible air crash on landing.

We were part of a large air show, with many guests down near Camp Lejeune. Targets were built, we planted explosives, and aircraft attacked with Bull-Pup missiles, bombs, napalm, bomblets, etc. We were supposed to blow the targets to smithereens as the ordnance landed. Well, the larger-than-life show was a bust as far as I was concerned. Rain shorted out some of the electric lines, most of the so-called trembler switches failed to operate, and the dropped ordnance failed to live up to the devastation expected of our TNT. This was my first experience with the bombing demonstrations where we had to fake the bomb hitting the target, and I didn't like it. On the other hand, our rigged atomic explosions were always a success, generating a large mushroom every time. Faking was a necessity in these cases. This demonstration maneuver took weeks, and I would come home with Venus Flytraps for my kids. That swampy area is one of the few areas where the cannibalistic plant grows in the United States.

My team subsequently drove down to the Engineer Stockade at Camp Lejeune to work with their EOD teams in detonating duds out on an island beyond the inland waterway. Besides their artillery duds, there were also many of our bombs and rockets. In our truck I included two cases of quart bottles of my home brew, as I knew the men would appreciate a cold drink or two after a hard summer day of dodging high-explosive fragments. They, of course, were fully provided with all of the housing amenities, so the beer was deposited in their large reefer along with pitchers.

The impact area at Camp Lejeune where we had been working had no cover to speak of. As the fuzes were lit, we skedaddled under automobile carcasses full of holes. We worked our tails off all day, and only one man was hurt. I ran all the way to an inlet and was able to signal someone for help. A Higgins boat arrived, and the man was safely hauled away. Back "at the ranch," finally the brew was opened, and I never expected the reaction. You must realize that EOD goes back to the British bomb-disposal squads of World War II and had quite a history. Many senior NCOs, WOs, and officers were manning EOD billets. Being a recent recruit in EOD with practically no experience and no time to speak of, I was not looked up to or trusted at all, and I could feel it every day. But now the Master Sergeants, "Gunnies" — Gunnery Sergeants, and others kept telling me how great the beer was, and that they had never tasted better. My stock rose a little that day it seemed. Incidentally, my home brew had a very high alcohol content!

When Marine Air Group 14 was ordered up to Oceana Naval Air Station, just south of Virginia Beach, Virginia, for operations in that area, a

Sergeant and I went along naturally as EOD support. I was given the additional duty as mess officer. But we had absolutely no problems whatsoever with the mess. The mess Sergeant was outstanding, as was his boss, Master Sergeant Emmehula. The name means "man killer" in Comanche. When I was called away for emergencies, the mess always ran smoothly. Sergeant Emmehula died a few years ago, and I believe that his widow is in charge of or is a "chief honcho" of the Department of Indian Affairs in Washington, D.C. I cannot imagine anyone more qualified for that assignment.

At this time, the worst accident we experienced was with an A-4 Skyhawk. The pilot bailed out, but he and his ejection seat landed hard in some trees and he was killed. My duty was simply to disarm any bombs, rockets, or other armament present, to make safe the explosive bolts used to blow the bombs away from the aircraft, and to make safe the ejection-seat rockets if they had not been utilized.

One day, Colonel Lewis W. Walt showed up out at our EOD shack and put on a demonstration with two new weapons: the Stoner-63 and the M-16 rifles. They both appeared to be futuristic weapons made by Mattel, not by Mr. Stoner. They had been rigorously tested in the tropics and the Arctic under all conditions. Some service units were to be armed with the Stoner-63, which had amazing adaptions, but the Marine Corps was to be equipped with the M-16.

Colonel Walt showed us the bullet for the M-16. My God! We all had fired .22s as kids, but this bullet appeared even smaller. Then the Colonel picked up a steel helmet and a cabbage and handed them to a Sergeant who placed them on the ground some yards away, with the cabbage inside the helmet. A volunteer was asked to step up. He was handed a .30-caliber M-14 rifle and told to shoot, which he did.

We walked over and observed a .30-caliber hole in the steel and, when the helmet was picked up, a .30-caliber hole in the cabbage, with a slightly larger hole in the back of the helmet. OK, we thought, the result was as expected.

Then a Marine, not a volunteer, was handed the light M-16 and told to fire at another cabbage-helmet target. The Marine braced himself and fired. There was a minimum of recoil and a "ping," compared to the blast by the M-14. The helmet toppled backward a skosh. We observed a tiny hole, and as the Colonel picked up the helmet, we saw a pile of coleslaw — and there was no back to the helmet! Colonel Walt described the high velocity of the small bullet, and how it tumbled when it hit something, taking everything with it like a shotgun blast. With a 15-round magazine, we all knew that the USMC had a new weapon, one that we never wanted to face.

The worst event while I was in North Carolina occurred as I was competing on a rifle and pistol team at Camp Lejeune. During the lunch break, the news came over the radio that President John F. Kennedy had been assassinated in Dallas. But, in contrast to that dark spot, the fishing in North Carolina was great, as well as on my leaves in Florida when we visited my mother.

The only other additional "dark spot" in North Carolina was the one assignment that we were called upon to do that I frankly did not approve of. Certain law enforcement officers would request the Marines to blow up and destroy the property of some North Carolinians. We were ordered to locations out in the forest where we would plant explosives in shacks, on large vats, stoves, and crockery. The resulting detonation would put the moonshiners out of business for a while in that location. Somehow or other it just didn't seem proper to me.

Then, suddenly, in 1965 I received orders to report to the EOD School at Indian Head, Maryland, as an instructor.

Somehow the seven of us — Erlinda, Reggie, Rolando, Karen, Lynn, Pup-Pups, and I — plus two autos, found ourselves ensconced in a nice second-floor apartment in the Riverview complex owned by the U.S. Navy at Indian Head. The EOD School was a few blocks away, fenced in as part of the U.S. Navy Propellant Plant.

What a great community we found there. With no more nervous 24-hour expectations of emergency telephone calls, we could now have a better social life, and did. My duty in the nuclear facility was interesting and satisfying, and Linda made many friends.

The closest PX/Commissary, however, was Cameron Station, a U.S. Army installation up Route 210, and west over the Wilson Memorial Bridge over the Potomac River, a few miles into Virginia.

But we had a theater on the base, and a drive-in a few miles up Route 210. La Plata, Maryland, had a great Chinese restaurant, as well as other good ones. Slot machines were also legal in Charles County, and there were many seafood — mainly crab — places, as well as a population of wagon-driving Amish.

Reggie attended Lackey High School in Indian Head, and later both he and Rolando joined the Boy Scouts of America. The Lackey "Braves" had a nearby rival in the Pomonkey "Indians." Karen enjoyed school, showing her talent early in art, and Lynn loved pre-school and made a good friend in Binkey Hobson.

We fished and picked berries, and at Christmas the kids and I would drive out to Stump Neck, where I was stationed the last year or so of my tour, to cut our Christmas tree.

Of my four children, only Karen decided to accept tennis as her sport, and the courts next to the swimming pool were where we got started. She later played on the San Pasqual High School team in Escondido, California, and the Palomar Junior College team in San Marcos, and was later recruited at a tournament in Ojai, California, by the men's coach of Oral Roberts University, receiving a partial scholarship.

While on the subject of tennis, I was unable to compete in All-Marine or Inter-Service matches, but the EOD School fielded a good doubles team, and we competed successfully in a government league. We played in my old haunts in D.C., including the 16th and Kennedy courts in northwest Washington. One time, as we were unloading from our van at the courts down in East Potomac Park near the 14th Street bridge, a motorcycle pulled up; the rider, dressed in black leathers, dismounted, removed the black helmet, and blonde tresses flowed down. A young U.S. Navy officer made some joking remarks, and guess what! . . . She was part of the opposing team, played the Navy officer and his partner, and whipped them good. I was pleased that the civilian ladies were asserting themselves in such a way — embarrassing the Navy.

In June of 1965 I won the National Propellant Plant Singles Tennis Tournament by defeating assistant management board chairman John Blanck, seeded number one, 6-4, 7-9, 7-5, on the court right in front of Commander Kenneth Ploof's residence, three days after he had relieved Commander James C. Peeler as Commanding Officer of the EOD School.

At Indian Head, we had a garden each summer and explored all over the area, which was quite wild. We encountered copperhead and cottonmouth snakes, and one time we messed with a large snapping turtle.

The two duties at Indian Head that I enjoyed the most were the "Boneyard," right at the school, next to the nuclear weapons sections, where we ran realistic problems for all new and refresher students on wrecked nuclear weapons, and a presentation of photos and facts on various nuclear accidents that had occurred over the past 25 years. I will mention only those that have appeared in newspapers and on television. (Interestingly, even recently on TV there was a reference to a nuclear accident that had occurred in New Jersey.)

One accident had occurred in England, one near San Francisco, one near Goldsborough, North Carolina, one near Chicago, one on the base at Shreveport, Louisiana, and others. By far the most interesting accident was the one near Palomares, Spain, in 1966, when a B-52 unceremoniously dumped four H-bombs, three in some tomato fields and one close by in the Mediterranean. The EOD reports and pictures taken in the tomato fields were good, but the ones taken in the Mediterranean by our Scripps Institute-based submarine *Alvin* and aboard the rescue ship were great. (A book about the incident, *America's Lost H-Bomb! Palomares, Spain, 1966*, by Randall C. Maydew, was also published by Sunflower University Press. The late author stated that the Palomares incident was but one of 32 such occurrences, and eventually led to a safer design philosophy for nuclear weapons.) The successful rendering-safe procedure (RSP) and mistakes made at these sites were impressed upon the students.

Two Vietnamese Captains and some enlisted men attended the basic course at the EOD School, and I got to be friends with both officers — one, by later beating him at Ping-Pong for the championship of Vietnam, and the other when he complimented me on Reggie's intensity in kicking him in a soccer game played at one of the picnics that Commander Ploof had scheduled for all hands.

The Commander and I also really kicked booty at horseshoes, and we played tennis once in a while on his court. One of the Vietnamese officers, Captain Viet, was stationed in the Central Highlands later on when I was in Vietnam, and I only managed to see the other, a Major by then, when I was in Saigon.

At Indian Head, there was a golf course on the base; I was on the EOD golf team, and loved it. We invited the Lartzes down one time, and Jack could not get over the availability of beer at each tee!

While I was at Indian Head, the old Boneyard, familiar to all EOD personnel schooled in nukes, was closed down — especially the final Top Secret nuclear problem entitled "The Monster." My crew saw the building of a new Boneyard and worked like dogs restocking the bays with improved problems. Speaking of The Monster, I only blew up my team four times when I had tackled it back in 1963. My crew consisted of senior ranks of the U.S. Marine Corps, Navy, Army, and Air Force, and presented great nuclear accident problems for the students. The new Boneyard proved to be a success and was still operating when I left for Vietnam in September 1967.

I received permission from Commander Ploof to invite Richard Basehart — who at the time was starring in the TV saga *Voyage to the Bottom of the Sea* — to visit the facility to add a little more realism in the show. As I noted earlier, Basehart and his wife had lived in the same duplex as my mother and I when we first had arrived in Hollywood in 1946. But to this day, I do not believe that Basehart actually read my letter, as all I received in return was the standard publicity response of a card with pictures of the cast and a printed signature. Basehart was a gentleman, had a great speaking voice, and passed away some years ago.

Chief Warrant Officer Bill Vick, instructing at the EOD School, and I were in charge of the 1966 Marine Corps Ball aboard the station. All I can remember of those days, however, is that Vick had less than two years to live — he would be killed in Vietnam — and that the Beatles' song "Yellow Submarine" was played over and over again.

At this time, Colonel Heinl, who had been my Commanding Officer in Haiti and was an accomplished author, telephoned Commander Ploof and arranged to contact me personally aboard the base. I was worried, to say the least. What could I have possibly done? We met at the Officers Club and he interviewed me about an episode in Korea. He was writing *Victory at High Tide*, and when it was published he sent me an autographed copy.

Heinl described the action that had taken place when we had delivered the tanks to Colonel "Chesty" Puller, which I noted earlier in this work, though Heinl's account had edited out any unflattering references I made concerning the officer who had suggested we "turn around rather than engage with the enemy in a firefight."

Later on, my buddy Jack Lartz was covering an uprising in the Dominican Republic. He and all the other newsmen were scrunched down when a bushy mustached civilian approached in coat and tie. Jack told me that they were receiving fire from somewhere and were prone. The gentleman removed his coat, turned his cuffs up, stood up, drew his field glasses, and in his distinguished English-type voice announced that the gunfire was coming from a nearby village. It was Colonel Heinl, then retired and representing various periodicals. Jack said that Heinl's actions that day instilled much respect for the brave man.

Incidentally, the Colonel had confided in me as to his worst day in the Marine Corps. He said he had been aboard ship a few days after Pearl Harbor in December 1941 transporting Brewster Buffaloes, Grumman Wildcats, and other needed aircraft to Wake Island. One day, the ship suddenly made a 180-degree turn; it was painfully obvious that the United States had given up on that unfortunate outpost. The Marines, sailors, and civilians there would subsequently be maltreated and starved, and an unknown number were beheaded.

During our stay at Indian Head, Maryland, my wife Linda had a friend, Irene, that she had met playing Bingo. The woman was from Luxembourg and had married a U.S. soldier soon after World War II. They resided in Ripley, Maryland, where we visited them frequently. Irene had the following interesting story to tell us about an experience in her home town during the war. It seems the American Commanding General in the area had ordered a soldier to escort home each of the girls who worked in his Headquarters, as the area was dangerous. Well, one evening as Irene and her escort were winding their way through the very narrow streets, a vehicle turned the corner and threw slush on them as they were flattened against a building to let it pass. The car stopped, backed up, and the passenger apologized. It was General George S. Patton! Irene said they all loved him.

During the time we were at Indian Head her husband was a mason at the propellant plant. He told me his main job was to replace the original bricks long ago used to build the installation. He and Irene visited her home town in Luxembourg while we were at Indian Head, and when they returned to the States, she gave me a gift, a small glass bottle covered with a basket. She told me that it was the national alcoholic beverage of Luxembourg, I believe called *kirsch*, sounding somewhat like *quiche*. I sampled the beverage, and on the next workday out at the Boneyard I invited Air Force Master Sergeant Hobson to our apartment. His daughter was Binky, my youngest daughter's friend. I served him the beverage, and the first words out of his mouth were "White Lightning!" He was from Kentucky, and I knew he would recognize the taste. He was amazed to learn that it was from overseas and made from cherries or plums.

After we had arrived at Indian Head, we acquired another member of the family, Tweetie, when he banged into the back window where we had bird seed deposited. That robin was, indeed, a pet; he was never caged, except in the car. He would fly around and almost every time come on back. I even had to climb a tree to rescue him on a couple of occasions when he was young and was too chicken to leave it.

Indian Head was really a very interesting place to tour. The nitroglycerine plant displayed beautiful filigreed large urns imported from Sweden, where Swedish chemist Alfred Nobel had invented nitro. I mention this also because regardless of the safety precautions, there have always been accidents with this dangerous explosive. That is the reason dynamite, which contains nitro, is not a military explosive.

When I was later in Vietnam, during 1967-1968, Erlinda was out back hanging clothes when the nitroglycerine plant blew up. She wrote me that the clothing almost went parallel to the ground with the concussion. No casualties were published, but the U.S. Navy had a difficult time replacing the plant, as the Swedish contractor had taken the plans with him many years earlier.

Another most unfortunate thing happened when my crew was out at the Stump Neck test area peninsula one Friday. The Indian Head Boneyard had been moved there. The crew told me that a well-known EOD refresher student, a Lieutenant, was missing after leaving the Gateway Tavern just outside the main gate. Well, I had my ideas about this so the next morning, Saturday, Pup-Pups and I went down to one of our familiar haunts, a 40-foot deep stream just across the road from the Gateway. The stream passed through a culvert a few yards from the main gate, and a couple hundred feet behind the post office, the only structure in the wooded area. Talk about horror. There lying in the shallow water face up was what appeared to be a wax dummy. Pup-Pups and I climbed down, and sure enough, it was a dead body. We quickly reported our discovery to the guards at the gate. There was an investigation, but I have no idea how it turned out. To me it seemed that he probably had been murdered, after a reported altercation at the bar; but he could have just wandered drunk in that direction and fallen. Someone certainly knows.

I recall many enjoyable experiences at Indian Head. In 1965, Linda and I dressed up and went to the 1st Marine Division reunion with Duck and Shirley Montgomery, at either the Wardman Park Hotel or the Shoreham out on Connecticut Avenue — I cannot recall which. Colonel Chesty Puller and the Commandant were on the stage. They were handed a Walkie-Talkie and spoke with General Walt in his tent in Vietnam! I was astounded, as was almost everyone else in the room. Duck said to me something like, "Don't sweat it, Reggie; the little radio only reaches the Pentagon, where it's relayed by single sideband to Nam." As usual, Chesty asked how the "old SOB" was, which brought much laughter. I wondered if the Commanding General of the 1st Marine Division was armed with an M-16 rifle.

I also remember when Master Sergeant Hobson and I were sent, First Class, on United Airlines to Albuquerque, New Mexico. We reported in to the Sandia Military Reservation and with some other EOD teams and civilians developed a workable rendering-safe procedure for a new hydrogen bomb.

I had attended one more Marine reunion before I left for Vietnam in 1967. General Ray Davis, at Quantico, had contacted me earlier, in 1966, to inquire whether I wished a ride on his plane to the 1st Marine Division Reunion in Detroit. At the airport, General Davis arrived with another General, and all sorts of aides. When he introduced me, I knew one of them, so I said to him, "I was a Masters' Bastard." You should have seen the faces of the Captains and Lieutenants; but General Davis just smiled, for I was speaking to General James M. Masters, Sr., who had been our Commanding Officer at Tauali, New Britain Island, in 1943. We then reminisced on that operation a little, and General Masters was interested to know that his younger brother had been my Commanding Officer at the 2nd Infantry Training Regiment in the 1950s.

Later arriving in Motor Town, and having heard my tale of running into Muzzy — Thaddeus Muszynski — there in 1945, General Davis asked me if I could possibly find Muzzy, who had been his Marine buddy when he had been a Lieutenant in Cuba. He wanted me to bring him to his first reunion. Harmon, the truck driver, and I went out to Dearborn and met Muzzy's whole family. I had seen Muzzy in 1945, after the Jap had blown him up with the anti-tank mine, but no one really knew just how seriously he had been wounded. This time I asked him if he would show us, and he did. Muzzy's right arm had been blasted — his baseball arm. We knew that the doctors had removed strips of skin from his upper legs to repair it. But the large, black wounds to his torso were unexpected. We wondered how had he worked for years operating some sort of huge press. His grown kids' faces were somewhat aghast as he showed us his wounds, but we were proud of him.

Muzzy enjoyed the Detroit reunion, spending most of his time hanging with the General at the Sheraton-Cadillac Hotel headquarters.

Amidst the intense work at Indian Head, I remained the singles tennis champion in 1967, when I again defeated John Blanck, late of Penn State, again 6-4, 7-9, 7-5, 8-6. I also defeated Dr. John Connelly for the number one position on the station ladder, and he and I won the doubles. He was a good friend and looked after my family's health while I was overseas.

In August of 1967 I received orders for Vietnam. My time was up enjoying a peaceful life with my family. The last movie that we saw at the Indian Head Drive-In was *Fantastic Voyage*, with Raquel Welch, which was excellent. I knew that I would have one soon.

I took the family up to D.C. to visit my old homes and schools, and Linda's friends from when she was stationed there as a WAVE during

World War II. We did not expect to be back in D.C., as the EOD people had told me that upon returning from Vietnam I would probably be stationed on the West Coast. Linda returned once, however, for a WAVE reunion. And I cannot believe that the city was able to build a subway system, considering the unstable, swampy land that Washington was built upon.

I left for Vietnam that summer of 1967. I was off to war again.

Chapter 9

Vietnam

I LEFT IN MY 1961 Mercedes for Camp Joseph H. Pendleton, California, once again, and was put into a replacement battalion commanding a few hundred men at Tent Camp #1, called Las Pulgas. We knocked ourselves out trying to get into condition by climbing old Sheep-Shit Trail, which had been famous from the days Pendleton had been put into commission back in the early 1940s.

The Mercedes was then stored in San Diego in a nice facility protected by guard dogs, and my charges and I were bused up to El Toro Marine Corps Air Station, near Santa Ana. A large blue-tailed jet (of Continental Airlines, I believe) was waiting for us out on the tarmac, and we began loading. Immediately, one of our troops came up to me and reported that someone had said that a man was carrying a gun. I alerted the MPs, who I am sure were there to guarantee that we all boarded the plane, and within a few minutes several men in suits and ties showed up and dragged the Marine off the aircraft along with his personal weapon, a pistol.

Sojourn in Vietnam

We arrived in Okinawa, Ryukyu Islands, and I spent September 1967 trying to get in shape by running to and fro from Camp Hansen to Blue Beach, which had been a Marine practice landing site for many years. My immediate future was to be an Explosive Ordnance Disposal (EOD) officer for some unknown outfit in Vietnam. My family — Erlinda, Reggie, Rolando, Karen, and Lynn — remained at the Naval EOD School in Indian Head, Maryland. They kept the '59 Volkswagen.

All of my charges that I had accompanied to Okinawa — replacements from Camp Pendleton — were duly turned over to the assignment section, and I was on my own. I recalled an old Spanish proverb quoted when going into the face of protracted danger:

Nada es verdad	Nothing is the truth
Nada es mentira	Nothing is a lie
Todo depende en el cristal	All depends on the looking glass
En que mira.	In which you look.

My assignment in Vietnam was with the 2nd Marine Air Wing at Chu Lai, about 56 miles south of Danang, where I had arrived by C-130 Hercules aircraft. We had a lovely cottage among the trees near the beach, and as I was a supernumerary — an extra "live body" — all kinds of weapons-disposal jobs were mine. The worst, and most scary, occurred in October when with Army EOD personnel, Arrendal, Boyce, and myself responded to a call for disposal of dynamite left by the SeaBees. There was so much, enough for approximately two large trucks, that we had to have help loading it. The explosives were in clear, 50-pound plastic bags. In each bag was about a pint of liquid, and you know what that was — nitroglycerine that had leached out of the dynamite sticks. All the movies I had seen of nitro being transported by burro, truck, train — whatever — flashed through my mind as the Marines were handing the bags up to us in the trucks. I just knew we all were going to disappear when someone stepped in the wrong place or dropped a bag. But the trucks were loaded, and we EOD personnel headed for the disposal area, outside the perimeter, about two miles down bombed-out Route 1 and a mile on a dirt road in "Indian Country." Our request to dispose of the dynamite by detonating it between the runways had been turned down by the ignorant powers that be. There would have been absolutely no danger of flying debris of fragments — only a big boom. We made a mushroom cloud where we had been instructed to, and the SeaBees were "on my list."

I ate my meals at the Officers Club on the beach, picked up seashells, and sighted in on the sand ramp — a ramp into the sea made so that the LSTs could unload their cargo. The man in charge of the ramp was Lieutenant Roger Staubach, soon to be the quarterback of the Dallas Cowboys of the National Football League. I played a lot of Ping-Pong in the club, mainly with the Korean pilots, and saw many good movies, of course being always on call for emergencies.

One day a Marine F-4 Phantom jet crashed just off the end of the runway. We waded in a swamp, recovering the bomb fuzes and other explosive devices from the plane and had to deal with pieces of the two pilots. It was just horrible. The debris had stopped short of a Marine in an observation post on the perimeter, and he was a basket case, unable to talk to us or give any information. After much searching, we were able to recover some 500-pound bombs, a hundred yards away out on the beach.

A cease-fire was proclaimed for Thanksgiving, and all flying and firing stopped. Then suddenly, a U.S. Army observation plane began buzzing and firing at the Viet Cong on the peninsula just south of us. The gooks fired back, and downed the American interloper. It was sort of a shock to hear American cheering coming from all over Chu Lai. Believe it or not, most

Hom & Harry
With Best Wishes
For
a Merry Christmas
and
a Happy New Year.
Love
Royjie

The author bought this Christmas card from a young girl of about eight years old, in Saigon, 1967.

MERRY
CHRISTMAS

While in Saigon, 1967, the author bought his two daughters, Karen (9) and Lynn (5), a traditional *ao dai* dress, similar to that of the two strolling Vietnamese beauties at left.

Americans supported fair play, and this was supposed to have been a cease-fire — no one was supposed to shoot at anybody.

⊷⇒◯⇐⊷

In early December 1967 I flew on a C-130 Hercules to Saigon for a refresher course and update on new munitions introduced by the Chinese. I stayed at the Hotel Myrakord (though I am not certain of that spelling) and that was where I met the movie star Martha Raye, who had been made an honorary member of the Army Special Forces. She really looked spiffy in her uniform, and we were able to talk twice. I remember congratulating her on her television show with Rocky Graziano and hoping that it would continue when she returned Stateside.

At the Saigon PX I purchased a beautiful jade stone surrounded by pearls, and when the beautiful young girl presented it alone, I was taken aback. I had thought that I was buying a pair of earrings for Erlinda, but instead I now owned a beautiful tie tack!

I also rendezvoused with Captain Ninh, the Commander of the ARVN detachment guarding the Saigon River front, right next to the statue of the Vietnamese George Washington, General Tran Hung Dao, who had saved Vietnam from a Chinese invasion. The Captain had attended the EOD School at Indian Head, Maryland, and immediately invited me back inside to his men's and his joint quarters. He apologized for the mean accommodations, but was quite proud when he opened up the small refrigerator next to his bunk and broke out a Bahmitybah beer, the Vietnamese brew of French heritage, called "33." He told me that he really had to have a "beer reefer" just like the ones in the BOQ at Indian Head. He informed me that the other Vietnamese officer that had been at the school with him, Major Viet, now had a battalion of ARVN up in the central highlands.

The statue of General Tran Hung Dao, situated on the Saigon River. Notice the General pointing down to the river. Centuries ago he prevented a Chinese invasion by having large pointed poles (large punji sticks) embedded in the river bottom, which destroyed the Chinese war junks and ensured victory.

The statue of two members of the Vietnamese Marine Corps in downtown Saigon, which the Communists destroyed immediately upon the capture of the city.

In Saigon, I also checked out the zoo and saw the magnificent statue of heroic Vietnamese Marines that just recently had been completed downtown. (In 1975 it would be seen on television being toppled and destroyed by the North Vietnamese, along with the complete destruction of the Cho Lon district, which had the large PX full of fine jewelry from all over the Orient.) I "did" Tu Do Street with an Australian Warrant Officer, and hung out with Jack Lartz, my boyhood buddy who was on duty with the American Information Service in Saigon. I helped Jack wash his Karman Ghia.

Then, after returning to Chu Lai, I was transferred over to the main airstrip and really got a lot of work, as the Lieutenant and Warrant Officer there simply wanted to live comfortably and contemplate their upcoming cushy new assignments back in Hawaii. It was at this time that I realized that EOD — this special little splinter group of the Marine Corps — was not for me. These people were more worried about returning to the States, just putting their time in. I didn't work that way.

But meanwhile, Bob Hope and Raquel Welch flew in on C-2A "CODs" (Carrier Onboard Delivery transport aircraft) from an aircraft carrier, for a show at the South Vietnamese Army stadium, and I stood the runway duty. The entertainers were not allowed to stay overnight in-country anymore, but were sure brave to take off from and land aboard a carrier. I would have liked to see Raquel, having just viewed *Fantastic Voyage* with my kids before arriving in Vietnam, and I loved her role in *One Million B.C.*

In 1944, on our way to Peleliu, I had seen the original star of *One Million B.C.*, Carol Landis, just for an instant, when I had been supported on a coconut by my buddy in the rear of thousands of "doggies" at Jack Benny's show on Banika Island, Russell Islands. However, I had not been impressed by Bob Hope and his ensemble on Pavuvu Island, Russell Islands, back in June of 1944. The performance was just too choreographed. Now when Gary Cooper had visited us on Goodenough Island, D'Entrecasteaux Group, on November

28, 1943, that had been an experience! He put on an excellent show. At the time we had been told that the entertainers had flown directly to Goodenough Island to visit the 1st Marine Division, and so they were presented with 1st Division patches, which we had been authorized to wear on our dress uniforms in Australia.

⋯⇒◯⇐⋯

One evening in Vietnam, just before dark, we got the word that two USAF F-4 Phantoms were coming in, mistaking us for Danang. As the Sergeant and I watched, they approached in echelon, almost side by side, onto our narrow airstrip. Of course the left plane went off the strip, with his right wing out on the runway. We responded in our truck and asked the Air Force pilot for the location of the safety pins to the ordnance he was carrying — napalm, bombs, sparrows, etc. Naturally, he did not know, so we opened all compartments on the bottom of the plane until they fell out. It was dark by then and really scary, as our returning planes just missed the armament-loaded Phantom. It was a relief to get all the weapons pinned, placed on dollies, and away from the landing strip. The Air Force sent a message for us to use the ordnance as we deemed fit! How different from the Navy.

Every morning we routinely drove down the runways in our pickup truck gathering the 20mm shells that had been ejected from the aircraft guns during hard landings. The tips were usually missing, leaving the high-explosive filler exposed. This was not TNT, but "tetra something" that would detonate from just a scratch. I would lean out the door as my driver eased on the accelerator, grab the round, and deposit it on a soft rag on the floor of the cab.

One day, back at Chu Lai on December 22, 1967 — I will never forget that day — the Lieutenant ordered me and two Sergeants to load Grade III munitions (Vietnamese, Korean, and U.S. duds and misfires) onto trucks and dispose of them.

I was appalled, as I surveyed this rain-soaked, sand-covered mess just out back of their "ranch." How many weeks — or months — had this existed?

Nevertheless, Sergeants Mueller and Claborn obtained a 6x6 truck and we began digging up trash explosives, duds, and who knows what. We went after the most dangerous items first, the 20mms. I spotted one in a water-filled ammo can next to a 60mm mortar shell, with its tail fin just above the water. As I carefully latched onto the 20mm shell, there was a terrific explosion. I was blown backward, was soaking wet, and noticed that two of the men on the truck went down. We called for corpsmen, and I recovered the red-hot tail section of the 60mm mortar shell. The 20mm was in my hand, so I knew it was the mortar shell that had detonated — luckily a low-order, opposed to a high-order detonation, which would be expected of the shell. Upon examination, we determined that the shell had been fired, failed to detonate upon impact, had been recovered, and then was simply dumped in the "back yard" at the EOD shack! Obviously the weather, water, and time had affected the fuze and firing pin, and with just the slightest movement it had exploded. The two men on the truck were not seriously wounded, and the doctor told me that I had a ruptured eardrum, but that it would grow back. I still have the tail of the 60mm shell on my mantle.

During the rest of December, the Sergeants and I loaded, transported, and destroyed over 60 tons of Grade III armaments. We sometimes cooperated with Army EOD and its radio-controlled detonations, which were experimental to say the least. We primarily used electrical blasting, but sometimes non-electric timed fuzes were called for, and we assured the safety of the Vietnamese in the area. The rockets, napalm, and various-sized bombs were usually no problem, but we never did discover just what items might explode as they were aboard the truck and when we were unloading them at the disposal site. It was very scary when you had tons of explosives stacked and nerve-wracking "pops" occurred.

⋅⟶⇐⋅

One foggy morning, all the sirens and horns went off, and the Sergeant and I raced out onto the airfield in our pickup, neck and neck with the crash crew. Everyone else stopped 50 yards short, as the Sergeant and I approached an A-4 Sky-hawk, a small attack bomber, which until a few moments previously had been screaming down the runway just behind its wingmate. Luckily, it was the leader who became airborne. This aircraft was sitting crazily in the middle of the runway amid the strong smell of gasoline. I recognized the pilot, who had just deplaned, as an old Ping-Pong adversary from the Officers Club, and asked him what had happened. He was very excited — who wouldn't be? — and told me that he had been making it down the strip in echelon behind his wingman when he had noticed a red light go on. He said he was just beginning to wonder what was happening, when . . . he then grabbed his stomach and bent over in front of us while grimacing and bugging his eyes out. The red light had signaled that his tail hook had become unlatched and at that instant it had caught the arresting cable, which lay across the runway. He was demonstrating how his seat belt had almost cut him in half, as he was stopped from a speed of about 100 knots.

He broke out a cigarette, and I quickly, warned him that the cable had bashed in the 750-pound napalm tank that he had been carrying. He paled and got the Hell out of there.

The Sergeant and I removed the always-acting (A/A) fuzed WP (white phosphorus) ignitors from the ends of the large napalm tank and motioned for the crash crew to take over. All in all the situation had been a little hairy for a while, but the pilot's reenactment of the action in the cockpit had really amused me, and I'll never forget it. In fact, I have a couple A-4 seat belts in my 1959 Volkswagen, and I remember that day every time I buckle up.

⋅⟶⇐⋅

One bright day in Vietnam the strident ring of the emergency phone sent a momentary chill down this Warrant Officer's backbone — a chill that is still with me whenever the telephone rings.

I answered, "EOD here."

"This is the tower. Navy A-6 aborting" (an Intruder attack bomber). "Hydraulic trouble," he said. "Ordnance Top Secret. It's all yours."

"EOD, aye."

Well, there it was. A couple more dry "Swab Jockeys." How they could log those missions over North Vietnam day after day and then return home to the carrier to just a cup of coffee was beyond me. Not rating even a cold beer after being chased all over the sky by deadly "flying telephone poles" — the surface to air missiles — was a crime!

I called my driver and told him to head for the MAG-24 (Marine Air Group 24) parking area, the closest one to the Officers Club. We jumped into the old light-reconnaissance truck — the "recon" — and raced up the taxiway. I told Gunny to pull up there; we could see the A-6 approaching. It was good landing — fast, but all right. The canopy was already up and the plane was not even stopped as the pilot, a Marine Major, was climbing down.

As we pulled up, the radio operator, a Marine Captain, climbed leisurely down from the aircraft and left the scene, after answering my query with, "*What* safety pins? I don't know anything about any stinkin' safety pins!"

The crews never seemed to know where, or even if, the pins were aboard. Incredible as it may seem, many pilots knew next to nothing about what they were delivering, and maybe that was for the best.

Six large bombs were slung underneath the plane. They were different from anything we had, with glass noses and extra-large fins amidships and aft. They sort of resembled the Bull-Pup missile, but were called "Wet Eyes"!

We removed the safety wires connected to the bomb racks,

inserted the "found" safety pins, and I called my buddy, "Stretch" Conners, the ordnance officer of Marine Air Base Squadron 14 at Chu Lai, for some dollies. His men down-loaded the "Eyes" and away they went for safe-keeping. I asked Stretch to guard them with his life.

Well, the next day, the Marine Air Group received a "Twix" (radio message) from the Navy asking for the location of the "Wet Eyes." No planes loaded with ordnance were allowed to land aboard carriers, but the Navy intended to recover them from wherever they had set down by any means possible.

Suddenly, the proverbial "stuff" hit the fan. The bombs were not down at MABS-14, Stretch Conner's bailiwick, despite what I had told the Colonel. Come to find out, Conners had loaded them aboard *our* Intruders that night to enable a pre-viously planned operation to go forward. The operation had been mapped, and *in the event* the Marine Corps ever came in possession of such weapons (which always had seemed an impossible scenario), it would be carried out. Some rivers of North Vietnam were thus certainly very dangerous places for a few days, courtesy of the 2nd Marine Air Wing. That there is a funding support difference between the U.S. Air Force and the U.S. Navy seemed pretty obvious to me.

In Vietnam, EOD personnel were requested frequently to inspect the bottom of aircraft for battle damage, as there was a medal in store for the air crew if any damage was found. And pilots would be chagrined when a lowly Sergeant or Warrant Officer would tell them that they had simply been too low and had received their own bomb fragments.

I frequently ate with a Coon Ass Captain from Louisiana. We connected because his name was Ferrington. My father had enlisted in the Marine Corps in 1916 with that spelling, but my mother had not allowed my brother and me to use it, as that spelling was incorrect in her mind. Anyway, the Captain

A U.S. Marine Corps A-6A Intruder, of Marine Squadron 533 at Chu Lai, Vietnam. The A-6A is loaded with twenty-eight 500-pound bombs, three at eight stations and just two at each of two inboard racks, due to the wheel doors.

The USS *Repose*, aboard which the author recuperated from an intestinal abscess surrounding his ruptured appendix.

The author's Vietnam Veteran patch.

flew an old Grumman F9F Cougar jet on reconnaissance missions, and he always buzzed a particular gook in the A Shau valley. Well, on this day he told me that the gook bastard had fired a rifle at him and had caused some disruption in his instruments. The Captain had to abort the mission and bring the Cougar back to base. He asked me to come on down to the flight line and take a look. Sure enough, in a wire cluster (a bunch of wires tied/taped together), I found a gook rifle bullet and presented it to Captain Ferrington with my congratulations.

⋅⊷═◑⊜═⊶⋅

My duties at Chu Lai came to an end the third week of January 1968, and I was transferred to Ground EOD up at Danang, where I became the Security officer before I was sent off to Khe Sanh. It became very clear to me that certain responsibilities were taken very lightly by whoever had put the land mines out. I had always been impressed with the necessity of mapping the location of all booby traps and land mines. However, this had not been done in the draws and routes of approach to Marine areas around Danang. I really had a bad time trying to secure the approaches to the EOD compound out near ammunition supply point #1 (ASP #1). Unmarked mines, trip wires, and booby traps were nothing to joke about. I pray that these horrible devices will be outlawed in the near future.

While in Okinawa in 1967 I had started the poem that follows. I added to it in Japan and Guam in 1968. The refrain is to the tune of "China Night," a song popular with the 1st Marine Division during the Korean War.

'Namese Replacement Blues

Leavin' this island, goin' down south,
Namese duty, shut ma' mouth.
Hate those VC, hate 'em like sin,
Left my *josan* [*girl*] in Wisconsin.

I'm a one man army, a walkin' grenade,
I'll call in some smoke and those Cong'll fade.
Twelve month's duty in the monsoon,
Chôtto matte [*just a minute*], I'll be home soon.
    Okinawa, Okinawa, Okinawa *kudasai* [*please*],
    Arigato, arigato, arigato gozaimasu [*thank you*].

Chu Lai airfield on the South China Sea,
MAGs 12 and 13 where I wanna be.
Green Knights and Bulldogs, Black Knights true
    [*nicknames for the squadrons*],
Skyhawks and Phantoms and Cougars too.

The Korean Marine Corps is here on the job,
When they hit the A Shau the gooks begin to sob.
Dud 20s on the runway, nitro hazardous,
Napalm, Sparrows, what is all the fuss?

Refrain
Up to Camp Monohan with old Major Lane,
I'm Security officer, ain't it a shame?

Grade III disposal, York's in charge,
No sloppy shots from that ex-Sarg.

Tet Offensive, my goodness sakes,
Incomin' rounds and you got the shakes.
Accident at Khe Sanh, one man dead,
Hop on a GV and northwest I head.

Refrain
Humpin' ammo into a hole,
Retrievin' duds and diggin' like a mole.
Our French bunker's hit by a 120 round,
Dust and blackness and not a sound.

The Major calls the roll and then says a prayer,
No one's hurt, a miracle I swear.
An 82 mortar duds near the tower,
EOD responds and I'm done within the hour.

Refrain
Medevac me man, take me away,
Hercules and helo to good old NSA
    [*Navy Support Activity*].
Starlifter AirVac north to Japan,
Out of country, hot damn man.

Beaucoup Tet wounded land PJ'd [*in pajamas*] in the
    snow,
Tachikawa Air Base hosts a bad show.
Leavin' old Nippon, goin' back in,
Encore duty, worse'n Chosin.

Konichi-wa [*good morning*], Danang, I'm not through yet,
Join the 3rd Ps [*MPs*] and begin to sweat.
Generators, water points, mess hall, drinks,
S-4 duty surely stinks.

Rotten timing in the combat zone,
Appendix breaks, now take me home.
Saddle block shot and pic of Raquel,
At 1st Hospital and all is well.

Refrain
Transient center down in Danang,
120 Rockets, bang, bang, bang.
I'm so close now to makin' it clean,
Damn you Viet Cong, don't be mean.

Hospital ship, good ole Repose,
Ray Davis visits, the "Babe" he knows.
Off Quang Tri, battle flares ashore,
All my worries are sea snakes galore.

Refrain
Hot Guam interlude, first Navy nurse,
Pelletier's his name, who carries no purse.
Star Lifter AirVac, mighty big jet,
Three doggie nurses, the best news yet.

Over the sea, man; take me away,
Back to California, I'm on my way.
Got my ribbons, got my stars,
Set up the cold beers in any old bars.

Gotta see a round-eye, a mini skirt too,
Want to see everything that is new.
We're comin' in now, I see the runway,
Take it easy, pilot, that's all I gotta say.
    Okinawa, Okinawa, Okinawa *kudasai*
    Arigato, arigato, arigato gozaimasu

At the air base down in Danang, I had been appalled at the many caskets arriving and the occupied body bags being unloaded from helicopters and other aircraft. Then, during the January-March 1968 Tet Offensive, I was sent off for duty at the Khe Sanh combat base on a small plateau in northwest South Vietnam near the Laotian border. I boarded a Hercules C-130 and after a hazardous landing at Khe Sanh and quick exit from the aircraft, I was in Hell.

My mission at Khe Sanh, as a Chief Warrant Officer-3, was to replace a fellow Explosive Ordnance Disposal trooper, a Corporal who had been killed the day before. I was to continue his job. I discovered later that there was also an EOD Lieutenant who was eager to leave the area posthaste. He had spent two days in the ditch next to the runway waiting to board a plane out. My assignment was to continue to collect all the scattered ammunition from the detonation of the main ammunition dump, to help with all misfires of weapons including artillery, and to disarm or detonate all friendly and enemy damaged shells and unexploded incoming ordnance (duds).

The Khe Sanh base was being defended by the 26th Marine Regiment of the 3rd Marine Division, commanded by Colonel David Lownds, and various other units of the 3rd Marine Division. Also present were American soldiers, sailors, airmen, SeaBees, and an Army of the Republic of Vietnam (ARVN) Ranger Battalion.

Professional Marines

We were ensconced in a French pillbox at Khe Sanh — a few Marines and sailors in a conglomeration of special troops who were in constant communication with the various commands that were surrounded by the North Vietnamese Army (NVA).

A Major was in nominal charge of certain communication

The label from "33," a French-founded Vietnamese-made beer.

personnel, engineers, corpsmen, two enlisted members of graves registration, an EOD Warrant Officer-3 (myself), and others in an "on call" situation.

We considered ourselves to be temporarily very lucky to be where we were, in the concrete bunker. The rest of the 26th Marine Regiment and attached units were only protected by foxholes, dugouts, and trenches from the enemy 120mm rockets, artillery, and mortars, which rained down incessantly. At that time, my favorite expression was *"Vive la France!"* — on account of the "33" beer and our bunker!

Anyway, it was pouring down rain, dark as the ace of spades, the 120s were coming in, and the phone rang. The Major received a report of two dead Marines. I know what ran through my mind; I don't know about the others: *"What the Hell, they're dead; get 'em in the morning!"*

It was "no-man's land" out there. No way should anyone be sent out into that! Nevertheless, we heard rustling, some whispers, and gear being assembled, and before long two figures left the bunker — the two graves registration troops.

A few hours later they safely returned, and we could smell the cordite, mud, and filth on them even above our own stench. As they settled in, they conversed softly. All hands were listening intently there in the dark, and immediately the role of the very large reefer outside was made abundantly clear: to store and refrigerate bodies. The two were hyped, their adrenaline was up; they were unable to sleep, and so were planning the next day's preparation of the bodies. To our horror, we heard of the draining of blood and the injection of formaldehyde, until finally the Major said, *"For God's sake, shut up!"*

They did, yet all hands knew that we had two very brave, qualified, and dedicated Marines in our bunker. I felt ashamed that I had been initially against the mission, as I knew full well that their action had indeed lifted the morale of the men at the death scene and had left our little group in awe of them.

The closest I can come to describing the Khe Sanh fire base is comparing it to the island of Peleliu in 1944. And yet, the battles we had at Peleliu with the Japanese were horrific, but they did not occur every day, all day, and all night as they did up there at Khe Sanh, on top of that isolated bull's eye. And many of us could not shoot back, but just had to take it.

There were hardly any structures of any size located above ground at Khe Sanh. The almost continuous incoming rounds of 120mm rockets, artillery shells of all calibers, mortars, and small-arms fire dictated that only the latrines were so placed. But it took a brave man to use those facilities, which were "air-conditioned," due to the many fragment holes in them. Many did not.

It was amazing when you got a chance to watch the U.S. Air Force, Navy, and Marine Corps airmen at work. The B-52 Stratofortresses, which were not visible, made the most unearthly sounds, and their carpet bombing was awesome. Their missions were called "Arc Light." The smaller planes — Phantoms, Skyhawks, and that large one-man F-8 Crusader — came in below us to ravage the valleys all around the plateau.

One day my Sergeant and I answered a call from an artillery battery. We arrived to find that a round was stuck in the barrel of a 105 howitzer. After flushing the barrel with oil and pushing and shoving to no avail, I will never forget the look on those gunners' faces when we advised them to shit-can the whole barrel. We simply could not detonate the loaded barrel with any degree of safety in that constricted area.

Another day we were in a revetment in the ammo dump when two mortar shells landed a few seconds apart in there with us. Mortar ammunition was stacked ten feet high, and the incoming high-explosive fragments did a job on them. We weren't even scratched, however, as we got the Hell out of there as fast as we could.

Fire in the Hole

At Khe Sanh, in February of 1968, I was laboring with a working party of highly trained reconnaissance Marines burying collected damaged artillery rounds from the ammo dump catastrophe and answering questions such as, "*Why is this shell smoking?*" I did not respond, but just took the round and hastily deposited it in a bucket of water for detonation later. It was a white-phosphorous round that had been split, and air was allowing the phosphorous to burn. If the detonator was overheated . . . well, you can guess the horrible result.

Suddenly, as we worked, the phone rang and I was summoned to the airstrip, as there was an emergency at the control tower. Upon arriving at the scene, ten yards north of the tower the problem was obvious. There in plain sight was a Chinese 82mm mortar shell, one-third buried upright, just where it had landed!

My December of 1967 TAD (temporary additional duty) in Saigon for updating on new enemy booby traps, shells, and other weapons was proving useful. The sight of the Chinese mortar shell sickened me. As I had learned in the orientation classes down in Saigon, this shell had been up-graded by the Chinese to include a chemical delay. In other words, the dud could detonate at any instant, so I knew time was wasting.

One of my Sergeants appeared, and I quickly dispatched him for something to electrically detonate the shell for the safety of all hands in the area. The location was very convoluted, with large packing cases everywhere, creating small alleyways and paths. It was extremely unsafe for a non-electric disposal, fuzed with a particular number of seconds of delay, as someone might appear in those seconds.

The Sergeant immediately left on his task, and I scrounged a large section of communication wire, tied it securely around the tail fins of the shell, and, using a sort of lever arrangement, tried my mightiest to pull the 82mm out of the hardpan. But it would not budge. This was the only time in my entire life that I had wished I were 200 pounds! I kept trying, but to no avail. And according to SOP (standard operating procedure), I had to get the Commanding Officer's approval for detonation.

The Sergeant returned with the firing device for a Claymore mine. I told him to begin collecting some sandbags, as I took off for Colonel Lownds' new rocket-artillery-proof bunker, which luckily was not far. The request was made, the reasons given, permission was granted, and I was back in a flash. We securely attached a TNT charge, primed with an electric cap, to the dud, sandbagged it, and I selected a hole in the ground for me to dive into, as I considered it would take too much time to reach the Sergeant's firing position from where he had to be in order to complete the safe detonation of the 82. I trusted the Sergeant implicitly and handed him the firing mechanism, which was a squeeze electrical generator. I was determined that no Marines, wandering or rushing by, would be in danger. But I realized that not having the firing device in my possession was not in the regulations; however, this was, indeed, a special case and the Colonel was counting on me.

The plan was for me to yell "*Fire in the hole!*" three times, and then the Sergeant would squeeze the generator three times.

"*Fire in the hole! Fire in the hole! Fire in the hole!*" . . . and a Marine stuck his head out of the fifteen-foot sandbagged tower to take a look! I yelled at him to get the Hell back in behind his sandbags, and I dived for my hole. I did not make it, however. We heard the large blast — a hit — and I was on my face in the hole with my eyes closed and blood all over my hands. I tried to open my left eye but couldn't. After a while, I fearfully decided to try my right one. It worked, thank God.

All in a haze, my next stop was "Charlie Med" (C Company, 3rd Medical Battalion) and then onto a stretcher being carried to the airstrip where for a while we hid in the ditch scrunched down during an incoming barrage. A large aircraft landed from the east and I could hear it slowing with its propellers in reverse, then turning around and coming back, again slowly, never stopping. The two corpsmen were seriously conversing as to when to make their dash. (I remembered the Lieutenant who, upon being relieved from duty at Khe Sanh, had spent two days in that ditch!)

Suddenly we were charging out onto the hazardous tarmac and up behind the moving C-130. The two brave corpsmen gave the stretcher a big shove up along the rear ramp of the aircraft. As I rode along the rollers into the plane, I could barely see two Air Force troops up ahead and was really thankful when they latched onto the front handles of the stretcher. I surely didn't want to roll back down onto the runway at Khe Sanh of all places!

Then it was simply "close up your rear port and pray" as the plane struggled for altitude through the enemy antiaircraft fire at the end of the runway. What a great relief it was to be safely stowed away in an Air Force Hercules, leaving that Hell-hole, and safely flying over Indian Country headed for Danang.

All I remember of my short stay at a hospital near the main runway at Danang was that one day I went into the head, stared in the mirror, and did not recognize myself. My face looked like a perfectly round, black, blue, and red bowling ball, with unshaven stubble sticking straight out!

Two Korean Marines were in the ward with me. One was a handsome Captain, in the bunk next to mine, and the other was an enlisted man with no legs, across the aisle. The enlisted man would not give up in his effort to recover, and day and night asked for *muhl* — water. Then the good-looking Captain, who appeared to be OK, just stopped breathing one day. I screamed for a doctor or nurse, and when someone finally arrived, the Captain was dead.

A plane ride to Tachikawa Air Force Base in Japan followed. We deplaned in pajamas and "Gators" (thonged Japanese shower slippers) into three inches of snow and trudged or were carried over to an old bus, which transported us to the hospital. The casualties from the Tet Offensive indeed were terrible. The fellow in the bunk next to me had been a military policeman in the U.S. Air Force guarding airplanes at Ton Son Nhut airfield on the outskirts of Saigon. He was paralyzed. My injury was a smashed left cheekbone, which was magically repaired/replaced with some sort of metal.

From Tachikawa I had a helicopter ride to Yokosuka Naval Station, a plane ride to Okinawa, and soon a plane ride back "in-country" to Vietnam.

Addendum to "Sojourn in Vietnam"

Upon returning to Vietnam in March of 1968 I submitted a request for termination of EOD duty, which I received. I was assigned to the 3rd MP Battalion of the 3rd Marine Division with my 0302 MOS in the Infantry and Marine Gunner designations intact. I settled in right across the road from my old EOD unit and was assigned S-4 (Supply or Logistics) duties. I was in charge of electricity, generators run by Koreans, the water supply — including the two engineers operating the purification site up in the hills — and food, which encompassed the mess hall, cooks and all.

Colonel Gambardella was the Commanding Officer of the 3rd Ps, as we were called. He had all of the 3rd Marine Division's scout dogs and guard dogs and their handlers. My hut was just outside the division brig, which was loaded with the worst criminals imaginable.

I had never been so busy in my life. Many trips were made to Danang to check on the MPs living in town and to locate and try to arrange for delivery of matériel needed for the upkeep and maintenance of our equipment. The Colonel wanted a new mess hall, so one day I contacted the SeaBees in Danang. I had been advised by my mess Sergeant that we needed a special generator, with extra power, to run the mess-hall reefers. Well, I got to see the head SeaBee and told him the story about a favor I did the SeaBees on Peleliu Island back in 1944 when my platoon had been slogging back into the hills of the island, and I realized that I had to get rid of the new Japanese .32-caliber rifle that I had. I told him how we saw a sign that read "CBs," so I rushed inside the tent and to my surprise saw only a few guys sitting on the bare dirt — no juice, no food, no nothing. I simply gave the rifle to them, and they gratefully said that they would repay me someday. Can you believe it?

The result of all this was that years later the powerful generator and expensive reefers were soon delivered to our Vietnam compound!

China Beach, on the bay near Danang, was on my itinerary also. What a place! I had never seen so much equipment, food, and supplies. It was an R&R (rest and recreation) center for the U.S. Army. I was impressed mainly by the terrific ocean waves, rip tides, and undertow. The sirens seemed to be sounding continually, as the lifeguards were overwhelmed trying to save all the helpless swimmers who were either unfamiliar with the ocean waters or were hopelessly drunk.

And meanwhile, all this time, day and night, the 120mm North Vietnamese rockets kept coming in, landing haphazardly. Sometimes, however, they could be deadly on target, as our tank battalion learned one night as we huddled in our bunkers a half-mile away.

-+=◐ ◑=+-

In addition to worrying about the enemy, whenever one of our 3rd MP Battalion dogs escaped, we all sought safety. The scout dogs were OK for the most part, but when one cracked up, he was either disposed of or became a guard dog with but one handler and one aim in life — to kill. The dogs were all German Shepherds, as the Doberman Pinschers had been replaced after World War II. Doberman lovers had been "up in arms," due mainly to General Puller's firsthand knowledge of their actions on Peleliu.

One day there was a riot in the brig that would not cease. The dogs were called in, with a drummer beating a rhythm (to me it sounds like "*el degüello* — attack with no quarter" — as at the Alamo). The leashed dogs were marched almost in step down the street to the brig gate. As we all watched in amazement, the gate was opened, the handlers and the dogs rushed in, and soon the dogs ended up slobbering over the faces of the prone prisoners. The riot was over.

At about this time, Colonel Gambardella called me in one day and said that the new Commanding Officer of the 3rd Marine Division, General Raymond G. Davis, was coming for a visit. I asked the Colonel if I could be present, as I knew the General. I had last seen him at the Marine reunion in Detroit, when we had visited with Muzzy. The Colonel (of what was called the "Afrika Corps," as the officers referred to the 3rd Ps because the Colonel reminded them of the Italian Generals in that stellar outfit during World War II) said, "Fine" — just as long as all the necessary coffee, tea, soft drinks, and battery acid (Marine Corps lemonade) were provided.

And so, we stood in the overpowering heat as a helicopter came in with all the attending debris. We saw some people disembark, and a figure finally got clear of the dust. He yelled, "*Babe, Babe Farrington!*" and rushed over and hugged me! It was as much a surprise to me as it was to Colonel Gambardella, who later said to me that he did not know that I knew the General that well! I explained that as a Private 1st Class, I had served with General Davis in the 1st Antiaircraft

Machine-Gun Battery in the 1st Marine Brigade, 1st Marine Division, as of February 1, 1941, at the naval base in Guantanamo Bay, Cuba. Later, as a Captain, General Davis had been the Commanding Officer of A Battery of the 1st Special Weapons Battalion, in which I had served on Guadalcanal during 1942-1943.

Anyway, the General graciously invited me to come along on his inspection of a special brig that the 3rd MPs operated, but which was semi-isolated and Top Secret. I could not believe it; there were the North Vietnamese sailors who had been captured in the Tonkin Gulf Incident, which put this war into high gear. They were really pampered, each having his own hooch, bunk, foxhole, and enrolled in any Marine Corps Institute courses requested. Some looked at you with hate-filled eyes; others spoke pretty good English and smiled a lot. I heard later that they were the first to be traded for our MIAs (missing in action), although I don't really know if this is true or not. I do know that they were in the Marine brig outside Danang in May of 1968.

I planted a garden and built a horseshoe pit just outside the Officer/Staff NCO Club, which was just a few yards behind the front lines, which were manned at all times and equipped with Claymore mines and even a few "Fougasse" (a 55-gallon drum of oil or gasoline with an explosive charge below and behind it).

During this period I joined Nancy Sinatra's Fan Club because she supported all the Americans in Vietnam, and I received an autographed photo. And also during this time, Senator Robert Kennedy was assassinated at the Ambassador Hotel in Los Angeles, and Martin Luther King, Jr., was murdered in Memphis. For many days the Armed Forces Radio played nothing but Soul music; it almost drove us out of our minds — too much of one thing.

We played volleyball, and it soon came time for the dedication of the new mess hall, which was nearly finished. But I was sick. I was sweating bullets every night, soaking my bedding. Finally I went to the doctor, who said I probably had malaria. He sent me for a blood test, and it was no surprise to me that the test was negative, as I had had malaria before, down in Australia in 1943.

The MPs assigned me as master of ceremonies for the mess-hall dedication, and I had to tell jokes and introduce Marine and Vietnamese groups for their presentations. The whole deal was a big success they told me, but I was still sick. That night, or a few nights later (I really have no recollection of the time intervals here), I woke up with my sheets wringing wet. I put my hand down to a pain on my right side, and felt a large lump. I quickly climbed out of the sack and headed for the Officers/Staff NCO Club, which was swaying in time to the loud music on the juke box and was all lit up. (Like many of the buildings there, it was on wooden stilts.) I entered, went behind the bar, took the drunken Chief Medic's hand, and put it on my side. He looked at me, we exited the club, jumped into his medical Jeep, and headed out. With the horn blowing and lights on, we exited the 3rd MP perimeter, traveled fast through Indian Country to ASP #1 (ammunition supply point #1), entered, passed through, exited, sped through more Indian Country, and finally arrived at the 1st Hospital Company, Reinforced, 1st Marine Division, located in some Vietnamese buildings. Upon entering, I was stripped, placed on a table, and given a saddle block (I remember my wife mentioning this when she gave birth). A board was mercifully placed over my stomach so that I could not see I imagine, and the surgeons started cutting. I could hear the sounds and the talking.

All this was acceptable as 30 feet above my head, at the very apex of the thatched roof, was a picture of Raquel Welch from the movie *One Million B.C.* It was great to have someone "familiar" present at my predicament.

From the conversation, I gathered that my appendix had ruptured some time (a week or so) before, and the large ball held all the dangerous material. They removed it, sent me to NSA (Naval Support Activity, I believe), which was a large Naval hospital complex down near the main Danang airfield. All my friends were left behind, and some were killed later on, mainly Private 1st Class Klusendorf, who had worked for me in the S-4 Section. After I had left Nam, ASP #1 was sabotaged. A tennis-playing Colonel, who investigated the incident a few weeks later, informed me at the 1969 All-Marine Tennis Tournament that the horrendous blast had completely leveled my new mess hall down to the cement pad. Fortunately, with advance warning due to the large fire, all the MPs and dogs had evacuated before the blast.

My new home was the USS *Repose*, a U.S. Navy hospital ship. There was nothing to do now but to drain my guts into a bottle and read. One day the nurse said that the Commanding General of the 3rd Marine Division was coming aboard to visit his wounded. As I was not wounded, and was feeling ashamed of my condition and of being *hors de combat*, I abandoned my bunk and was safely relaxing up on deck reading and listening to my radio when all of a sudden I heard, "Attention on deck!" I looked up and there was a Navy Chief with General Davis and a Navy Captain. General Davis said, "No, no, don't get up Babe! I never thought that I'd see you in this condition!" He introduced me to the ship's Captain, who reminded me of Slim Sommerville of the movies.

A while later, a person walked up and plunked himself down on the wooden deck beside me. It was the ship's Captain. He told me that General Davis had talked about our time on Guadalcanal, and seeing as how the Captain also had been in the area aboard ship at the same time, we had a long conversation. He was a nice guy.

The *Repose* cruised along the coast of Vietnam, even up to Quang Tri near the DMZ (demilitarized zone). My only worry was that I needed to get stronger and that poisonous sea snakes might climb aboard ship, which I dreamed about every night.

I don't remember how, but I ended up in what we considered "hot" Guam. The Naval hospital was really nice (no 120mm shells landing in the vicinity), and I had as a nurse Lieutenant Pelletier, the first male Navy nurse. The bunk next to me was occupied by a Philippine sailor whose ship had caught fire; he had been rescued by the U.S. Navy. One day he asked me if I would like a San Miguel beer, from the Philippines. To my rejoinder that San Miguel beer was not exported, he answered that it was now. We went to a club on the beach and had a few. I remember going outside and seeing acres and acres of beachfront and a large part of the bay cordoned off with barbed wire. Duds and explosives were still there from World War II! I knew that some EOD teams were in for trouble.

I was finally airlifted to the States via a C-141 Starlifter transport, and was not off-loaded in California but taken all the way to Andrews Air Force Base, outside of Washington, D.C. Following an ambulance ride, I was deposited in the U.S. Naval Hospital at Quantico, Virginia. The next few months were really hazy. I spent time in the hospital at Quantico, and when able traveled home to Indian Head, Maryland, either by hitchhiking, or by taking a train to D.C. and then a bus to a rendezvous with my wife at the Naval Research Laboratory just outside the Naval Housing Area next to Bolling Field — or I was sometimes speeded by special-services boat across the Potomac River to the dock at Indian Head.

It was a sad time for me, as I felt like I was *persona non grata* around Indian Head. You see, I had not only blown myself up under questionable circumstances, but I had also quit EOD for very personal reasons.

One day I was hitchhiking just outside the Quantico main gate when a Lieutenant Colonel picked me up in his Volkswagen Beetle. We conversed on the way out to Triangle, Virginia, and up the Shirley Highway. It seemed he was on his way to England to set up the finances for the purchase of several of the newest British aircraft for the U.S. Marine Corps — the Harrier, a vertical takeoff and landing (VTOL) aircraft. As we started tooling up Highway 1, the Colonel was upset; I noticed that we weren't going over 45 miles per hour and it was dangerous with all the heavy truck traffic. The Colonel then told me that he had recently purchased the VW for a good price, as the parking area at the Naval Annex near Marine Corps Headquarters and Arlington National Cemetery had been flooded and all the cars had been inundated. He didn't seem to know what was wrong with the car, so I quickly informed him that it was simply the clutch, which was slipping, and that the cost of repair was reasonable and easily done. He had been thinking of getting rid of the Beetle, but promised to have it repaired upon his return from England. His dealings overseas evidently paid off, as the Marine Corps was using the Harriers to good effect. They operated successfully for the British in the Falklands.

It was at about this time that I learned that Chief Warrant Officer Vick, a Captain, and a 1st Sergeant, all EOD men, had been killed in an incident outside Danang involving a 120mm gook rocket. I recalled how Vick and I had made Warrant Officer together, he from Master Sergeant and I from Technical Sergeant, when we had been stationed at Middle Camp, Fuji, in the 3rd Battalion, 3rd Marine Regiment, during 1955-1956.

But meanwhile, the doctors at Quantico asked if my appendix was still present, and I said yes. They asked if I could prove it. Being an officer and a gentleman had no effect, and they set up a barium test for me. I immediately wrote to 1st Hospital in Danang, and the following letter arrived the day *after* the test:

CWO Arthur C. Farrington
USMC 070916/0302   04 AUG 68
U.S. Naval Hospital   NNL/lnr
Quantico, Virginia.

Dear CWO Farrington
You are 100% correct. Your appendix was not removed. The only thing we did was drain the large abscess that resulted from perforation of an acutely inflammed appendix. Normally it is recommended that the appendix be removed 6 to 8 weeks after the drainage ceases and the wound is healed, however, this is not always necessary and is a matter of medical judgement. I'm sure that LCDR Garrett will recommend the best and safest course for you and I urge you to accept his decision with confidence.

Our records show that a copy of your Narrative Summary accompanied you to the USS Repose, so apparently it was lost somewhere in the transaction. I am enclosing another copy of the Narrative Summary and will send one to LCDR Garrett as well, and perhaps one of them will get through. It's still kind of warm over here and our business is sporadically busy.

Good luck!

Sincerely,
N. N. Llewellyn LCDR MC USNR
Chief of Professional Services
1st Hospital Company, Rein.
1st Marine Division, Rein., FMF
FPO San Francisco, Calif., 96602

Incidentally, you must avoid a barium test if at all possible.

I was not able to. The film *A Few Good Men* demonstrates how terrible it is.

Thank God that Quantico Town is just a few blocks from the hospital. I would usually stop off for a couple beers before reporting in to the doctors, which made everything easier, but there was nothing in this world that could lessen the discomfort of the test.

After the Quantico doctors had removed the encapsulated appendix, I was recovering in the hospital where in the cubicle next to me was a Marine Lieutenant with no legs. We had heard that the TV program *Laugh In* was to be broadcast, and he invited me over to watch it. It was the first time we had seen the program, and everything was fine until the end, when the program had just one person clap. I could not stand it; I was laughing so hard I had to wheel out into the aisle before my stitches would break. The Lieutenant seemed to enjoy the program as well, though I knew he would not find much to amuse him for the rest of his life.

Finally I received orders to report once again to Marine Corps Base, Camp Joseph H. Pendleton, California, in January of 1969. Seeing as how I had earlier driven our 1961 Mercedes across country and stored it in San Diego, Linda and I decided to make the trip in the VW. We loaded into our black Bug and "hauled ass," as the boys would say, on the Marine Corps birthday, November 10, 1968, with a rented container on the roof. "We" consisted of myself, Linda, Reggie, Rolando, Karen, Lynn, Pup-Pups, and Tweetie, the Robin we had had for a couple years already and who was as happy as anyone when I returned from Vietnam.

Once on the road, our first dalliance was at Quantico, to bid *adios* to EOD Sergeant Becker and his family. We were happy to babysit for the children so that the Beckers could attend the

Marine Corps Birthday Ball there. The Sergeant had been a very good friend of mine while in EOD.

Our next stopover was Norfolk, Virginia, to visit Benton R. Montgomery (Duck) and his wife, Shirley, our friends for many years. By this time Duck was a Lieutenant Colonel, still working in counterintelligence.

Our next stop was Ormond Beach, Florida, where my mother was living with her husband, then on to Luling, Texas, my wife's hometown. We had spent most of our 30-day leaves there during the 1950s and stopped over whenever driving coast-to-coast.

At the highway rest stops, we burst out of the Bug. The kids and Pup-Pups would take off, and Tweetie would happily fly around. Everyone would end up, with no problem, back in the car. We did Las Vegas, Lynnie winning a package of psychedelic flowers at "Circus-Circus," which we immediately pasted all over the VW. (You must remember that this was 1968, and as a military family we had been remote from most of the counter-culture goings-on.)

It snowed one night near Flagstaff, Arizona; the temperature dropped to nine degrees, and when we piled into the car in the morning, it was in a state of shock and would not start. The VW was a "tropical" auto, and this was too much for it to handle! It had served us well in Haiti, North Carolina, Maryland, and crossing the country thus far — but nine degrees was the limit.

Luckily for us at this juncture, a road crew staying at the same motel poured out of its rooms and laughingly shoved us on our way. Later that day at a gas station, a similar VW pulled up to the pumps, heading in the opposite direction, with a U-Haul on its roof just like ours. We stared at the two girls, they stared at us, we exchanged pleasantries, and both Bugs moved out.

Finally after logging 5,200 miles, we arrived in Oceanside, California, and were ready for what was to be our last two years in the U.S. Marine Corps.

Chapter 10

California —
and Retirement

W E SPENT CHRISTMAS of 1968 in a nice apartment in south Oceanside, California, right on the beach. One day the kids and I saw a ten- to twelve-foot shark just a few feet from shore, which dropped suddenly right there — no swimming for us. He was leisurely swimming parallel to the shore in plain sight. I sure didn't envy surfers.

We soon obtained housing, and I picked up the Mercedes in San Diego. I was assigned to the 2nd Infantry Training Regiment again. My duties were many, but the most distasteful was as Legal Officer. Day after day I had to deal with people who should never have been enlisted in the U.S. Marine Corps. The letters necessary to the parents when their son was "over the hill" for ten days were bad, but the one when their son was declared a deserter after thirty days was worse.

I will never forget the time I stood in front of the Colonel with a Marine and his father. We intended to court-martial the boy, but first we listened to the father. Briefly this is the gist of what he had to say. His son had come home from Vietnam with all those ribbons and had been working for him in his business ever since up in L.A. The Colonel looked at me and I said, "Sir, your son has never completed

The Farrington family and their beloved 1959 Volkswagen Beetle, when they were newly arrived at Oceanside, California. From left to right: Front row, Tweetie, Karen, and Rolando; Back row, Linda, Reggie with Pup-Pups, and Lynn.

Unloading the VW at Oceanside. From left to right: Rolando, Reggie, Tweetie (in cage), Karen, Lynn, and Linda with Pup-Pups.

the training here at 2nd ITR, has never been to Vietnam, has earned no medals whatsoever, and is a deserter from the United States Marine Corps." You should have seen the gentleman's astonished face.

Our Casual Company — the place people are sent when they have done something wrong, the "extra" people waiting for court-martial, or whatever — was always full of miscreants, not Marines. Coordination with the Provost Marshal was necessary, and I had to be present when the undercover operatives, dressed as sharp PFCs or sloppy Privates, arrested suspected drug dealers and hauled them away. But I knew I had had enough of this; I was getting depressed. I didn't talk about my day, and didn't wish to go to work. I had a great rank and wished to stay in the Marine Corps, but this duty was getting to me.

One day a Lieutenant who had served with me in Vietnam mentioned that he had just been assigned burial detail for some Colonel. I asked him the particulars, and lo and behold the deceased had been one of my Commanding Officers at 2nd ITR back in the 1950s. We had played golf on Thursdays and Saturdays with two other compatible officers. He was not a large man, but he claimed that he could hit a drive over 300 yards. Captain Cahoon, an instructor at the 2nd ITR at Pendleton, had told me one day that the good Colonel had done that in Panama, on baked fairways where the golf ball would roll at least 100 of those yards. Anyway, the Colonel had been a nice gentleman, so I took the Lieutenant off the hook and with the help of a good crew we accomplished a ceremony in Eternal Hills. The Colonel had retired there in Oceanside, and had lived in a gated community. One night a ruckus had occurred, the Colonel had gone outside to investigate, and he was shot and killed. You never know.

In the summer of 1969, after the Western Regional Tennis Championships, we flew to Beaufort Marine Corps Air Station (MCAS) in South Carolina for the All-Marine competition. We hard-court players from California could never get in the proper condition for playing back in the hot and humid East on the Har-Tru surface, no matter how much we tried, so we had to rely on the doubles for any trophy hopes.

I recall a tournament in Little Creek, Virginia, where the two finalists in the open singles were an odd pair. One was a U.S. Navy SEAL in his thirties from San Diego, and the other was a Navy Lieutenant who had been ranked first on the U.S. Naval Academy tennis team. He had graduated a year or so before and had been stationed in Holy Loch, Scotland, with the nuclear subs, in non-tennis-playing weather shall we say. For you not familiar with Har-Tru courts, they are much slower than regular red clay and the points go on forever. After hours of play, the SEAL won. We all agreed that conditioning did it for him.

I recall other incidents as well. While we were at the MCAS Officers Club one night in Beaufort, South Carolina, the American astronauts had landed on the moon. And about that time, a movie called *Candy* was shown aboard the station, starring the British Beetle Ringo Starr. I am sure that the movie was the beginning of realistic sex scenes in films.

One day I visited downtown Beaufort and met and talked to some members of a very special group of black Americans, called Guliah (pronounced Gulla). They lived mainly on St. Helena Island, between the Parris Island and Beaufort Marine Corps bases. Their culture was interesting, to say the least.

We then traveled up to Fort Myer, Virginia, where we were billeted while engaged in the Inter-Service Tennis Tournament at the Army and Navy Country Club, a little way down the Shirley Highway from the Pentagon. The Army always had the #1 singles player it seemed. First it was Arthur Ashe, then Stan Smith; at that particular time, it was Charlie Pasarell. Our team consisted of Colonel Cummings, Gunnery Sergeant Voyles, Major Hofinga, 1st Lieutenant Parkerson, Dental Technician 3rd Class Young, Private First Class Geder, Major O'Brien, Master Gunnery Sergeant Eppinette, Lance Corporal Bruder, and myself.

While in the D.C. area for the tournaments, one day I hiked over to the headquarters of the Arlington National Cemetery, picked up a map, and found my buddy Chief Warrant Officer Vick in Section 30, grave number 656. After looking around and seeing that the coast was clear, I carefully collected a small ivy plant. Today and every day when I walk outside my home here in Escondido, I remember Gunner Vick, for there, growing tall, is the ivy.

Also in 1969, I won the singles and doubles horseshoe tournaments held in the main area back at Camp Pendleton. The beautiful trophies outshone anything I had ever won in tennis.

⊹⇒ —·— ⇐⊹

The 1969 Marine Corps Inter-Service Tennis Team. From left to right: Colonel Cummings, Dental Technician-3 Young, Master Gunnery Sergeant Eppinette, Gunnery Sergeant Voyles, Private 1st Class Geder, Lance Corporal Bruder, Major Hofinga, Major O'Brien, Chief Warrant Officer Arthur C. Farrington, and 1st Lieutenant Parkerson,

The year 1970 rolled around, and the All-Marine Tennis Tournament was held in California, on the courts next to the Commanding General's ranch house down on Vandegrift Boulevard. I succeeded in winning the Senior (45 and up) Singles and, with my partner, the Senior Doubles championships.

The 15th Naval District then sent the team, headed by U.S. Navy Commander Stan Potts, to the Inter-Service Tourney in Texas. We were billeted at Randolph Air Force Base and played the matches at Trinity College in San Antonio.

Later that summer, I was beaten by a Marine Captain for the base horseshoe championship, but teamed up with a PFC for the doubles win. It was so hot that everyone had their shirts off except my partner. He would not remove his. Back in my VW, I asked him if he wanted a Coke, and after he had declined, I began to realize the situation. When I returned, with my

Arthur C. Farrington, ready for his "Last Hurrah" in "Mess Dress" at Camp Joseph H. Pendleton, California, just before his retirement in 1970.

drink and an orange for him, I asked if he would take his jacket off. Sure enough, just as Linda had told me about the Mormon Samoan girls she had played volleyball with, he was a Mormon. He was pleased to show me the undergarment he wore, as a member of the Inner Temple. It was stitched with the five wounds of Christ, and he did not wish the other horseshoe players to make fun of him or criticize him.

Our house on Dolphin Drive in Camp Del Mar, a section of Camp Pendleton, California, was fine, and the beach was nearby. We fished off the breakwaters, at Lake Pulgas, and at Lake Margarita near the hospital when it was stocked, but our favorite getaway was Casey Springs. To get there you had to turn off Basilone Road, pass through the Camp Pendleton artillery impact area, and climb the mountains. It was almost your private place with great fishing, exploring, and cooking out. The only worry was when Tweetie was flying all around. I would worry that some type hawk would scoop him up.

Upon returning one time from Casey Springs, Tweetie became sick and we took him to a veterinarian. The diagnosis was probable pneumonia, but an antibiotic shot did not help. What a great pet that little Robin had been. He's buried on U.S. Marine property.

Meanwhile, during this tour of duty, Karen and I perfected her tennis and she was ready for high school, area, and college competition, and a lifetime of enjoyment and exercise. During these last two years in the Marine Corps I had attended night school operated by Chapman College, from Orange, California, held at our amphibian tractor compound at Del Mar across Interstate 5 from Camp Pendleton. These classes enabled me to receive a teaching credential, and after my retirement, I substituted in all subjects (including once in girls Physical Education), kindergarten through high school, adult school, and with Native American Indians, to enable them to obtain a GED necessary for government employment. I taught from 1971 to 1988.

I was promoted to Chief Warrant Officer-4 in the fall of 1970, and part of me would have loved to remain in the Marine Corps. But, to make a long story short, I retired on December 31, 1970.

Nevertheless, *once a Marine, always a Marine.*

— Semper Fidelis.

Index

by Lori L. Daniel